Essentials of Retirement Planning

Essentials of Retirement Planning

A Holistic Review of Personal Retirement Planning Issues and Employer-Sponsored Plans

Eric J. Robbins

business**expert**
Press

First published in 2014 by
Business Expert Press, LLC
222 East 46th Street, New York, NY 10017
www.businessexpertpress.com

ISBN-13: 978-1-63157-031-5 (paperback)
ISBN-13: 978-1-63157-032-2 (e-book)

Business Expert Press Finance and Financial Management Collection

Collection ISSN: 2331-0049 (print)
Collection ISSN: 2331-0057 (electronic)

Cover and interior design by Exeter Premedia Services Private Ltd., Chennai, India

First edition: 2014

10 9 8 7 6 5 4 3 2 1

Printed in the United States of America.

Abstract

This book provides the quintessential information needed to understand the financial side of the retirement planning coin. You'll begin by learning about the various plan types employers may offer their employees. Topics related to compliance testing will be thoroughly discussed as well as strategies used to legally shift benefits in favor of highly compensated employees (HCEs).

However, some employers do not sponsor a plan. In this instance, retirement savers will need to understand the options available within the world of individual retirement accounts (IRAs). This book is not intended to provide investment advice, but rather to guide how different retirement savings vehicles function and how they can be effectively deployed.

Many financial professionals find that their clients ask questions about all aspects of their financial life. For this reason, this book also discusses non-investment-related topics such as housing options, Social Security planning, Medicare planning, and a few other basic insurance-based issues faced by all retirees.

Keywords

employer-sponsored plans, medicare, social security, retirement plan compliance testing, retirement planning

Contents

Preface ix

Acknowledgments xi

Part I   Retirement Plan Overview 1

Chapter 1   Crisis of Financial Unawareness and a 30,000-Foot
            View 3

Chapter 2   The Retirement Landscape 11

Chapter 3   Initial Concerns in Retirement Planning 19

Chapter 4   Defined Benefit Plan Types and Money
            Purchase Pension Plans 29

Chapter 5   The World of Defined Contribution Plans.................39

Chapter 6   Plans for Small Businesses and Nonprofits................53

Part II   Retirement Plan Design 61

Chapter 7   Coverage, Eligibility, and Participation Rules..................63

Chapter 8   Designing Benefit Offerings 75

Chapter 9   Plan Loans, Vesting, and Retirement Age Selection..........85

Chapter 10 Death and Disability Planning 97

Chapter 11 Plan Funding and Investing......................................105

Chapter 12 Fiduciary Responsibility 119

Part III   Retirement Plan Administration 131

Chapter 13 Plan Installation and Administration 133

Chapter 14 Plan Terminations 141

Part IV   Special Plan Types 151

Chapter 15 Nonqualified Deferred Compensation Plans..................153

Chapter 16 Equity-Based Compensation 169

Chapter 17 Introduction to IRAs 181

Chapter 18 IRAs in Depth 195

Part V   Comprehensive Retirement Planning 207

Chapter 19 A Holistic View of Retirement Planning........................209

Chapter 20 Social Security 221

Chapter 21 Retirement Needs Analysis 239

Chapter 22 Housing, Medicare, and Long-Term Care Concerns......251

Chapter 23 Retirement Distribution Planning 263

Chapter 24 Managing Distribution Options 281

Appendix...291
Notes...293
References..297
Index 303

Preface

I am an Eagle Scout. Why is that important? Well, the Boy Scout motto is "Be Prepared." And, when it comes to retirement, the sad reality is that most people are not. Most people live their lives spending most of what they earn and sometimes more than that. The state of retirement in America for the majority of people is not what Hollywood portrays on TV, and this worries me greatly.

How do we work toward a solution? Only through education, discipline, and a strategic rewrite of the status quo can we hope to reshape our own futures and the futures of those that we, as financial professionals, help. I have worked in private wealth management since 1998, and much of that time has been spent helping those who did plan well. Individuals in this category will need a trained financial professional.

It is imperative that the next generation of financial professionals receives the highest level of training possible. It is also important that they subscribe to a clear ethical standard, perhaps by becoming a Certified Financial Planner or perhaps by becoming a Chartered Financial Analyst charterholder. The industry desperately needs individuals who are willing to leverage their training to benefit their clients first and foremost.

I wrote this book because I was asked to teach a course on Retirement Planning at Penn State Erie, the Sam and Irene Black School of Business. I was immediately impressed with the rigorous program in place and the high quality of both the faculty and the students. The textbook being used was *Planning for Retirement Needs* by Littell and Tacchino and it is an excellent teaching tool for those students studying for the CFP® exam or for those who want a very in-depth review of retirement planning. But some of my students were still considering their career paths and did not require the full intensity of a CFP® prep course. I chose to create this book to be a thorough review of all of the major topical areas, but in a more condensed format. My students appreciate this format and relish the fact that the price of this textbook is so budget friendly.

This book covers all of the core topics. It crosses the spectrum of employer-sponsored plans, compliance testing concerns, individual retirement accounts (IRAs), Social Security, Medicare, and retirement distribution planning. There are discussion questions at the end of each chapter, which I use myself in the classroom to get students thinking about the core topics from the chapter. There are also online resources available on the book's webpage for interested educators.

Acknowledgments

I would like to thank my wife, Joy, and both of my kids, Hope and Nathanael, for their patience and support as I finished this book.

I would like to thank my professional mentor, Dr. Greg Filbeck, for without his guidance I would not have entered the wonderful world of higher education.

PART I

Retirement Plan Overview

CHAPTER 1

Crisis of Financial Unawareness and a 30,000-Foot View

Introduction

The reality is that most Americans are underprepared for retirement. The current plan deployed by many is to spend what you make, save as little as possible, and fall back on Social Security when it is time to retire. This is a broken philosophy that is both wrong and approaching the end of its potential realistic use. We need a new level of awareness. Further, we need to understand the amazing benefits offered by tax-advantaged retirement savings opportunities. Some employers offer retirement benefits, and some employers do not. We will explore exactly why an employer should consider offering a plan in this chapter.

Learning Goals

- Understand the current state of an average American's retirement preparedness
- Identify why tax-advantaged retirement plans are beneficial
- Identify general characteristics of tax-advantaged plans
- Explain how employer-sponsored plans benefit large employers
- Explain how employer-sponsored plans benefit small business owners

Financial Awareness (or Lack Thereof)

A recent study found that out of 100 people who begin working when they are 25 years old, by the time they attain age 65, only four percent will have stockpiled adequate savings for retirement, and 63 percent will be completely reliant upon Social Security, friends, relatives, or a charity for their subsistence needs.[1] According to the Federal Reserve Bank of St. Louis (St. Louis Fed), American's personal savings rate is almost at its lowest point since 1959 when it began tracking the measurement.[2] With this as a backdrop, it should not be too surprising that according to a Harris Poll, 34 percent of Americans have nothing saved for retirement.[3] This is partly because employer-sponsored plans are not offered by all companies. According to the Bureau of Labor Statistics (BLS), only 68 percent of all workers have access to an employer-sponsored plan, and of those who have access, only 54 percent participate.[4] This same annual report from the BLS shows that those least likely to have access to a plan are service workers, part-time workers, and nonunion workers. If this information does not make your jaw drop, then you need to check your pulse.

We cannot blame the average American too much. We have been programmed to spend, spend, and spend. We need a reboot, and we need a plan because without proper retirement planning, the potential of retirement security will remain as elusive as it is today. Throughout this textbook, you will learn various facets in the retirement planning process and about the different types of tax-advantaged plans available to a business and the types available to individuals privately. You will learn about specific regulations and limitations inherent in the system. You will also learn about unique employer-sponsored plans like stock options and employee stock discount programs.

To begin our correction of the crisis of financial unawareness, there are two main categories of tax-advantaged retirement plans. The first category is known as a *qualified plan*. A qualified plan meets certain government requirements to be tax deferred. Examples of qualified plans are defined benefit plans, cash balance plans, money purchase plans, target benefit plans, profit-sharing plans, 401(k)s, stock bonus plans, and employee stock ownership plans (ESOPs). Some investors misuse the term *qualified plan* to include all tax-advantaged retirement savings accounts including individual retirement accounts (IRAs), which are the primary retirement savings vehicle for those without an employer sponsored plan. The term *qualified plan* only applies to a very specific list of account types.

Table 1.1 Qualified versus other plans

Qualified plans	Other employer-sponsored plans
Defined benefit plans	SEP plans
Cash balance plans	SIMPLE plans
Target benefit plans	403(b) plans
Money purchase pension plans	
Profit-sharing plans	
401(k) plans	
Stock bonus plans	
ESOPs	

Abbreviations: ESOP, Employee stock ownership plans; SEP, Simplified employee pension
SIMPLE, Savings incentive match plan for employees individual retirement account.

The other account types fall into a second category, which does not have a fancy name, and so we will simply call them *other* plans. Specifically excluded from qualified plan status are individual retirement accounts (IRAs), 403(b)s, simplified employee pension (SEP) plans, and savings incentive match plan for employees (SIMPLE) plans. You will learn about SEPs, SIMPLEs, and 403(b)s in Chapter 6. Table 1.1 summarizes the list of those employer-sponsored plans that are considered qualified and those that are considered other.

Tax-Advantaged Plan Attributes

You can see from the data presented in Table 1.2 that utilizing a tax-advantaged savings account to prepare for retirement will enable a significantly larger account balance to be compiled. The magic of tax-deferred (or tax-free) compound interest simply cannot be ignored.

Regardless of whether a tax-advantaged retirement plan is technically qualified or not, they all share several characteristics. If the plan is sponsored by an employer, like a defined benefit plan or a 401(k), then the employer gets a tax deduction for the tax year in which the contribution is made. The employer's deduction is not influenced by the employee's level of income. Employers can deduct every penny that they contribute to a retirement plan.

Table 1.2 Comparison of tax-advantaged savings versus nontax-advantaged savings

	Tax advantaged	Regular investment account
Savings	$17,500.00	$17,500.00
Less taxes owed @28%	$0.00	$4,900.00
Available to invest	$17,500.00	$12,600.00
Investment earnings @7%	$1,225.00	$882.00
Less capital gains taxes @28%*	$0.00	$246.96
End-of-period result	$18,725.00**	$13,235.04

*Twenty-eight percent assumes the gains are short-term capital gains.
**Taxes will be paid on the tax-advantaged savings when ultimately withdrawn from the account and theoretically at a greatly reduced tax rate.

From the employee's perspective, taxes are deferred typically until money is withdrawn from the account in retirement. This is a significant benefit to employees as their marginal tax rate while they are working is almost always reasonably higher than their marginal tax rate during retirement. Because of this amazing tax deferral benefit, municipal bonds and other tax-sheltered investments should not be held within an already tax-deferred plan. Tax-sheltered investments usually have lower returns because the tax benefit attracts investors, but someone with an IRA or a 401(k) would already receive favorable tax treatment. They are free to look for higher yielding investments since there is no benefit from double tax deferral.

Employees do not need to withdraw their entire account balance, thus triggering a taxable event, when they retire. They have the option of rolling their employer-sponsored plan into a different type retirement account like an IRA. This step will further defer taxes beyond the employee's retirement date. We will also discuss this process in detail later in this book.

An interesting and creative feature of qualified plans is that a life insurance policy can be included as an investment within the plan. Again, we will discuss details later, but understand that the use of life insurance is only available within qualified plans and not in the other category.

General Requirements of Tax-Advantaged Plans

Qualified plans must have broad participation from within the pool of employees. A scenario where the business owner is the sole participant in the company's retirement plan is not an acceptable way for owners to save for their own retirement if there are other employees of the company. The rank-and-file employees must also be included. Related to this requirement are the nondiscrimination rules, which state that an employer cannot discriminate against the rank-and-file and offer relatively better benefits for highly compensated employees. We will spend an entire chapter later, discussing nondiscrimination testing.

In the world of employer-sponsored plans, *vesting* refers to the amount of time employees must work for a company before they own all of the employer's contributions into their account. Employees always own the contributions that they themselves have contributed, but the employer's portion is subject to a vesting schedule, which is simply a certain percentage that becomes fully owned by the employee at certain time intervals of employment tenure. Employers are permitted to select either immediate vesting or gradual vesting based on certain timetables.

Another general requirement is that employers must communicate effectively to all of their employees the benefits available to them. This seems logical and straightforward, but employers cannot pick and choose whom they wish to tell about the availability of benefits.

Plans will commonly have a plan document, which covers all of the legal intricacies of the plan. The plan document satisfies the requirement that all plan terms must be clearly stated in writing.

Introduction to Nonqualified Deferred Compensation and IRAs

There is a way for employers to contribute additional money to their highly compensated employees. These nonqualified deferred compensation plans are sometimes generically called *457 plans,* although this is technically only the name for nonqualified deferred compensation plans offered to nonprofit organizations. As you will learn, these plans can be used to discriminate legally in favor of a select group of executives. There are very few design restrictions involved with nonqualified deferred compensation plans. We will spend a full chapter discussing these plans later, but the general nature of these plans is that the employee does not get a tax deduction because the contributions are made from after-tax earnings. However, there are options available for an employee to delay reporting the additional income. The employer will wait to claim a tax deduction for his or her contribution until the employee has claimed the additional compensation as taxable income.

Individual retirement plans are entirely managed and operated by the taxpayer. The employer is typically not involved in this process. Common examples of individual retirement plans are SEPs, a SIMPLE IRA, traditional IRAs, and Roth IRAs. Each of these four savings vehicles are funded using IRAs.

Taxpayers can make both tax-deductible and nontax-deductible contributions to their individual retirement accounts. However, most taxpayers use only tax-deductible contributions. There are specific contribution limits for each type of individual retirement accounts.

The Employer's Need for a Plan

It is easy to see that employees need retirement savings plans because the plans help them save for retirement, but what does the employer gain other than a tax deduction?

Of course, employers could simply offer retirement plans to their employees because they are good corporate citizens. One notorious example of a company exemplifying this trait is Starbucks who offers retirement contributions even to part-time employees. However, most companies need additional inducement to provide retirement benefits to their employees.

Employers who offer retirement savings plans have a carrot to dangle to both attract and retain valuable employees. Top talent should be drawn less to companies without retirement savings plans. The plans also boost morale, which in theory should increase efficiency and output.

What impact might unions have on this topic? Unionized employees often have a comparably better retirement package because unions include retirement planning in their collective bargaining agreements.[5]

Stalemates on the issue of retirement packages have caused lost productivity and lost jobs.

Another reason that offering a retirement plan can benefit an employer is to ease the transition for older employees into retirement. This makes jobs available for younger workers. This is a double-edged sword in a sense. On one hand, the employer will be encouraging seasoned workers to leave the company. But on the other, younger workers will save the company money in both wages and health insurance premiums.

A small business has its own set of reasons to offer a retirement plan. Recall that small business owners cannot initiate an employer-sponsored retirement plan with the intention of only contributing for themselves. However, they can use several legitimate methods to transfer money from their business to their retirement nest egg in a tax-favorable way.

Other than the tax benefits, small business owners might want to establish a retirement plan to shelter assets from business creditors and the potential of bankruptcy. Assets within the owner's personal retirement account are personal assets, and business types like a corporation or a limited liability company (LLC) offer protection of personal assets in the event of a business collapse.

Also, small business owners might offer retirement benefits because it will mean that they can pay their employees less in wages because the retirement benefits enhance their overall compensation package. When it comes to large employers, think attraction and retention. When it comes to smaller business owners, think maximization of tax shelter and protection of assets.

Discussion Questions

1. What are the tax advantages common to all types of tax-advantaged retirement savings plans?
2. Do tax-advantaged plans need to invest in tax-favorable investments to remain tax advantaged?
3. What common requirements do all tax-advantaged retirement plans share?
4. What are some nontax-related benefits of participating in an employer-sponsored retirement plan?

5. There is a small smartphone supplier with mostly young employees. The industry is highly competitive. How could offering an
employer-sponsored retirement plan help this company compete
better with its rivals?

CHAPTER 2

The Retirement Landscape

Introduction

Many people are honest in their intentions and their actions. Some are not. The presence of this "some" necessitates an entity to create rules and to monitor them. The purpose of the rules is to ensure that participants in employer-sponsored plans are not being taken advantage of. The American government enacted the Employee Retirement Income Security Act (ERISA) in 1974 and the Pension Protection Act (PPA) in 2006 to help with this need to level the playing field and to keep all of the players honest. There are three primary governmental organizations that have influence over pension regulation. You will learn about each of them and what they do in this chapter.

Learning Goals

- Explain how ERISA reshaped the world of pension
- Identify the four titles of ERISA
- Understand the major trends in post-ERISA legislation
- Understand the implications of the PPA of 2006
- Identify the agencies involved in regulating tax-advantaged retirement plans
- Explain the purpose of an advance determination letter (ADL)

Introduction to ERISA

Regulation adds a great deal of complexity to any system. The world of employer-sponsored retirement plans is no different. The presence of regulation means that employees are theoretically safer and that consultants who thoroughly understand the regulation can benefit from this knowledge.

The **Employee Retirement Income Security Act (ERISA)** is a federal law that protects the employer-sponsored retirement assets of millions of Americans. Its primary purpose is to protect participants in employer-sponsored plans by helping them to understand and ultimately receive the benefits that have been promised to them.[1]

ERISA made some key changes that will be discussed throughout this book. First, it imposes requirements on vesting schedules and measures of employee participation. Second, it provides options for a company that has not fully funded its promised pension obligations. Third, it establishes a safety net for workers if the company should file for bankruptcy. Fourth, it imposes certain standards, called fiduciary standards, on those who manage the pension assets. Fifth, it removes the monopoly that employer-sponsored plans had on the retirement savings market, before ERISA. Before ERISA was enacted, employer-sponsored plans were the only mechanism for employees to save for retirement. ERISA also created the individual retirement account (IRA), which enabled workers to save for retirement outside the purview and limitations of their employer.

It is important to understand that ERISA does not require employers to establish a pension plan. However, it *does* require that those who establish plans must meet certain minimum standards.

ERISA is organized under four titles, or sections, that establish the minimum standards applicable to employer-sponsored retirement plans. **Title I** of ERISA establishes the requirement to disclose an employee's right to collect the promised benefits. Disclosure is the key word. **Title II** of ERISA establishes parameters on the tax deferral of contributions. Certain requirements and vesting schedules must be in place, or the contributions are no longer considered to be tax deferred. If compliance is not strictly followed, then the plan could be deemed not a "qualified" plan, which would retroactively affect both the employee and the employer who may need to undo several years' worth of tax deductions if the tax status of the retirement plan were to be reversed. **Title III** of ERISA creates a regulatory framework for implementing ERISA. The duties are split between the Department of Labor (DOL) and the Internal Revenue Service (IRS). **Title IV** of ERISA is very important! This title establishes the Pension Benefit Guaranty Corporation (PBGC).

Post-ERISA Trends

In the years following the adoption of ERISA, several trends have emerged in the world of employer-sponsored retirement plans. The first trend is a reduction in taxation benefits. At one point, pension benefits received extremely favorable tax treatment. For example, they were once not subject to estate taxes. This is no longer the case. Each favorable tax treatment has been gradually removed so that today, pension benefits are taxed as ordinary income (just like earned income). This trend clearly has benefited the federal government more than the pension recipients.

The second trend relates to the use of IRAs. At the time that ERISA was enacted, IRAs permitted very limited contributions. Their boundaries have gradually been expanded to encourage more private saving. Now, investors benefit from higher contribution limits and the introduction of Roth IRAs.

The third trend is related to the second, and it deals specifically with contribution limits. Immediately follow the passing of ERISA, legislation began to appear that limited deductible contributions for highly compensated employees. This legislation had the effect of increasing the use of nonqualified deferred compensation plans, like a 457 plan. In 2001, this trend began to change, and the income limits were gradually made less restrictive. This was done both to encourage saving and to incentivize small business owners to open plans. An ongoing trend has been to give all business types equal access to employer-sponsored retirement savings plans.

A fourth trend has been the limits placed on tax deferral. The federal government realized that the tax inducement to save in a retirement plan was tremendous and that the government was losing out on a revenue source for too long a period of time. In 1986, legislation was passed that requires distributions to begin by the attained age of 70½ to correct this revenue oversight.

A fifth trend relates primarily to small business, but it also applies to other business types. To ensure that small business owners were not giving themselves retirement benefits to the exclusion of their rank-and-file employees, top-heavy rules were instituted. We will discuss the top-heavy rules in detail in Chapter 6, but they essentially prevent discrimination.

Another rule inspired by small business abuses is the affiliation requirements. Some businesses were forming separate entities to avoid retirement regulations. Now, they must aggregate all related businesses with common ownership to eliminate this loophole. People can be very creative, and as new loopholes are found, new regulations will likely emerge to plug the leaks.

PPA of 2006

The PPA of 2006 is legislation that was designed to protect employer-sponsored plan participants further and to improve the pension system in general. It mandates an accelerated funding schedule when a defined benefit plan does not have enough money to meet its projected obligations. It also mandates accelerated vesting schedules for defined contribution plans. Both of these requirements protect employees (participants) from an employer's poor judgment.

Another requirement that protects employees is a requirement to offer more than mere employer stock in a defined contribution plan. Can you imagine a scenario where you work for a large company and have a substantial portion of your 401(k) invested in your employer's stock only to have your employer go bankrupt? Now, the employees are without jobs, and their retirement savings have been decimated. This exact nightmare played out in the lives of countless former employees of Enron. Lives were forever altered because employees failed to diversify their employer from their retirement savings. People invest in what they know...or what they think they know.

The PPA also made several improvements to the pension system. From 1983 to 2001, total 401(k) contribution limits had been held level, but legislation enacted in 2001 temporarily increased these limits.[2] PPA made the previously temporary higher contribution limits a permanent incentive for additional savings. It also encouraged the autoenrollment feature that many plans now incorporate. This feature will automatically enroll new employees in the respective retirement plan of the employer unless they specifically opt out. There is also now an option for employees, who are unaware of the basics of asset allocation strategies, to seek investment advice from a representative of the defined benefit plan.

Who Is the Regulator?

Regulation may be wisely designed to protect consumers and encourage proper behavior, but someone must implement and oversee the laws, or they will not be applied correctly, if at all. There are three agencies given regulatory oversight over different corners of pension law.

The first in the pension regulation triad is the IRS. Before an employer begins to fund a tax-advantaged retirement plan, it is a good idea if they request an **ADL** from the IRS. This letter is *NOT* mandatory, but it is highly recommended. If a company begins to fund a retirement plan in September of a given year, but in June of the following year, the IRS audits the company and determines that its retirement plan does not meet the requirements of ERISA, then all contributions into the plan would need to be reversed, and both the company and the employees have a tax issue on their hands. The employer will need to restate their previous year's tax return to eliminate the tax deduction that they claimed. They will also need to reissue W-2s for each affected employee, and the employees will all owe taxes potentially with interest and penalties to the IRS on a personal level. The path of least resistance is to simply apply for an ADL, which will bestow the IRS's seal of approval on establishing the plan.

The IRS also holds the task of auditing tax-advantaged plans. Each year, employers must fill out a special form called a 5500 form, which helps the IRS determine ongoing compliance with pension law.

In addition to these two regulatory responsibilities, the IRS may also issue interpretations of the law to help companies determine compliance with the expanding body of legislation. The IRS may issue a **proposed regulation**, which is merely an idea that the IRS has had. These regulations cannot be relied upon until they explicitly state that they can. The IRS may also issue **regulations,** which apply to all taxpayers or it may issue **revenue rulings,** which only apply to very unique situations. Occasionally, they may issue a **private letter ruling,** which is an exclusive interpretation for one company's unique situation.

The second pension regulator is the DOL. One key area of purview for the DOL is the enforcement of Title I of ERISA (disclosure rules). One thing that they look for is the distribution of the **summary plan**

description (SPD) to all participants. The SPD discloses all relevant facts to the employees in a somewhat organized fashion.

The DOL also polices the use of investment choices within tax-advantaged retirement plans. There is a list of prohibited transaction types that the DOL monitors. We will discuss this list of prohibited transactions in detail in another chapter. They also monitor adherence to the **exclusive benefit rule**, which states that all plan assets must be invested for the exclusive benefit of the employees (participants). The purpose of the exclusive benefit rule is to prevent a company from buying shares of another company to attempt to influence their actions in the marketplace, which would be a manipulation of the forces of competition and not a sole benefit for the plan participants.

In addition, the DOL also monitors the actions of the plan's fiduciaries. The fiduciary is the person or group with responsibility over the employer-sponsored plan. Every plan has a fiduciary. They are held to a standard known as prudence, which means that they must act as a prudent person would be expected to act. It should go without saying that the fiduciary would act in a prudent way for the exclusive benefit of the plan's participants, but sadly, reality points to a different outcome unless the DOL looks over its shoulder. The DOL can sue a plan fiduciary if they breach their duties. We will discuss fiduciary responsibility later in this book as well.

One confusing element is that the DOL can potentially issue interpretations of the laws just as the IRS can.

The third regulatory body is called the PBGC. The PBGC can issue interpretations of the law in a similar way that both the IRS and the DOL can. It would probably be simpler for the field of retirement planning if only one of the three issued interpretations of the law, but for now all three are able to do so.

The PBGC is essentially an insurance plan for defined benefit plans. Most employers with defined benefit plans can pay an "insurance fee" of $35 per participant to PBGC, and then the plan participants have a layer of protection, should the employer go bankrupt before all of the participant's benefits have been paid out to them. However, they only guarantee benefits up to $4,500 per month. This threshold is sufficient for most retirees.

If a defined benefit plan ever desires to terminate, then it must first notify the PBGC. This type of termination is considered a **voluntary termination** where the company has a defined benefit plan that is fully funded, but desires to shut it down and switch to a different plan type (perhaps a DC plan) to reduce cost or streamline plan administration (oversight and logistics). It is possible for the PBGC to find that a defined benefit plan is so underfunded that it needs to be forcibly terminated. This is known as an **involuntary termination.**

Given the regulatory backdrop, it is easy to see why many employer-sponsored retirement plans use a prepackaged (or **prototype**) plan, which is predesigned to meet all regulatory hurdles. Occasionally, employers will still desire to customize certain features of their plan. These customized plans do provide more flexibility, but they are more costly to administer and more difficult to establish.

Discussion Questions

1. What were the major reforms instituted by ERISA?
2. Describe post-ERISA trends in the world of retirement planning.
3. What role does an ADL play in the creation of a new employer-sponsored tax-advantaged retirement plan?
4. What is the role of the IRS in the retirement market?
5. What is the role of the DOL in the pension process?

CHAPTER 3

Initial Concerns in Retirement Planning

Introduction

When facing something new, sometimes the most difficult aspect to figure out is where to start. Have you ever encountered a business situation where you felt that the person on the other side of the table was merely trying to sell you something that would benefit him or her more than it would you? This is a huge hurdle that financial professionals need to overcome because those who apply this "me first" thinking have tarnished the industry's reputation. The first place to start is the client relationship. Build a relationship with clients or prospective clients. Get to know them, and get to know what challenges *they* need to solve. Then offer suggestions to meet their need. Suggestions should always come second. But to make suggestions, a financial professional needs to understand thoroughly the various options that are available solutions. This chapter will introduce you to the basic characteristics that separate a defined benefit (DB) plan from a defined contribution (DC) plan. One more tool in the toolbox to help a client or prospective client meet his or her needs.

Learning Goals

- Describe how the fact-finding process is used in choosing between the available plan types
- Understand the usefulness of an employee census
- Understand the fundamental differences between DB and DC plans
- Understand what a "Keogh" plan is

Preliminary Concerns

It is an unfortunate reality that far too many people approach retirement without proper preparation and with unrealistic expectations. It is the job of the financial professional to reeducate them on their assumptions. This can be done at any point, but preparations should begin as early as possible to achieve the highest probability of achieving the desired result.

To help those saving for retirement best, a retirement professional needs to understand the ins and outs of each plan type. Since there is so much information involved, attaining this specialized knowledge can give you a competitive advantage in the job market. In this chapter, we will explore a few of the plan types in more detail. But first, you need to understand how to begin a relationship with any client.

Always initiate a client relationship with the sole interest of finding out how you can help prospective clients solve a problem. Sometimes, they don't even know that they have a problem. This is where you become the teacher and educate them on the benefits of retirement planning, the magic of compound interest, and so on. One mistake that many in the financial services industry make is to treat the prospective client as a sale. He or she becomes only a means to an end. People can typically see right through this mindset. It would turn you off if someone tried it with you, and it is one of the fastest ways to sour a potential client relationship. Focus on the person. Focus on the relationship. Help them as you would want someone to help a person that you genuinely care about, and you will succeed in the world of personal finance.

Once you have established a relationship, you can begin the data-gathering process, which we call the **fact-finding process**. The first step in this process is to identify the client's goals. What is he or she specifically trying to achieve? It is best to be as specific as a certain level of retirement income or a specific estate goal. To simply say, "I would like to have the best retirement possible" is not very quantifiable. If you aim at nothing, you will hit exactly that except by chance. That is worth saying again. If you aim at nothing, you will hit exactly that except by chance.

The next step is called **due diligence**, which basically means that you check to see if the goal is physically attainable. You may find a scenario where a business owner wants to save a substantial sum for his or her own retirement using an employer-sponsored plan, but leave out the employees. After all, they only have a certain amount available to save and don't they deserve it all since they own the company? Due diligence would reveal that this is a violation of the law and cannot be done. Back to the drawing board for this prospective client...the process of due diligence will help to determine if the desired plan is both legal and appropriate.

It is also important to coordinate retirement planning objectives that you are working on with other financial professionals already in use by the client. I am specifically taking about any attorneys who would be familiar with legal issues and any accountants who have a handle on tax concerns.

If your prospective client is a business, then part of the fact-finding process is identifying the company's budget. Businesses must balance the trade-off between the benefits they desire to offer and the cost of providing those benefits. An **employee census** is also a valuable source of information. This document will provide a list of all employees, their ages, and relevant compensation information. You will see how valuable this information truly is, once we learn about compliance testing methods.

Overview of DB Plans

DB plans and their cousins, the DC plans (which we will discuss in the next section), offer numerous design options. However, the associated flexibility makes these plans costlier to administer than some other options like a simplified employee pension (SEP) or savings incentive match plan for employees (SIMPLE), which are lower in cost, but offer fewer design choices.

Under the umbrella of the "defined benefit" plan stand two different plans, the straight DB plan and the cash balance (CB) plan. In a **straight DB plan**, the employer promises to pay a certain benefit to their employees during their retirement. As you can imagine, this open-ended obligation can become very burdensome to employers as benefits accrue over time. The employer bears all of the investment risk because they must make prespecified payments to their retirees. This focus of risk is one key distinction about a DB plan. Another key distinction is that unlike DC plans, a DB plan can award benefits for past service.

A **CB plan**, which is extremely rare to see in practical use, is a subset of a defined benefit plan where each employee has a separate "account" where their benefits accrue. This is different from a straight DB plan, which has one master account from which benefits are paid to the entire pool of retirees.

Overview of DC Plans

While a **DC plan** is offered through an employer, it is very different from a DB plan in some very important ways. First, a DC plan typically involves deducting (or deferring) compensation from an employee's gross pay and depositing the money into a retirement savings account. The most common types of DC plans are money purchase plans, target benefit (TB) plans, profit-sharing plans, 401(k)s, stock bonus plans, and employee stock ownership programs (ESOPs). We will discuss each of these in detail in later chapters, but the following discussion will provide a good overview.

Money purchase pension plans (MPPPs) are retirement savings accounts where both employers and employees can deposit contributions based on a percentage of annual earnings. Upon retirement, the entire cash balance in the employee's account can be used to purchase an annuity, which becomes a stream of retirement cash flow.

A **TB plan** is an account for which a specific retirement benefit is targeted. Contributions are then adjusted periodically to attempt to make this target become a reality.

At the most basic level, a **profit-sharing retirement plan (PSRP)** is a way for employers to contribute a portion of their profits to each employee's retirement savings accounts. We will discuss specifics in another chapter.

The **401(k)** is perhaps the most well-known type of DC plan. In this plan type, employees will make a contribution into their retirement account. Most employers will match the employee's contribution, thus amplifying the savings impact. Various investment options are available within a 401(k). The 401(k) plan type will be discussed in detail in Chapter 5.

With a **stock bonus plan**, the employer will make their contributions in the form of employer stock. Another version of a stock bonus plan is called an **employee stock ownership plan (ESOP)**. An ESOP will typically involve selling shares of a company to its employees at a discount within the framework of a tax-advantaged retirement savings account. These two types of plans will create more demand for the company's shares. One catch is that these plan types are only available to companies who have publically traded shares. These plan types will link employee motivations to stock performance, which can be both good and bad.

Another common form of a DC-like plan is a **403(b)**, which is only available to employees of nonprofit organizations (i.e., schools and hospitals). We will discuss the 403(b) in Chapter 6.

Differences Between DB and DC Plans

Table 3.1 provides a great overview of this section. It points out that DB plans have an inherent limitation called the *415(b) benefit limit*. This limit is designed to set a cap on the amount of benefit that can be paid to any given employee during retirement so that highly compensated employees cannot be unfairly favored. The benefit available to an employee offered through a straight DB plan cannot exceed whatever balance it would take to purchase a life annuity at age 65 equal to the lesser of 100 percent of the highest consecutive three-year average compensation OR $210,000 (2014 limit). The monthly benefit at $210,000 equals $17,500 ($210,000/12). The proximity to this upper limit is determined by an actuary. During the period of attained age equal to age 62 to 65, there can be no actuarial adjustments to these thresholds. If a retiree is younger than 62, then the upper limit is reduced below $210,000 by an actuary, and if he or she is older than 65, then the limit could be raised.

Table 3.1 DB versus DC: Major rule differences

DB plans	DC plans
415(b) benefit limit	415(c) contribution limit
Subject to PBGC	Not subject to PBGC
Longer mandated vesting period	Shorter mandated vesting period

Abbreviations: DB, Defined Benefit; DC, Defined Contribution; PBGC, Pension Benefit Guaranty Corporation.

On the other hand, DC plans are subject to 415(c) limits. Note that DB plans have a "b" in their respective benefit limit, and DC plans have a "c." For DC plans, the annual limit to contributions is the lesser of 100 percent of compensation or $52,000 (2014 limit). The exception to this rule is for those employees who are age 50 and older. There is something called a *catch-up contribution*, which enables an additional $5,000 to be contributed. We will discuss aggregation rules in another chapter, but for now, you need to understand that this limit applies to all compensation to an employee from an employer. The employer cannot "hire" the employee through multiple companies with common ownership to raise the limit for that employee.

DB plans are also subject to the supervision of the PBGC, whereas DC plans are not. Another distinction is that DB plans have minimum participation (from the pool of eligible employees) requirements, whereas DC plans do not. DB plans typically also have longer vesting periods than do DC plans.

Table 3.2 provides an easy glimpse of the key differences that exist between the two primary plan types. In a DB plan, the benefit is specified, while in a DC plan, it is the contribution or sometimes the employer's contribution match that is specified. Benefits earned within a DB plan can be heavily weighted toward an employee's final salary, while DC employees contribute throughout their career, and their benefits have nothing to do with final salary. Employees with a DC plan always know what is being contributed, but the ultimate benefit is at the mercy of their investment selections over time.

Table 3.2 Key difference between the DB and DC approach

DB plans	DC plans
Specifies the benefit to be received	Specifies the contribution to be made
Assets are usually pooled together	Assets are held in individual accounts
Investment risk borne by the employer	Investment risk borne by the participant
Unpredictable cost for the employer	Predictable cost for the employer
Costly to administer	Less costly to administer
Provision for past service	No provision for past service
Not portable between employers	Portable between employers

In a straight DB plan, the plan assets are allocated to one master account and not to individual participants (employees). In contrast, all participants have their own uniquely identified account in a DC plan.

In a DB plan, all investment risk is borne by the employer. They must provide a specific benefit, and if the plan assets take a substantial hit in the stock market, then the employer must make up the shortfall out of operating income. In a DC plan, all investment risk is borne by the participant. The company's only obligation is to contribute any matching dollar amounts, which are not adjusted for inflation. If the participant chooses investments that appreciate substantially, then they will benefit, but they also will directly feel the pain of any losses.

From the employer's perspective, a DB plan has very unpredictable costs. If the investments tank, then they may need to incur a substantial unplanned expense. The employer must weigh the reality of these costs with their desire to provide certain benefit levels for their employees. On the other hand, DC plans have a very predictable cost for the employer. They will pay their matching contribution plus any administrative costs.

The administrative costs for a DB plan are significantly higher than for a DC plan. There is simply more work that needs to be done in checking compliance, calculating actuary assumptions, and determining employer contribution levels.

As mentioned earlier, a DB plan allows past service to increase an employee's ultimate benefit, while a DC plan does not.

A DB plan is not portable, which means that the employee's share of the plan assets cannot be transferred into a separate account if the employee leaves the company. A DC plan, as you will learn, can be transferred to various types of retirement accounts if an employee terminates employment.

Special Plan Type: The Keogh Plan

A **Keogh** (pronounced Key-O) plan is an old plan type that was offered to self-employed individuals and those in partnerships. You will not see any new offerings of this plan type, but there are still some floating around from when they were once well used. They are pension-type plans and therefore have the same limitations and regulatory oversight that would apply to any other pension-type plan.

The calculation of allowable contributions for a Keogh plan has multiple steps. Let us assume that a self-employed prospective client approached you and told you that he or she makes $200,000 per year and would like to contribute 25 percent into their Keogh plan. He or she asks you how much the allowable contribution is because it is unfortunately not as simple as merely multiplying 25 percent by their compensation. The first hurdle to cross is compensation. Is this his or her salary or the net business earnings? As a self-employed individual, all of the earnings of the business are attributed to the owners, not just their respective salaries. For simplicity, let us assume that $200,000 is their net earnings. The next step is to calculate the *Keogh contribution rate (KCR)*. The KCR is calculated by dividing the planned contribution rate (in decimal form) by 1 plus the planned contribution rate. In this case, the KCR equals 0.20 (0.25/1.25).

Self-employed individuals can deduct from their net earnings 50 percent of the Social Security tax that they pay. This is because they pay both the employee's tax (which you already pay if you have or have had a job) AND the employer's half, which your employer pays perhaps without your knowledge. In the case of this example with $200,000 in net earnings, the applicable Social Security tax deduction is $7,049.40. Don't concern yourself with the calculation of this number. We then subtract the Social Security tax deduction ($7,049.40) from the net earnings ($200,000) to arrive at our adjusted Keogh earnings of $192,950.60. We then multiply the KCR (0.20) by this number to arrive at our estimated allowable contribution amount of $38,590.12 (0.20 × $192,950.60). We are not done quite yet...our prospective client can contribute the lesser of the number we calculated ($38,590.12) or $52,000, which is the cap for 2014. Under this scenario, this client could contribute up to $38,590.12.

This is not very complicated at its core, but it does involve a multistep process. Given the perceived complexity of this process, you can understand why business owners might be willing to pay a financial professional to calculate their allowable contribution.

Discussion Questions

1. What are two typical roadblocks that financial professionals face when helping clients plan their retirement?
2. Answer these potential client questions:
   a. Can a DB plan pay the owner of a small business $210,000 (2014 indexed) per year, beginning at age 60?
   b. Is it true that if an individual works for a company and participates in two separate 401(k) plans (through different subsidiaries) he or she can contribute $17,500 (2014 indexed) into each plan for a total contribution of $35,000?
3. John Smith, the owner of Smith's European Delicacies has expressed an interest in establishing a qualified plan for his employees. His goals are to (1) provide a meaningful benefit for his employees, (2) help out a few long-service employees who have been with him for over 15 years, (3) and encourage employment loyalty to his company. Would you recommend a DB plan or a DC plan to Mr. Hopkins and why?
4. Is there a scenario where an employer might choose to combine a DB plan and a DC plan?

CHAPTER 4

Defined Benefit Plan Types and Money Purchase Pension Plans

Introduction

Data from the Bureau of Labor Statistics confirms that an employee is nearly twice as likely to have access to a defined contribution (DC) plan as to have access to a defined benefit (DB) plan.[1] Why is that? Here is a hint…the answer directly relates to an employer's responsibilities and potential liabilities under both plan types. In Chapter 4, you will read about the various types of DB plans and why each might be chosen by an employer. You will also see the different formulas that could be used to calculate a certain benefit level within a DB plan. You will also be introduced to money purchase pension plans (MPPPs) and find out why they are not exceptionally popular in practice.

Learning Goals

- Identify the difference between a pension-type plan and a profit-sharing type plan
- Understand why an employer might choose to offer a DB plan
- Identify how benefits can be calculated using a DB plan
- Describe the basic features of a cash balance (CB) plan and its potential usefulness
- Describe a target benefit (TB) plan and its potential usefulness
- Describe the basic features of an MPPP and its potential usefulness

Table 4.1 Qualified plan types

Pension-type plans	Profit-sharing-type plans
Defined benefit plans	Profit-sharing plans
Cash balance plans	401(k) plans
Money purchase pension plans	Stock bonus plans
Target benefit plans	ESOPs

Abbreviation: ESOP, *Employee stock ownership plan*.

A Pension-Type Plan Versus a Profit-Sharing-Type Plan

Just like all qualified plans are either a DB or a DC plan, all qualified plans are also either a pension-type plan or a profit-sharing-type plan.

Table 4.1 lists the categories different retirement account types fall into. There are three primary distinctions that separate these two categories. The first distinction is the obligation level for contributions. Employers who offer a pension-type plan are obligated to make a certain annual contribution. However, employers who offer a profit-sharing-type plan are not required to make specified contributions. The second distinction relates to the allowable timing for distributions. Pension-type plans have specific limitations on when withdrawals can be made. Generally, the rule is that an employee must be of retirement age to receive a distribution (withdrawal) from their pension-type asset. On the other hand, profit-sharing-type plans permit *in-service withdrawals*, which are distributions while the employee is still working. Certain restrictions apply to in-service withdrawals, and we will discuss those in Chapter 6. The third area of distinction pertains to the use of company stock in the investment pool. Pension-type plans are limited to no more than 10 percent of the assets being invested in employer stock. This measure prevents a pension plan from owning a considerable amount of voting shares and potentially influencing the actions of the company, which endowed it. Profit-sharing-type plans have no restriction on ownership of employer stock.

Why Choose a DB Plan?

There are numerous reasons why an employer would choose to offer a DB plan. One of the key phrases most often cited that might lead a professional to recommend a DB plan is a request to provide an "adequate retirement benefit for long-service employees." The second key distinction is that straight DB plans can account for past service. *This concept is paramount for a straight DB plan.* You will learn more about this concept in the next section.

A DB plan will also maximize the tax-sheltering potential for older business owners. When we learn about the benefit calculation formulas in the next section, you will see how older, longer service employees can receive higher allocations of contributions, which create a more significant tax shelter.

The increased ability for a tax shelter has another side—increased costs to the employer. Sometimes, the cumulative effect of this increased cost can become unmanageable over longer periods of time. Companies usually establish a DB plan with the best of intentions, but the long-term effect is often missed. For example, Ford recently had to use a new issue of corporate debt to meet its DB obligations.[2] It is not the healthiest option to swap one form of debt for another, although it is admirable that Ford takes its pension obligations seriously. Employers need to understand the potential costs that offset the potential benefits. As with everything in life, there will always be a trade-off that needs to be understood.

Another strategic feature of the DB plan is that the company can build a "years-of-service cap" into their formulas. This means that the company could elect to stop accruing benefits after 30 years of service have been provided to the company. Why would they knowingly provide an incentive for long-service, well-experienced employees to consider either retiring or switching to a competitor? Simple...money. Longer service employees typically are paid considerably more than a recent college grad. The company might use its pension plan benefit formulas to alter its wage costs overall.

DB Formulas to Determine Benefits Paid

By now, you should already know what distinguishes a DB plan from a DC plan. With a DC plan, the investment risk resides with the employee, while the investment risk is borne by the employer with DB plans.

The common element to each formula for calculating DB benefits is that the ultimate benefit will be less than the employee's final salary.

The most widely used method is called the **unit benefit formula**. Because it is the most widely used in practice, we will spend more time discussing this formula than the others. The first hurdle is to define "compensation" because it is the basis for applying the formula. Are wages compensation? Yes. What about bonuses? What about overtime? The key here is that if the company defines compensation as wages plus any bonuses but they exclude overtime, then they could have an issue on their hands. Bonuses are typically paid to executives and managers, while the rank-and-file employees receive overtime. Including bonuses while excluding overtime is considered discriminatory to the rank-and-file employees.

The company also needs to establish how they will calculate the employee's **final average compensation (FAC)** because this is a key factor in the unit benefit formula. This could be defined as the highest three years of compensation while employed at the company. They could use the highest five years or the highest three of the final five years. The company can choose how they want to calculate FAC, but they must be consistent across all wage categories.

Another factor for the unit benefit formula is years of service. How will the company decide what length of time has earned the employees a credited year of service? If they work for 25 hours per week for nine months, have they given enough service to qualify as a "year of service"? The benchmark is typically 1,000 hours of service. An employee working only 25 hours per week for nine months falls just short of this benchmark. Recall that one distinctive advantage of a DB plan is that it can provide credit for past years of service. This most often applies if the company decides to add a DB plan in a given year, and an employee has already worked there full-time for 10 years. The DB plan can provide value for that employee for the past service provided to the company. This feature greatly increases the cost for the company, but it is a great advantage for the employee.

A factor for all forms of DB plans is the method through which the ultimate benefit will be received by the participant. The most common form is called a **life annuity**, which is a stream of payments (calculated by an actuary) that will last for the life of the participant. Once the participant dies, all benefits stop. Any money left in the DB plan is forfeited unless the company has made specific alternative arrangements with their employees. I know that this can be difficult to digest, but it is true, nonetheless. You will learn about special mechanisms to protect surviving spouses (like a qualified joint and survivor annuity) in another chapter.

Some plans will provide an additional layer of benefit known as **10 year certain and continuous**. Under this provision, the benefits are guaranteed for at least 10 years. After 10 years have elapsed, the benefits become a life annuity. This option is costly for the company to offer, but it does provide some additional benefit to the spouse of the participant. If the participant dies during the first 10 years of retirement, then there will at least be a benefit for the 10-year guaranteed time frame.

Another universal consideration is the definition of who qualifies for a "normal retirement age." A typical definition is that an employee must be at least age 65 with no less than five years of service to the company. This means that if someone begins to work for a given company at age 63, then he or she must wait until age 68 to retire with benefits.

The actual calculation of the unit benefit formula is very simple. The company will select a certain percentage and then apply it to the FAC with an adjustment for years of service. Consider an employer who desires a 45 percent income replacement ration in retirement with a 30-year service cap. This means that employees will accrue 1.5 percent per year worked up to a maximum of 30 years (30 × 1.5 = 45). So, an employee with a monthly FAC of $10,000 and 22 years of service would have an accrued DB plan benefit of $3,300 per month [0.015 (1.5%) × $10,000 × 22 years].

While the unit benefit formula is the most widely used method of determining a participant's benefits, there are three other formulas that could be used.

The first alternate formula is called the **flat percentage of earnings method**. Under this method, the ultimate benefit is simply a chosen percentage of FAC. This method is required to reduce the benefit received if the participant has less than 25 years of service. There is no explicit incentive to work any longer than 25 years. The only incentive is to qualify for the plan and to maximize monthly FAC. If the company chooses

40 percent for the same employee whose monthly FAC was $10,000, his or her monthly benefit will be $4,000 per month (0.40 × $10,000).

The next alternative formula is called the **flat amount per year of service method**. This method will provide a given dollar amount for every qualifying year of service given to the company. This method does not give any weight to the FAC. It treats the executives potentially the same as the rank-and-file employees. For this reason, this method is a popular choice of union-negotiated deals. If the company elected to pay $100 per year of service, then the employee with 30 years of service would receive $3,000 per month ($100 × 30 years).

The last alternative method is called the **flat benefit method**. This method simply sends the same dollar amount to every qualifying employee. Every qualifying employee might receive $1,500 per month. There is no adjustment for length of service or FAC. This method provides the lowest level of incentive to the employee. For this reason, it is not recommended for use except if cost containment is the primary company objective.

Special DB Plan Types

A **CB plan** is really a DB plan that is designed to look a lot like a DC plan. It is a type of DB plan, but it offers accounts for each participant. These "accounts" are completely hypothetical. They do not hold any real money. They are simply book entry line items on the balance sheet of the company. The accounts are then credited with the actuarially determined required return and not the actual return of the plan assets. If the actual return exceeds the actuarially determined return, then it is the company, *not* the participant who benefits. One special feature of the CB plan is that it must include a *three-year cliff vesting schedule*. This means that after three years, all benefits accrued in the CB plan must be fully owned by the participant.

CB plans are usually reformations of what was a DB plan. A DB plan can simply be altered into a CB plan if the company so chooses. Why would a company choose to establish a CB plan? Perhaps they like the benefits of a DB plan, but they want their employees to have more transparency in the process (like a DC plan).

The disadvantages of offering a CB plan follow the same logic as a DB plan. Unlike a straight DC plan, the company will need to pay for *Pension Benefit Guaranty Corporation* (PBGC) coverage. They will also have higher administrative costs than a DC plan while also incurring a required contribution level. CB plans are still perfectly legal to offer, but they are not widely used because they involve these inherent disadvantages when compared to straight DC plans.

A **TB plan** is a hybrid plan type. It is technically a DC-type plan where each employee has his or her own account, but it feels like a DB plan because the employer makes all of the contributions. The actual contribution is determined by actuarial calculations of the contributions that would be necessary to provide a certain annuitized benefit (the target) in retirement. The actuary will calculate a contribution level, and then that contribution will become fixed. The attainment of the target benefit will be 100 percent, reliant upon investment performance. There are no guarantees from the employer that the target will be reached. The sole purpose of the target is to give the actuary a starting point for determining the initial contribution level. The actuary will use both the employee's age and his or her compensation in determining the employer's contribution.

The contribution limit for a TB plan is the lesser of 100 percent of compensation or $52,000 (2014 limit). The actuary will calculate the contribution, but it is limited to the above-mentioned limits.

Why would an employer choose a TB plan? One reason is if the company has a high percentage of older employees at the time the TB plan is established. Because the older employees have less time for their employer's contributions to compound, the actuary will suggest a significantly higher employer contribution, given a certain target benefit. Following the same logic, older owners will receive a higher allocation than younger rank-and-file employees, should that scenario fit a company's demographics. TB plans are rarely used in practice because other plans offer more flexibility for the employer's contributions.

Money Purchase Pension Plan

An **MPPP** is by definition a type of DC plan. It derives its name from the fact that upon retirement, the entire account balance (the money) is typically used to purchase some form of annuity. Participants are not required to do so, but they usually select this option because this is the option most commonly presented to them. Money purchase plans are being discussed so close to DB plans for two reasons. First, money purchase plans have a very rigid contribution scheme much like a DB plan. Money purchase plans are among the only plan types with required contributions. Second, money purchase plans are becoming as rare in practice as DB plans. A profit-sharing plan, which you will learn about in the next chapter, offers much more flexibility than an MPPP without the constraint of a required contribution. Some employers have chosen to offer money purchase plans because they are contractually obligated to provide a certain benefit...so the required contribution is a moot point.

Unlike DB plans, there is no provision for the past service. All contributions are based on each year's gross compensation. The employer's contributions into an MPPP are always based on a certain percentage of annual compensation. If the employer selects to contribute 3 percent of compensation for an employee who earns $50,000 per year, then the annual contribution will be $1,500 (3% × $50,000). The employer is limited to a maximum of 25 percent of gross compensation.

With an MPPP, all participants will have their own account where their employer's contributions are deposited. They then have the potential to benefit from any increases in investment performance that their investment selections may produce. However, this means that the employee will bear the full risk of the performance of the investments. They could gain from outperformance just as they could be hurt by underperformance.

There is no provision for in-service withdrawals with a MPPP. The balance cannot be withdrawn until retirement. However, MPPPs are permitted to offer plan loans. From the employer's perspective, the costs of administering an MPPP are predictable.

After the enactment of the Economic Growth and Tax Relief Reconciliation Act (EGTRRA) of 2001, which among other things raised the pretax contribution limits, many employers chose profit-sharing plans over MPPPs unless they had contractual obligations to provide a certain benefit anyway. In this instance, they could always employ an MPPP and then add a profit-sharing plan to add an additional year-by-year discretionary benefit if they so choose.

Discussion Questions

1. The owner of a regional car dealership would like to establish a DB plan that helps to retain and reward experienced employees. He also wants to give a meaningful reward to both himself (owner) and other highly compensated employees. His goal is to replace 60 percent of the employees' working wages in retirement.

   a. What type of benefit formula should be used? Why?

   b. Given an example of how the benefit formula could be written.

2. Most employers want to minimize their costs while still offering some benefit to their employees. Why would an employer want to account for past service in a DB plan?

3. Why would a flat dollar amount per year of service be more attractive to union-based employees?

4. A group of construction companies has established a small business with one full-time employee and one part-time employee. The purpose of the small business is to manage union negotiations within the local construction worker population. They would like to establish a retirement benefit for the one full-time employee, and they are willing to make regular but small contributions. What plan type would you recommend? Why?

5. A 54-year-old rural dentist realizes that he has waited way too long to begin planning for retirement. He wants to establish a qualified retirement plan for himself and two younger employees (both in their mid-20s). They are only able to afford an aggregate $20,000 annual contribution. What type of pension plan would you recommend? Why?

CHAPTER 5

The World of Defined Contribution Plans

Introduction

You should already have an awareness that defined contribution plans shield the employer from investment risk. Some plan types provide the employer with the flexibility of discretionary contributions. Others enable the employees to get involved actively in saving for their own retirement. This is a great way to encourage people to understand better and to engage in planning for their future retirement needs. There are also some creative solutions to help small business owners cash out of their business in a tax-favorable way. A financial professional should understand the broad opportunities available under the various plan types and be able to help clients choose which type is best suited to their stated needs.

Learning Goals

- Describe the basic features of a profit-sharing plan and its potential usefulness
- Describe the features and rules that apply to a 401(k) plan
- Identify the difference between a hardship withdrawal and a safe harbor withdrawal
- Understand the compliance tests required within a 401(k) plan
- Describe the rules that pertain to stock bonus plans and employee stock ownership plans (ESOPs)
- Understand how an ESOP loan could be applied

Profit-Sharing Plans

A **profit-sharing retirement plan (PSRP)** offers a very valuable benefit to both the employee and the employer. The employee receives a retirement contribution from the employer, which is always a good thing. A PSRP is treated like a defined contribution plan in that all investment risk resides with the employee. The employer simply makes a contribution, and the ultimate outcome is up to the participant's investment selections. The employer will benefit from discretionary contributions.

The board of directors of the company has discretion over whether contributions are made for any given year. The board can allocate a portion of the business's profits to the employees using a PSRP. However, the company is not required to post a profit to make a contribution. A lack of profits could trigger the temporary suspension of employer contributions. This suspension should not last for multiple years in a row, or the regulators could view the plan as not being active, which could be a problem for reinstating contributions.

Contributions into a profit-sharing plan are based on a level percentage of compensation. The upper limit for contributions into a PSRP is 25 percent of aggregate compensation with a cap of $52,000 (2014 limit). A profit-sharing plan can be integrated with the employee's Social Security benefits. This feature will be discussed in detail in Chapter 8. We will also discuss later the ability to either "age-weight" or "cross test" a PSRP, which are two techniques for shifting a higher percentage of the company's contribution to **highly compensated employees (HCEs)**. Both of these techniques can be used legally to discriminate in favor of HCEs. Pay attention later in this book for a detailed discussion on these techniques.

Consider Johnson's Hobby Warehouse who wants to make a $50,000 contribution to its company's profit-sharing plan. The company has three employees. Employee A (the business owner) earns $100,000, while employee B earns $60,000, and employee C earns $40,000. In the most basic profit-sharing calculation, employee A will receive an allocation of $25,000 {$50,000/[$100,000/$200,000 (total compensation)]}.

Unlike defined benefit plans, a PSRP permits in-service hardship withdrawals. *Hardship* does not mean that the participant is dying to go on a trip. This term is reserved for unforeseen financial emergencies.

In the case of true hardship, employees can access their retirement savings to help lighten the burden. We will talk in detail about this concept later.

Employees are also eligible to take loans from a profit-sharing plan. They can also take a loan from a 401(k) or a 403(b) plan. For money to be eligible for a hardship withdrawal or a loan, it must meet two tests. First, the employee needs to have at least five years' tenure with a given company. Second, the money being withdrawn must have been in the account for at least two years. In July of 2014, a long-tenured employee could access money that was contributed as recently as June of 2012, but nothing contributed in between until the two-year window has moved past a given contribution.

The most important benefit of a profit-sharing plan is that the employer has complete flexibility. Remember this benefit! The two biggest arguments against it are that (1) the company cannot provide for a targeted replacement ratio for its retirees, and (2) there is no adjustment for past service.

401(k)

One of the most well-known retirement savings accounts is the **401(k) plan**. It is often offered to employees as part of a cafeteria plan (where they get to choose which basket of benefits they want to accept from their employer). It receives such prominence because most employers offer a plan of this type. An employer can elect to contribute to both a profit-sharing plan and a 401(k) if they so choose. But unlike a profit-sharing plan, the 401(k) requires the employee to contribute money out of his or her gross compensation. In most cases, the employee's contribution is then matched by the company. According to a recent report by the Internal Revenue Service (IRS), matching contributions are offered by 68 percent of employers, and larger employers are more likely than smaller employers to offer a match.[1] This same report found that 15 percent of employers either suspended or reduced their matching contributions.

The concept of a match effectively creates a retirement partnership between the employee and the employer. The employer's contributions can be either fixed or discretionary. The employer might say that they will match an employee's contributions dollar for dollar up to a maximum of five percent of compensation, but then the employer could also make a discretionary additional contribution if the company's board so chooses, based upon profit targets or some other internal metric. However, sometimes the company will not match dollar for dollar. Some companies choose to match $0.50 on the dollar (1 dollar from the company for every 2 dollars contributed by the employee), while some choose custom-matching combinations.

Employees are always able to make non-tax-deductible contributions. They might consider doing this if they have already contributed the entire threshold amount of $17,500 (2014 limit). You will learn more about nondeductible contributions later. A typical 401(k) will offer an assortment of various mutual funds, annuity products, and perhaps even the employer's stock.

Recall the concept of vesting, which is the point when an employee owns the contribution into their account. The employee is always 100 percent (fully) vested in his or her own salary deferrals (contributions) from day one. It is the employer's contributions that are typically subject to a sliding vesting schedule. For example, an employer might have a policy that employees fully own the employer's contributions after three years of service have been completed.

We will discuss individual retirement accounts (IRAs) in detail later in this book, but you do need to know that 401(k)s have a substantial advantage over IRAs...a higher contribution limit. A 401(k) offers a contribution limit of $17,500 (2014 limit), while an IRA is much lower at $5,500 (2014 limit). A 401(k) also has the added benefit of an employer's matching contributions.

A **hardship withdrawal** is a government-sanctioned way for an employee to withdraw money from the retirement account in the event of an unforeseen emergency. Within a 401(k), employees always have access to hardship withdrawals on the money that was deferred from their gross wages. This access is not limited by the two-year rule, which is imposed on profit-sharing plans. However, the portion of the account that results from the *employer's contributions* is not available for hardship withdrawals.

To access a hardship withdrawal, the IRS has mandated that a hardship event must (1) be because of an "immediate and heavy financial need" and (2) be limited to the amount necessary to satisfy that financial

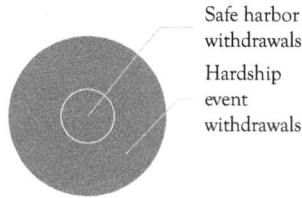

Safe harbor
withdrawals

Hardship
event
withdrawals

Figure 5.1 Safe harbor vs. hardship withdrawals

need.[2] Companies can exercise some discretion in determining what constitutes a hardship event, but the federal government has created a subset of hardship withdrawals that provides a list of events, known as **safe harbor events**, that MUST be considered a hardship event. The company can be more generous than this list if they wish, as long as they remain within the two IRS guidelines mentioned previously.

Figure 5.1 illustrates visually that safe harbor events are truly a subset of the larger basket of hardship withdrawals. The IRS has provided a list of safe harbor events, which includes medical care for an employee, his or her spouse, or dependents, costs related to the purchase of a principal residence, college tuition and related educational expenses, payments to prevent eviction or foreclosure on a principal residence, funeral expenses, and some home repair expenses. Disability is also a common safe harbor inclusion.

Most withdrawals from a retirement account, before age 59½, will result in a 10 percent early withdrawal penalty. Hardship withdrawals are no exception, although there are a few designated safe harbor events that are also 10 percent penalty free. This group of penalty-free withdrawals include needs such as disability, medical expenses that exceed 7.5 percent of adjusted gross income (tax terminology for taxable income), certain payments related to divorce, employment termination after age 55, and a series of substantially equal payments (you will learn about this special feature later). However, 401(k) plans are always permitted to allow employees to take loans from their accounts. We will discuss loans in detail in another chapter, but according to a recent IRA report, only 65 percent of employers have enabled loans within their 401(k) plans.[3]

It should be mentioned that preretirement withdrawals from retirement savings accounts should be avoided except as an absolute last resort. If the money is not in a participant's retirement account, then it is not compounding tax-free, and their retirement well-being may be put in jeopardy as a result.

Most 401(k)s offer a series of mutual funds from which participants may choose. Some funds offer education on investment allocation, while others leave the participants to their own fate. Some 401(k)s also offer something called a **brokerage window**, which is a potential opportunity for diversification if the participants either know what they are doing with investments or they have hired a professional to help them. A brokerage window involves switching some of the participants' funds out of the constraints of the limited pool of investments offered within the 401(k) and into a brokerage account (perhaps at Charles Schwab or TD Ameritrade) where the participants can purchase stocks or *exchange-traded funds* (ETFs) with their 401(k) assets.

As we move forward in human history, the 401(k) will likely be an area that experiences changes. Some employers have stopped offering matching incentives. Others, like IBM, have not gone this far, but they have decided to only make a matching contribution once per year.[4] This has the negative side effect of participants missing out on several months' worth of compound growth, and if they change jobs before the annual contribution is made, then they may miss out on the employer's match altogether.

401(k) Compliance Testing

To prove that they do not unfairly benefit HCEs, 401(k) plans must past a nondiscrimination test called the **actual deferral percentage (ADP) test**. The ADP is simply the percentage of an employee's salary, which is deferred [contributed into his or her 401(k) plan].

The first step in conducting the ADP test is to establish the definition of HCEs. They are anyone who own at least 5 percent of the business either in the current or prior year OR someone who earned more than $115,000 in 2013. Anyone who is not an HCE is by default called a **nonhighly compensated employee (NHCE)**.

Each 401(k) plan must pass one of two tests to satisfy nondiscrimination regulation. To conduct both of these tests, a financial professional will need to know the average ADP for the HCEs and the average

ADP for the NHCEs. The first test is called the **ADP 1.25 test**. With the ADP 1.25 test, the average ADP for HCEs cannot exceed 125 percent of the ADP for NHCEs. For example, if NHCEs have an average ADP of 6 percent, then HCEs cannot have an average ADP higher than 7.5 percent (6% × 1.25). Anything higher than 7.5 percent for HCEs would present a violation of nondiscrimination laws. The second test is called the **ADP 2.0 test**. With the ADP 2.0 test, the threshold is that HCEs must contribute no more than 200 percent of what NHCEs contribute, with the added provision that the difference between the two groups' average cannot exceed 2 percent. That is a lot to digest! Consider a situation where the average ADP of HCEs is 8 percent while the average ADP of NHCEs is 6 percent. The HCEs' rate is less than 200 percent above that of the NHCEs, and it is exactly 2 percent away... so they pass the ADP 2.0 test. What if the NHCEs' average ADP drops down to 5 percent? Then the HCEs are still less than 200 percent above the NHCEs, but they are more than 2 percent different. In this case, the HCEs would be forced to reduce their savings to 7 percent.

Under a rule known as **prior year testing**, the percentage of average ADP for NHCEs in a given year will determine the allowable percentage rate for HCEs in the next calendar year.

The ADP test is used for 401(k) plans that do not have a matching contribution. If the employer offers matching contributions, then the appropriate test is called the **actual contribution percentage (ACP) test**. Both the ADP and the ACP tests follow the same logic. The ADP test calculates percentages based on the employee's contributions only, while the ACP factors both the employee's and the employer's contributions.

It seems almost counterintuitive, but opening eligibility to all employees might create an issue in passing the ADP (or ACP) tests. Consider a company that is very generous on eligibility for 401(k) plan participation. If there is a group of NHCEs that are eligible but elect to contribute 0 percent, then that will dramatically lower the average percentage for the NHCE universe, which will result in a lower percentage of allowable contribution for HCEs.

There is one valuable exception to adherence in passing either the ADP 1.25 or the ADP 2.0 test. The company can make what is called a **safe harbor contribution** to a 401(k) plan. Under a safe harbor contribution, the employer can pick one of two contribution types that would completely eliminate the need for costly annual ADP testing. The first safe harbor choice is for the company to match dollar for dollar all employee contributions up to 4 percent of each employee's compensation. This is the most popular choice. The second safe harbor choice is for the company to contribute 3 percent of each employee's compensation whether or not the employees contribute any money themselves. When an employer contributes regardless of whether employees also defer some of their salary, it is called a ***nonelective contribution.***

According to the IRS, 43 percent of all 401(k) plans are organized as safe harbor plans.[5] This study also found that smaller employers are more likely to offer a safe harbor contribution than larger employers. This makes sense because the managers of a smaller company are more likely to also be the owners or decision makers of the firm, and they are most interested in providing a safe harbor plan to enable themselves to continue to have a retirement benefit and get around coverage testing requirements.

Why would an employer want to make a safe harbor contribution to a 401(k), which locks them into making a certain contribution? If they do make a safe harbor contribution, then they escape coverage testing (ADP or ACP). An employer might not pass the ADP test, but if they are willing to make at least a 3 percent nonelective contribution, then they could establish a safe harbor plan and be able to make contributions for the management and perhaps the owners if it is a smaller employer.

According to the final Treasury regulation T.D. 9641, an important caveat is that if the employer ever decides to stop making safe harbor contributions and just makes normal 401(k) matching contributions, they have a few hoops to jump through.[6] First, all safe harbor contributions due through the cancelation of the safe harbor concept must be made. Second, the plan will now revert to being subject to either the ADP or the ACP test for the full plan year. If an employer who is operating under a plan year from January to December decides to stop making safe harbor contributions in November, then they will be tested for coverage compliance for the entire plan year and not just the remainder of the plan year not yet passed.

Stock Bonus Plans

A **stock bonus plan** is very similar to a profit-sharing plan in that the employer has discretion over the contributions. However, the contributions do not need to be based on corporate profitability. When the employer does make a contribution, it is either in the form of company stock or in cash, which is then used to purchase company stock. A stock bonus plan can include a 401(k) feature, which allows employees to contribute as well. Distributions from a stock bonus plan will ultimately be in the form of company stock.

Stock bonus plans are somewhat unique in that they require accelerated distributions in retirement. Distributions must begin no later than one year after retirement, OR the time period could be extended to six years if the employee separated from service (changed jobs) prior to retirement.

Unlike 401(k)s, a distribution from a stock bonus plan is not rolled over into an IRA to extend the tax deferral further. Distributions from a stock bonus plan can take two forms. The first is a lump sum distribution. In this case, the employee has a unique tax benefit called the **net unrealized appreciation (NUA) rule**. This basically means that the employee can take a lump sum distribution of shares out of the stock bonus plan, but do not pay any taxes until he or she eventually sells the shares. When the shares are eventually sold, the employee will receive the more favorable capital gains tax rates! The other distribution option is to receive what is called a *series of substantially equal payments* over no longer than five years. A series of substantially equal payments will be taxed at the typically higher ordinary income rate.

The NUA rule is a great benefit, but this concept assumes that there is a public market for the company's stock. What if the company is not publically traded? In this case, the stock bonus plan must come with a required put option feature. This means that the employer must offer to buy the nonpublicly traded shares back from the employee at a reasonable valuation. Companies will often purchase insurance to help offset the costs associated with a put option liability.

One of the very important features that is inherent with stock ownership is the standard voting rights. Employees who own shares of stock through a stock bonus plan will retain all voting rights associated with the shares that they own.

The primary advantages of a stock bonus plan are that the employer receives a tax deduction at the tie that shares are contributed to the plan. It also provides the employee a vested interest in the well-being of the company. It is amazing what an ownership interest can do for employee motivation.

There are, however, some challenges that this plan type creates for employees. They now bear the risk of having an undiversified retirement portfolio. Whatever happens to the company's stock happens to them. Now, both their retirement and their livelihood are dependent upon one company's prosperity.

Employee Stock Ownership Plan

An **ESOP** is another form of defined contribution profit-sharing-type plan. This type of plan involves the employer establishing a trust to own shares of the corporation. The shares are then allocated to eligible employees' individual accounts. The company might fund the trust with shares that it owns (treasury stock), with cash from its balance sheet that will be used to purchase shares or from the proceeds from borrowings that will be used to buy shares. More on ESOP loans in a moment.

Stock bonus plans and ESOPs are both designed to encourage the employees to invest in their employer. These are both defined contribution plans that create more demand for the employer's stock. These are both tax-deferred savings options, which means that any growth in the account is not taxed until distributed.

ESOPs are certainly used as a motivational tool for employees, but the real benefit comes from the ability to liquidate a departing owner in a tax-favorable way. The ESOP could be used to purchase shares from an owner who is leaving the company.

One funding method that was mentioned is creating an **ESOP loan**. This is a scenario in which the ESOP will borrow money to purchase shares of stock. The company guarantees the loan, and the ESOP buys shares from a departing owner, from a specific group of investors, or from the open market (secondary market). The company will then hold the shares as collateral against the loan, while they are making loan payments. As loan payments are made, the company will transfer blocks of shares into individual employee accounts.

The ESOP concept and the loan feature, in particular, create a unique tax situation for the company. Any contributions that the company makes into the account are tax deductible. It does not matter if the contributions are cash, stock, or cash for ESOP loan repayment. All inflows into the account are deductible! Recall that profit-sharing-type plans can only deduct up to 25 percent of gross compensation for an employee. ESOPs have a provision that extend the allowable deduction beyond 25 percent if the additional money is used to repay the ESOP loan. *This increased deduction is a tremendous tax benefit for the company and its owner(s).*

Dividend-paying companies can also pay a dividend on the shares held in trust within the ESOP (not yet distributed to employee accounts). The previously nondeductible dividends are now transformed into being tax deductible! Additionally, if the company is organized as an S corporation (meaning pass-through of profits like a partnership but with benefits of a corporation), then whatever portion of the profits are attributed to ESOP ownership are not taxed in the current year! Those profits are taxed as the employee's account balance is taxed upon ultimate distribution.

The most significant ESOP tax benefit is called **unrecognition of gains**. Internal Revenue Code §1042(3) states that the owner who is selling shares to the ESOP can defer paying capital gains tax on their shares *if* the ESOP owns 30 percent or more of the company *and* the proceeds from buying out the owner are used by the departing owner to purchase shares of other domestic corporations.[7] The replacement securities will then have a basis commensurate with the business that was sold to the ESOP. The departing owners will then pay capital gains taxes on the gain in the business they sold when they eventually sell the new replacement securities. Consider a business owner who sells all of his shares to an ESOP, which, after the sale, owns 35 percent of the company. The departing owner's basis in the company was $250,000 and he received value of $3,000,000 from the ESOP transaction. Assuming that the departing owner uses the $3,000,000 to purchase the shares of a domestic corporation(s), then the capital gains taxes due on the gain of $2,750,000 will not be due until the replacement company is eventually sold. The replacement domestic company does not need to be a privately held company. It could be shares of a publically traded company like Procter & Gamble or Hershey Foods. This is a distinct benefit because it permits the departing owner to select the timing of taxation, which can help to manage tax brackets.

ESOPs share the requirements of a stock bonus plan with the exception of a diversification rule. ESOPs must be invested primarily in the issuing company's stock. However, once employees reach age 55 (theoretically 10 years prior to retirement age), they must be given the option for the company to diversify their holdings within their ESOP account. The diversification could be anywhere between 25 and 50 percent of the account depending upon their age.

Unfortunately, ESOPs are not available for partnerships. Another potential caveat applies to privately held companies. Private companies will incur additional expense to maintain an ESOP because they must pay to have the company valued annually and in the event of an ESOP participant leaving the company, they will need to pay the employee cash for the value of the shares. Another concern is the potential dilution effect of new shareholders. If the company issues new shares, then existing shareholders will still own the same number of shares, but with a reduced voting and ownership percentage. The vast majority of companies that offer an ESOP plan are small businesses (S corporations) and the data suggest that those with an ESOP in place perform better financially than their peers who do not have an ESOP in place.[8]

Discussion Questions

1. An employer approaches you for advice on which type of retirement plan might be best for them. After completing a fact-finding meeting with the employer, you learn that the company has highly unpredictable cash flows. They do not want to assume any investment risk, but they do want the ability to provide retirement value to their employees. The executives also want the ability to take plan loans, should the need arise. They don't have any interest in accounting for past years of service. The employer simply wants to offer a benefit to retain their most valuable employees. Which type of plan would you recommend to the business owners? Why?

2. A surgeon for a hospital system in rural Kentucky contributes $17,500 in salary deferrals into the 403(b) account at his hospital. This doctor also operates a private medical practice. He is considering establishing a 401(k) within the medical practice to shelter even more money from taxes. How much can this doctor contribute to the new 401(k) plan if it is established?

3. A company has adopted a 401(k) plan. The participants, their respective compensation, and their applicable percentage contributed (including employee and employer match) are as follows:

Eligible employee	2013 compensation	ACP
Employee A (CEO/75% owner)	$150,000	8%
Employee B (VP/21% owner)	$80,000	8%
Employee C (4% owner)	$60,000	5%
Employee D	$40,000	5%
Employee E	$30,000	9%
Employee F	$20,000	5%
Employee G	$20,000	5%

Abbreviation: ACP, Actual contribution percentage. For 2014, who are the HCEs, and what will be their maximum allowable contribution percentage?

4. An employee who is covered by a 401(k) plan mentions to you that she is planning on taking a $15,000 hardship withdrawal from her retirement plan to pay for an unforeseen emergency to renovate their kitchen before the holidays. What would you tell her?

5. A closely held company has an original owner who is about to retire. The company has a defined benefit pension plan, which has already served the purpose of providing benefits for the current owner. Assume that the owner does not have any family members interested in the business and that the employees have worked for the company for a long time. The owner considers his employees to be potential buyers of the company.

6. Having heard that you took a class on retirement planning, your cousin approaches you with a question about ESOPs. Your cousin owns a portion of a regional engineering company, and he is planning on selling his interest to the ESOP sponsored by his employer.

The ESOP currently owns 52 percent of the company, and your cousin acquired his 10 percent ownership interest 15 years ago for $50,000. The company has done very well, and now that your cousin's portion of the company has risen to $1,000,000 he feels ready to retire at his current age of 66. What advice would you give him?

CHAPTER 6

Plans for Small Businesses and Nonprofits

Introduction

Retirement planning is anything but a one-size-fits-all process. There are so many different types of plans available. There are even plan types that are best suited for small businesses. These plans offer reduced flexibility, in terms of plan design, but they also are much easier and more cost-effective to administer. Nonprofit organizations have their own category. Some nonprofits choose to offer a 401(k) or some other plan type that we have already discussed, but they are the only business type that can use a 403(b). Exhibit A, at the back of the book, summarizes all of the various contribution limits for the plan types discussed throughout this book.

Learning Goals

- Understand what makes a simplified employee pension (SEP) plan unique and when it might be useful
- Describe the savings incentive match plan for employees (SIMPLE) plan and discuss when it should be used
- Determine when a plan is top heavy and what this indicates for the plan in question
- Describe the features and restrictions of a 403(b) plan

SEP Plans

A **SEP plan** is offered through an employer, but is not a qualified plan. It is funded using an individual retirement account (IRA), and it is part of the "other" category mentioned in Chapter 1. From one point of view, it is like a person dressed up at Halloween. IRA on the inside...SEP on the outside.

A SEP is very easy to establish and maintain because of lower regulatory hurdles. This ease makes a SEP a favorite among small businesses. It is very similar to a profit-sharing plan, in that a SEP offers employers the flexibility of discretionary contributions.

When it comes to the contribution allocation formula, a SEP will differ from a profit-sharing plan. Recall that a profit-sharing plan is permitted to contribute, based upon a level percentage of compensation or integration with Social Security, which we will thoroughly describe in Chapter 8. SEPs also can use both of these methods. However, profit-sharing plans can also use age-weighting schemes or cross testing, both of which will be thoroughly described in Chapter 8. The SEP cannot use either age-weighting or cross-testing. This makes it harder for SEP plans to be tilted in favor of older, higher salary employees (owners).

Because a SEP is funded with an IRA, SEP participants are granted the ability to withdraw money whenever they need it. This does not mean that distributions will be tax-free or penalty-free. There may be penalties and tax consequences for preretirement age withdrawals. The point is that SEP participants will have much easier access than in most other retirement account types, and they will not need to be reliant upon plan loans and hardship withdrawals to access savings before retirement like they do with a 401(k). In fact, a SEP participant is not permitted to take a plan loan because it is funded with an IRA.

One distinguishing feature that employers really need to be aware of is the vesting requirement. Within a SEP, employees must be immediately 100 percent vested. If that is a problem for a given employer, then they need to consider alternative plan types.

A SEP has some applicable rules that mimic qualified plans, while others are very similar to IRAs. Like a qualified plan, SEPs can contribute up to 25 percent of gross compensation, subject to a maximum contribution of 52,000 (2014 limit). While 401(k)s are subject to actual deferral percentage (ADP) compliance testing, SEPs adhere to top-heavy rules, which will be thoroughly described in a later chapter.

To summarize our discussion on SEPs, these plan types are most often chosen by small businesses because they are easy to establish and lower cost to operate. The simple allocation formula is also attractive to small business owners. One caveat is that they must make participation available to any employee who is at least 21 years old and has worked for the company for three out of the last five years with at least $500 per year in earnings in each tax year. This means that part-time employees will potentially be covered by an SEP, while they would not be eligible for many other plan types. If a 25-year-old employee has earned only $1,500 in each of the last three years, then he or she must be included in the plan.

SIMPLE Plans

A **SIMPLE plan** is available to any employer with fewer than 100 employees. They must cover any employee who has earned at least $5,000 in any previous two years and is reasonably expected to earn at least $5,000 again this year. If an employee earns $4,000 in year 1, $5,000 in year 2, $3,000 in year 3, $5,000 in year 4, and is reasonably expected to earn at least $5,000 during the current year, then he or she is eligible for coverage by a SIMPLE plan. The years of $5,000 earnings need not be consecutive for eligibility to apply. Like a SEP, a SIMPLE plan will also be available to many part-time employees.

Employees covered by a SIMPLE plan can defer up to $12,000 (2014 limit) of their salary, which is subsequently matched by the employer. Notice that this deferral amount is less than a SEP and also less than a 401(k). The employer match must be either (1) a dollar-for-dollar match up to 3 percent of total compensation *or* (2) an employer match of 2 percent of an employee's total compensation regardless of whether or not the employee contributes out of the gross pay. This second option is known as a nonelective contribution. One neat feature is that if the employer picks option 1, then they could drop their match from 3 to 2 percent for any two years during a five-year period. This gives the small business a little flexibility.

Because SIMPLEs are funded with an IRA, they have IRA-inspired limitations. SIMPLEs cannot offer loans or insurance products. They have certain asset class restrictions, which follow IRA asset class restrictions, and they share tax rules with IRAs. Again, we will explore each of these traits in detail when we discuss IRAs in another chapter.

While SEPs are often compared to profit-sharing plans due to their discretionary contribution feature, SIMPLEs are sometimes compared to 401(k)s because they offer employee salary deferrals and employer matching.

Both SEPs and SIMPLEs must cover part-time employees, assuming that they meet a very low threshold of hours worked ($500 for SEPs and $5,000 for SIMPLEs). Traditionally, we think of SEPs and SIMPLEs as plan types for small employers. However, some large employers, like Starbucks, do offer retirement plan access for their part-time employees. They obviously have more than 100 workers; so they are offering a 401(k) and not a SIMPLE. The SIMPLE mandates that part-time employees must be covered. A 401(k) *could* cover part-time employees, but there is no mandate to do so...this provides a larger employer the flexibility to cover part-time employees now, but they could eliminate this option if business conditions necessitate.

A SIMPLE is easier to administer than a 401(k), albeit with more rigid contribution rules and lower employee deferral limits. Unlike 401(k)s, SIMPLEs also eliminate the possibility for loans. SIMPLEs offer reduced flexibility for the employees, but the lack of a loan provision is actually healthier for their long-term retirement potential. **One important distinction is that an employer who offers a SIMPLE plan cannot offer any other form of retirement savings account.** For example, an employer cannot offer both a SIMPLE and a profit-sharing plan.

Top-Heavy Rules

The Tax Equity and Fiscal Responsibility Act of 1982 (TEFRA) added another layer of compliance testing for coverage of rank-and-file employees. This testing is called **top-heavy rules,** and it is very simple to apply. We defined *highly compensated employees* (HCEs) in Chapter 5. This category of employees was used for the ADP and actual contribution percentage (ACP) testing applicable to 401(k) accounts. Now, we have a new category of elite employees. For top-heavy testing, the upper echelon of employees are called **key employees.** Key employees meet one of three criteria. The first criterion is that they are 5 percent owners. This threshold is the same as for an HCE. The second criterion is that a key employee may only own 1 percent of the business but earn at least $150,000 in salary. The third criterion of a key employee is reserved for officers of the company who earn a salary of at least $170,000 (2014 limit), irrespective of ownership interest. These last two criteria are different from an HCE. Someone earning $120,000 per year could be considered an HCE but not a key employee!

A defined benefit (DB) plan is deemed to be top heavy if 60 percent of the present value of the expected future benefits is allocated to key employees. A defined contribution (DC) plan is deemed to be top heavy if 60 percent of the current account balances are allocated to key employees. At least the percentages are the same as a memory cue!

What happens if a plan is deemed to be top heavy? In this instance, the plan must do two things: have a special vesting schedule and implement a special contribution system.

A top-heavy DB plan must have a vesting schedule that is at least as generous as a three-year cliff vesting schedule or a six-year graded vesting schedule. That should sound familiar because those are already the mandated vesting schedules for a DC plan. They do not have any extra vesting requirement if they are deemed to be top heavy. The DB plans, on the other hand, must adopt a vesting schedule at least as generous as a DC plan.

A top-heavy DB plan must offer a contribution scheme that is at least as generous as 2 percent for each year of service with a service cap of 10 years. This means that the minimum benefit in a top-heavy DB plan is 20 percent of final average compensation (FAC). In a top-heavy DC plan, the contribution scheme must be at least as generous as 3 percent of compensation unless the percentage for key employees is less. There is a special contribution scheme if the employer offers both a DB and a DC plan for their employees. If the employer chooses to satisfy the top-heavy rules with the DB plan, then all is the same, but if they choose to satisfy the rules with the DC plan, then the minimum contribution is now increased to 5 percent of compensation.

Typically, it is small companies that have top-heavy issues. It would be very difficult for a large company, like General Electric, to have 60 percent of the benefits reserved for key employees when the number of nonkey employees greatly outnumbers the volume of key ones.

You will notice that much of the compliance testing is aimed at preventing small employer abuses. Specifically, top-heavy rules apply to SEPs and SIMPLEs.

403(b) Plans

The universe of nonprofit companies has a unique plan available for only them…the 403(b) plan. Examples of nonprofit companies are hospitals, schools, and charities. Sometimes, you will hear nonprofits referred to as 501(c)(3)s. This is simply the location in the Internal Revenue Code that affords them special status. A 403(b) plan is available to any full-time employee of a nonprofit organization. However, it is not available to any contractors who work for the nonprofit. They must technically be employees, and they must be willing to defer at least $200 from their gross pay. If they meet those two simple requirements, then they are eligible.

A 403(b) can offer either employer matching or nonelective contributions. Recall that nonelective contributions means that the employer contributes regardless of whether the employee does or not. Much like a 401(k), loans are allowed, and so are in-service hardship withdrawals.

Employees can defer as much as $17,500 (2014 limit) from their gross pay, while the maximum total contribution (including the employers contribution) is limited to the lesser of (1) 100 percent of total compensation OR (2) $52,000 (2014 limit). A unique feature of a 403(b) is that employees who have at least 15 years of service with an employer are also eligible for an additional catch-up contribution of $3,000 annually.

It is important to understand that salary deferral limits are aggregated among SEPs, 401(k)s, and 403(b) on the chance that employees would have more than one plan type available to them.

Some 403(b) plans are exempt from the Employee Retirement Income Security Act (ERISA), which means that they are exempt from nondiscrimination testing and therefore lower cost to administer. Plans offered by governments, churches, and plans without a provision for employer contributions do not need to comply with ERISA. Noncompliance does not mean that they can do whatever they wish. They still must provide their eligible employees with documentation that contains the material terms of the plan being offered and clarify who is responsible for administering the plan. If a nonprofit is not expressly exempt from ERISA, then it will still apply. If ERISA does apply, then the 403(b) plan will need to pass a coverage test called a 410(b) test. The 410(b) test is a little complex, but basically it says that you must cover a certain percentage of nonhighly compensated employees (NHCEs) (somewhere between 60 percent and 70 percent) to avoid compliance issues. The actual calculation of the 410(b) test is beyond the scope of this book. If matching contributions from the employer are involved, then the ACP test will apply, and if the employer offers nonelective contributions, then they must satisfy a 401(a)(4) test.[1] The actual calculation of the 401(a)(4) test is also beyond the scope of this book. Just be aware that these tests are special for 403(b) plans.

A 403(b) plan can include either mutual funds or annuity products as investment vehicles. If they chose mutual funds, then ERISA is back on the table, even if they are an exempt entity. This is a very important rule.

Discussion Questions

1. A company wants to establish a tax-advantaged plan for its employees. The company is relatively new, and profits are unpredictable with a meaningful amount of variability. The employer would like to reward employees when the company does well and is somewhat concerned that the company has no retirement plan at all, which might make it difficult to attract experienced people to work there. Due to the inherent uncertainty of their profits, the company is extremely concerned about minimizing the costs of maintaining the plan.

2. A small employer wants to offer a tax-advantaged retirement plan to only their full-time employees. Is a SEP plan a good idea to recommend?

3. A small company with 75 employees already has a profit-sharing plan in place for its employees. It is trying to be a good corporate citizen and considering also adding a SIMPLE plan following the 3 percent dollar-for-dollar matching formula. What advice do you have for this company?

4. A company with very stable earnings and cash flow has had a modest money purchase pension plan for a long time. Participation in the plan precludes employees (87 employees) from participating in other plan types. The company wants to encourage its employees to save for retirement themselves. They also want the employees to have access to plan loans.

5. A very small S corporation has four employees. The owner realizes that competing employers are sponsoring 401(k) plans. To compete with the other employers, the owner would like a similar plan, but is not willing to pay significant administrative expenses.

6. A church-based nonprofit organization wants to install a retirement plan that could cover everyone who works at the organization. They have 3 full-time employees and 10 self-employed subcontractors. They are planning on allowing their workers to choose from a list of 15 mutual funds. They are trying to keep administrative costs as low as possible. What advice would you give them?

PART II

Retirement Plan Design

CHAPTER 7

Coverage, Eligibility, and Participation Rules

Introduction

Shouldn't employers be able to offer whatever benefits they want to whichever employees they want? In a perfect world where employers always have their employees' best interests in mind, this could be left to self-supervision. The reality is that left unchecked, many large employers would probably continue to offer a plan for attraction and retention purposes, but they would slant the plan in favor of the executives. Small businesses would certainly slant the plans in favor of employee owners. Knowing these tendencies, and seeing them in practice, regulators have installed a series of checks and balances to ensure that plan offerings are fair for the little guy and that offerings are properly disclosed so that employees know what benefits are available to them. There also must be a mechanism for providing common benefits if common ownership is shared between multiple companies.

Learning Goals

- Explain why the adoption agreement is necessary
- Understand the application of the 410(b) coverage test
- Identify opportunities created by the coverage requirements
- Understand the impact of a controlled group, an affiliated service group, and a leased employee on employer-sponsored retirement plans

Initial Core Concepts

All plans will have a formal document called an **adoption agreement**, which outlines who is eligible for the plan, the vesting schedule for participants, the nature of the benefits, the timing of the benefits, and any miscellaneous options that the participant(s) may have. This document helps to organize the design process. You might see a template (premade generic version) adoption agreement in use, but it is also possible to customize one based on an employer's unique objectives. Adoption agreement design is a natural outflow of the fact-finding and due diligence process. This document is used internally within the plan and is not submitted to any regulator for approval.

We used the concept of a highly compensated employee (HCE) in the actual deferral percentage (ADP) and actual contribution percentage (ACP) compliance testing. Now we will define it clearly. An **HCE** is technically only someone who meets one of two criteria. The first criterion is that the individual owns at least 5 percent of a given company in either the current or prior year. The second criterion is that their income level is above $115,000 (2014 limit). In lieu of this second criterion, the company could choose to use the top 20 percent of wage earners. They might choose this alternate method if they do not have people making above $115,000 (2014 limit).

A company has an employee who owned 4 percent of the business last year and 6 percent this year with a salary of $100,000. Is this person considered an HCE? Yes, this employee is considered an HCE. The same company has an employee who does not own any portion of the business, but the salary was $120,000. What about this employee? This person is also considered an HCE.

410(b) Testing

The **410(b) minimum coverage test** is a form of nondiscrimination testing applied to qualified plans to verify that the rank-and-file employees are not being treated improperly. It is easy to mix up the 410(b) minimum *coverage test* with the 415(b) defined benefit *contribution limit test.* Think of the 415 test being a higher number and therefore associated with the word "limit" as in "contribution limit."

With the 410(b) test, an employer must satisfy *one* of three rules. The three tests are the percentage test, the ratio test, and the average benefits test. If they satisfy at least one rule, then they pass the test and do not have a compliance issue. If an employer has separate business lines, then the tests can be applied to each business line separately with the proviso that the separate business lines exist for legitimate business reasons and they have at least 50 employees. General Electric could legitimately have separate business lines for kitchen equipment, locomotives, and jet engines among others. These are legitimate business lines and could have 410(b) testing applied separately.

There are certain types of employees that can always be excluded from 410(b) minimum coverage testing. These employees would not pass standard eligibility requirements. Examples of this type of employee include union (collective bargaining agreement) employees, employees who have worked less than one year, employees who work less than 1,000 hours in a given year, and employees who are younger than 21 years old.

The **percentage test** is the easiest to conceptualize. At least 70 percent of the eligible nonhighly compensated employees (NHCEs) must be covered by the plan. Simple to understand. Simple to apply. Consider a company with 24 employees of which four are part-time. Their current plan covers 12 of the HCEs and six out of the eight eligible NHCEs. Does this company pass the percentage test? Yes! They cover six out of eight of the eligible NHCEs. This is 75 percent (6/8) coverage. Since 75 percent is greater than 70 percent, they pass the test. No further testing required for this company!

The **ratio test** is also fairly straightforward. The percentage of covered eligible NHCEs must be at least 70 percent of the percentage of covered eligible HCEs. Thankfully, the regulators kept the percentage at 70, which makes it easier to remember given the previous test. Consider a different company whose employee census reveals 100 eligible employees. There are a total of 30 eligible HCEs and 15 of them are currently covered by the plan. There are therefore a total of 70 eligible NHCEs and 40 of them are covered. Does this company pass the ratio test? Since we need to determine the compliance threshold percentage for the NHCEs relative to a percentage of the HCEs' percentage, the first step is to calculate the HCEs' percentage. We know that 50 percent (15/30) of the HCEs are covered. Therefore, the NHCE compliance threshold is 35 percent (50% × 70%). We also know that 57 percent (40/70) of the NHCEs are currently being covered. Since 57 percent is greater than

35 percent, this company will pass the ratio test! But only 57 percent of eligible NHCEs are covered by this company's plan. They do not pass the percentage test. Is this company compliant? Yes! They only need to pass one of the three tests.

The percentage test and the ratio test are sometimes viewed as one percentage coverage requirement where you pass either one or the other. We will consider them as separate tests for ease of discussion.

The third test is called the **average benefits test**. The average benefits test differs from the percentage-style tests in that it examines both the *percentage* of NHCEs covered and the *level of benefits* that they receive. In §410(b) of the Internal Revenue Code, the description of the average benefits test is somewhat vague. The Department of the Treasury has issued several clarifying statements. What we know about this test is that the employer must base eligibility upon objective job classifications like job grade or hourly versus salaried employees. The "group the owner likes" is not an acceptable job classification. The second hurdle for this test is related to the benefits available under the plan. The average benefits of the NHCEs must be at least 70 percent of the benefits of the HCEs. This test is more complex to apply due to the various Treasury Department statements. A company will hire a firm that specializes in this type of testing if it becomes necessary. This test is designed for large employers who cover employees under several different plan types.

401(a)(26) Testing

Defined benefit (DB) plans must pass a second layer of coverage testing, which is found in §401(a)(26) of the Internal Revenue Code. This DB plan-specific testing requires that employers cover the lesser of 50 employees or 40 percent of all employees. There is a caveat that if the company has only two employees, then both must be covered. There is no reference to HCE or NHCE in the 401(a)(26) testing.

Consider a company with 50 employees. How many must be covered? The answer is 20 employees (50 employees × 40%). What about a company with 1,000 employees? The answer is 50 employees! Remember that it is the lesser of 50 employees or 40 percent of the workforce.

Notice that there is no mention about dollar amounts in either the 410(b) or the 401(a)(26) testing. These tests are only concerned with discrimination as it relates to the percentage of eligible NHCEs who are covered by a plan.

Planning Opportunities

One option that a company has is to cover all its employees. Since coverage creates another layer of expense for the business, companies typically want to keep coverage as limited as possible, but still offer enough incentive to attract and retain key talent. This is a complex trade-off.

As a general rule, companies can exclude a few groups of employees without any issue: employees under the age of 21, those with less than one year of service, or part-time workers with less than 1,000 hours of service in a given year. The company can always exclude HCEs and not have a compliance issue. Most testing revolves around discrimination against the rank-and-file employees. Employers can discriminate against the HCEs and not have a compliance issue.

Another option for the employer is to exclude as many as 30 percent of the NHCEs. This would pass the testing that has a 70 percent threshold. As more and more HCEs are removed, the compliance threshold from the ratio test will become lower and lower. In the previous example, if only 40 percent of HCEs were included in the plan, then the compliance threshold to pass the test would be 28 percent (40% × 70%) instead of the 35 percent as given in our example.

The real challenge for the company is to find the optimal level of benefits whereby the company is not paying anything more than what it needs to and the employees feel valued, motivated, and committed to give 110 percent to the company for as long as they intend to work. Starbucks is an excellent example of corporate leadership in valuing their employees.

One additional nuance that can work in the company's favor, while at the same time appearing to be a responsible corporate citizen, is that the company can delay coverage by up to six months once an employee first becomes eligible for an employer-sponsored retirement plan.

Analogous to the decision of a company's level of generosity is the matter of who is required to be able to participate in a plan.

One important rule for participation is called the **"21-and-1" rule**. It is fairly easy to guess what it means. Employees must be eligible for coverage once they have attained age 21 and they have worked for the company for at least 1 year. The exception to the 21-and-1 rule is that the employment tenure requirement can be extended to two years IF the employee is 100 percent fully vested from the moment he or she becomes a participant. We would call this *immediate vesting*. Remember that after an employee becomes eligible for benefits, the employer can wait up to an additional six months before benefits begin to accrue and be contributed for the employee.

Everything involved with legislation and regulation is open to interpretation. The regulators have gone as far as to define what they mean by "one year of service." A full year of service is technically the completion of 1,000 hours of service to the company in any consecutive 12-month period. Technically, completing 600 hours in the first six months of the year, then taking two months off, and then working another 400 hours does not qualify as a year of service. As a bonus to the employee, "hours worked" also includes time, for which the employee is entitled to be paid (holidays).

Aggregation Rules

Regulators put in place aggregation rules to prevent one individual from establishing multiple businesses and then contributing up to the stated plan type maximum contribution limit in each separate plan. If someone could do this, then they could theoretically shelter a tremendous amount of money each year from current taxation.

It has been decided that entities that share common ownership should be aggregated together for purposes of compliance testing and determining contribution limits for participants. Any violation of the aggregation rules could result in plan disqualification, which is when the Internal Revenue Service (IRS) revokes the tax-deferred status, and all contributions need to be unwound with lots of corporate and individual tax consequences.

Related to this concept is what is known as a controlled group. There are two types of controlled groups: a parent–subsidiary relationship and

Table 7.1 Aggregation rules illustration

Shareholder	Company A ownership	Company B ownership	Identical ownership
Tim	20%	11%	11%
John	45%	14%	14%
Rachelle	20%	65%	20%
TOTALS	85%	90%	45%

a brother–sister relationship. In a **parent–subsidiary-controlled group**, one entity owns at least 80 percent of another entity. It is possible for company A to own 80 percent of company B who in turn owns 80 percent of company C. All three companies are now aggregated together as a parent–subsidiary-controlled group. The **brother–sister-controlled group** gets more complex. A brother–sister group exists when the same five (or fewer) individuals own 80 percent or more of each entity AND "identical ownership" is greater than 50 percent. The concept of identical ownership is best explained using an example. Consider the data presented in Table 7.1.

The identical ownership is essentially a tally of the smallest ownership percentage held between two companies in question. In this example, Tim, John, and Rachelle do own more than 80 percent of each company, but their identical ownership is less than the 50 percent benchmark. This means that they are NOT considered a brother–sister-controlled group.

If any two (or more) companies are considered to be in a controlled group, then all entities within the group need to have access to the same retirement plans. If the data in Table 7.1 had instead indicated that Rachelle owned 26 percent of company A, then the identical ownership would have crossed the 50 percent threshold and they would be a brother–sister-controlled group. In that scenario, company A could not offer a plan while company B offers no plan whatsoever. This is an incentive for these owners to monitor their ownership percentages closely to avoid a retirement plan offering issue.

Family Attribution and Affiliated Service Groups

Another loophole that some have tried to exploit in an attempt to avoid percentage of ownership tests inherent in the consolidated group rules is to have their spouse, or their child, "own" a portion of the business on paper to such an extent that they fall below a compliance threshold.

Under the concept of **family attribution**, the regulators have closed this loophole. A spouse is deemed to own the other spouse's percentage of the company for compliance testing unless one of three events occurs. Attribution would not be applied if the spouses are divorced. Attribution would not be applied if the spouses are legally separated. Attribution would also not be applied if one of the spouses has no involvement with the operations of the business.

Another layer of family attribution is applied to ownership by minor children. The CEO's second grader might be an honor roll student, but probably not contributing much for new product launches and global competitive pressures. The ownership interest of a minor child is attributed back to the parents.

The third layer of family attribution is for adult children, grandchildren, and parents of the owner. If the owner holds more than 50 percent of the outstanding shares, then the ownership interests of adult children, grandchildren, and the owner's parents will be attributed back to the owner for compliance testing purposes.

There is a separate category for companies that produce a service and do not rely on investments in fixed assets to produce a return. These companies are known as **affiliated service groups**. If there is a scenario where a few businesses work together to produce a common product, they share common ownership and at least one of the companies is a service organization, then they are considered an affiliated service group. Affiliated service groups are treated just like a controlled group in terms of compliance testing.

Leased Employees and Coverage Rules for Other-Type Plans

Some companies prefer to lease employees from a third party like you might lease a car. Use their services for a period of time and then turn them back in for a different model year. Think of temporary workers. It is possible for a company to take advantage of their NHCE population by leasing a substantial percentage of that category of employees and thereby excluding them from any retirement plans offered by the company.

To be considered a leased employee, an individual must meet three criteria. First, he or she must be working under a signed agreement between the service recipient (hiring company) and a third party (employee-leasing agency). Second, the leased employee in question must be working full-time. In this case, *full-time* is defined as 1,500 hours per service year unless the company's normal employees commonly work less than 40 hours per week, in which case the 1,500-hour benchmark will be reduced to reflect the culture of the company. Third, the leased employee's services must be under the control of the service recipient.

If someone meets all three criteria, then he or she is deemed a "leased" employee. Leased employees can legally be excluded from a company's retirement plan, assuming two events occur. The first qualifying event is that leased employees cannot comprise more than 20 percent of the NHCE population of the service recipient. The second event is that the company must offer a specific safe harbor plan to its nonleased, regular employees. The safe harbor plan must be a money purchase pension plan with the contribution set no less than 10 percent of covered compensation AND with immediate vesting. If the company does not meet these two criteria, then the leased employees will need to be included in the company's retirement plan, whatever that may be.

Throughout this chapter, you have been learning about coverage testing requirements for qualified plans. Recall from Chapter 1 that there is a second category of tax-advantaged retirement plans simply called *other* for lack of a better term. The other category includes simplified employee pensions (SEPs), savings incentive match plans for employees (SIMPLEs), and 403(b) plans.

With a SEP plan, the employer can exclude employees from the company-sponsored plan for the first three years of their employment. As we described in Chapter 6, anyone who is not a union member, is at least 21 years old, and has earned at least $550 in three of the last five years must be included in the plan. The very low dollar threshold will mean that part-time employees will be included in the plan along with the full-time employees, assuming that the part-timers have been with the company for a long period of time (3 years).

A SIMPLE is very similar to a SEP. Recall from Chapter 6 that employees can be excluded for up to two years. SIMPLEs must include all employees (even those under age 21) who have meet the two-year tenure requirement and have earned at least $5,000 per year during their employment and are expected to earn at least $5,000 in the current year as well.

In the nonprofit world, employers use the 403(b) plan, which is treated much like a qualified plan. All employees subject to a 403(b) plan must be given access to salary deferrals (which are commonly matched by the employer) if they could make at least a $200 contribution. A special exception is made for those working less than 20 hours per week. If the employer is not a church or a governmental body and they offer a 403(b) plan, most of their employees will likely be eligible for participation.

Discussion Questions

1. You approach the CFO of a small company about adding a retirement plan for the employees. The CFO tells you that your timing is perfect. The company is actively considering adding a SEP plan. He further tells you that he has already put together an adoption agreement and has sent it to the Department of Labor for approval. Once the official approval comes in the mail, the company would be happy to talk with you about your ideas for implementing a SEP plan. What would communicate to the CFO before you leave his office?

2. Why do you think that a company might choose to define its HCEs as the top 20 percent of wage earners?

3. A plastics company is trying to find a loophole for 410(b) coverage testing. They have separated their production department from their materials acquisition department. The idea is to only offer a plan to the materials acquisition department which mainly comprises skilled workers, while the production department is mainly hourly employees that are easily replaceable. What advice would you give them?

4. A company has 20 retirement plan-eligible HCEs, and 16 of them participate. They also have 75 eligible NHCEs, and 37 of them participate. Does this company pass the ratio test?

5. Is it correct that a company can extend the normal eligibility rule of 21 years of age with 1 year of service to 21 years of age and 2 years of service if they offer full vesting within 2 years of inception of contributions?

6. You are the HR manager at a small company. A mid-tier manager who earns $150,000 annually requests a meeting to discuss his lack of access to the company's 401(k) plan. He appreciates the other benefits and the stock option grants, but by the tone in his voice over the phone, you get the idea that he is frustrated. In fact, he even mentioned that he is being discriminated against because he does not have access to the plan. What would you tell him when he comes to your office?

7. Consider the scenario below where three individuals have differing levels of common ownership over two separate companies. Company A offers a retirement plan, while company B does not. From the perspective of a controlled group, is there any issue here?

Shareholder	Company A	Company B
Tim	20%	15%
Susan	42%	15%
Roger	23%	60%
TOTALS	85%	90%

8. In the previous example, Roger has transferred 10 percent of his ownership interest in company A to his 12-year-old daughter. Could he use this technique to avoid any potential issues with controlled group status?

9. In the previous example, assume that Roger only owns 13 percent of company A, while his wife, who manages the sale team at company A, owns the other 10 percent. Does this new information change the potential issues with controlled group status?

10. A company is in the habit of hiring long-term temp workers for its manufacturing plant. They only use temp workers for noncore production jobs. Of the 400-member population of NHCEs, there are typically about 95 long-term temp workers with the remainder being full-time employees. The company's policy is to exclude temp workers both from health benefits and retirement plan benefits. The temp agency provides those services for the workers, albeit a lesser benefit than the company itself would have otherwise provided. Are this company's actions justified?

CHAPTER 8

Designing Benefit Offerings

Introduction

Talk with any prospective new employee and one of the first considerations on his or her mind is how much he or she will be compensated for employment services. Compensation comes in various forms: wages, bonuses and commissions, overtime, and various other soft forms of compensation. For retirement planning purposes, what comprises compensation is *very* important for discrimination testing purposes.

What would you think if I told you that there are ways to legally skew benefits in favor of either those who are considered highly compensated employees (HCEs) or those who are older employees? Nuts…not entirely. You will learn about these options and more in Chapter 8.

Learning Goals

- Explain why accrued benefits are important in a defined benefit (DB) plan
- Explain why the definition of *compensation* is so important
- Understand how an employer can use integration with Social Security, cross testing, or age weighting to provide either highly compensated or older employees an additional benefit allocation
- Discuss the role of voluntary employee after-tax contributions and the rules that apply to them

Nondiscrimination Requirements

In practice, executives get a lot of additional benefits. The key is to figure out a way to properly incentivize the executives and other exceptional employees while not minimizing the vital contributions from the pool of nonhighly compensated employees (NHCEs).

Retirement plans have great flexibility in designing contribution formulas, but they must adhere to nondiscrimination testing. One of the great challenges of plan design is to give the HCEs as much benefit as possible, while still passing the relevant nondiscrimination testing. Internal Revenue Code §401(a)(4) is the guardian of the NHCEs. It tests nondiscrimination with either benefits or contributions. If benefits are involved, then the benefits provided in a given year are what is tested and not the ultimate benefit to be received. Remember that it is important to distinguish between nondiscrimination testing and contribution limits [§415(b) and (c)].

It is also important to distinguish between an accrued benefit and a projected benefit. An **accrued benefit** is the amount earned up to a given point in time. In a defined contribution (DC) plan, this would be the plan balance. In a DB plan, it would be the benefit earned based on salary and tenure up until the current day. A projected benefit is estimated future value if the current trend continues and various assumptions prove true (actuarial assumptions, asset returns, etc.).

Another question that must be grappled with in considering nondiscrimination testing is: When must a year of service be credited for an employee? For a DC plan, the answer is straightforward. An employee covered by a DC plan will be credited with one year of service after completing 1,000 hours of service in any calendar year. The answer is much more customizable for a DB plan. An employer offering a DB plan can select their own definition of a *year of service* as long as it meets three criteria. The first criterion is that the standard must be both reasonable and applied consistently to all employees. The second criterion is that the standard not be set so high that a typical worker in that industry might not qualify. The third criterion is that anyone who worked at least 1,000 hours must be given at least partial credit. A typical DB definition of one year of service could be 2,000 hours in one calendar year. That translates into 50 weeks of 40-hour workweeks. If this were the standard chosen, then a company has created a window from 1,000 hours to 2,000 hours where employees will need to be given a pro rata partial benefit.

Companies can change their benefit formulas whenever they like with the caveat that only future benefits will be altered. Any benefits earned under the prior benefit formula must remain in place. This is known as the **anti-cutback rule**, because prior benefits earned cannot be taken away.

What Is Compensation?

Another component of employer-sponsored retirement planning that needs a consistent internal definition is *compensation*. Will the company only include wages? What about stock options, bonuses, and overtime? If they include bonuses, but exclude overtime, then this would be considered discriminatory since the HCEs are more prone to receive bonuses and stock options while the NHCEs typically receive overtime. Whatever their definition, compensation is capped at $260,000 (2014 limit) for benefit calculation purposes. This cap enables the HCEs to receive more benefit than the NHCEs, but not the extreme HCEs.

Consider an employee who earned $500,000 in a given year. The employer contributes 10 percent of compensation for all employees into a money purchase pension plan (MPPP). This employee notices that he only received an allocation of $26,000 for this calendar year. He is frustrated that he did not receive $50,000 [$500,000 (compensation) × 10%]. How could this be explained to him? The reason for the allocation being capped at $26,000 is that he has crossed the income cap of $260,000 (2014 limit). The employer simply applied the 10 percent figure applied for all employees to the income cap to factor the retirement plan allocation.

You have heard the term *safe harbor* in other chapters, but we will now begin to apply it to multiple plan types. In general, a safe harbor plan is an allocation scheme that if applied will avoid the need for nondiscrimination testing. A safe harbor plan will require a uniform retirement age applied to all employees and a uniform vesting schedule. The employer cannot have different standards for the HCEs and the NHCEs.

Safe harbor designs could offer one of three basic templates. The first template is a level percentage of compensation. The second template is a level dollar amount. You are about to learn about the third template, which is a plan that is integrated with Social Security.

Integration with Social Security

As previously mentioned, the third safe harbor template is a plan integrated with Social Security. These are sometimes simply called *integrated* plans. The overshadowing concept is that employers can contribute an additional amount for employees whose income is higher than an internally selected integration level. The **integration level** is usually set at or near the taxable wage base (TWB), which is established by the Social Security Administration. Essentially, the Social Security Administration says that they will only tax (social security tax) an employee's wages up to $117,000 (2014 limit). Any money that an employee earns above that number does not result in any social security taxes being withheld from their gross pay or the resultant employer match. This limits the amount of money being paid into the government's retirement savings program for all workers. In this sense, the Social Security system discriminates against HCEs.

Both MPPPs and profit-sharing retirement plans (PSRPs) can use an integrated formula. The caveat is that if the employer offers both an MPPP and a PSRP, then they can only integrate one of the two plans. The other must remain nonintegrated.

Let us assume that a company establishes an integrated PSRP for its employees with the integration level equal to the TWB ($117,000 for 2014). The way that the integration process works is that any employee (typically only the HCEs) who has earnings above the integration level can receive an additional contribution by the employer.

An employee subject to an integrated plan could receive an additional contribution equal to as much as 5.7 percent of their compensation! This is huge for HCEs! There are always caveats…first, the additional compensation to which the 5.7 percent could be applied is capped at $260,000 (2014 limit). The maximum additional contribution that an HCE could receive in 2014 is $8,151 [($260,000 − $117,000) × 5.7%]. Another caveat is that the figure of 5.7 percent only applies if the employer already contributes at least 5.7 percent for all other employees. If the employer only contributed 5 percent in an MPPP, then their additional contribution under an integrated MPPP would be limited to 5 percent. The other caveat relates to the integration level chosen by the company. If the company chooses an integration level equal to the TWB ($117,000 for 2014), then the full

Table 8.1 Schedule of integration levels and the maximum additional contributions allowed

Employer's integration level	Maximum additional contribution
@ TWB	5.7%
80–99.9% of TWB	5.4%
20–79.9% of TWB	4.3%
< 20% of TWB	5.7%

Abbreviation: TWB, Taxable wage base.

5.7 percent can apply, subject to the previous caveats mentioned. If, however, they set their internal integration level below the TWB, then Table 8.1 provides the maximum additional employer contribution at various levels of integration.

Notice the sliding scale of available maximum additional contributions for various integration levels shown in Table 8.1. You might be wondering why at the lowest integration level the percentage jumps back up to 5.7 percent. The reason is because at this low of an integration level, the NHCEs will likely be included as well, and therefore discrimination is not a concern.

Cross Testing

If an employer does not use a safe harbor plan, then they still have two other legitimate ways that benefits might be skewed to the older employees who are also often HCEs. The first method is called **cross testing**, which favors older workers through an annuity simulation process.

Cross testing is a means of testing *benefits* within a DC plan. An actuary will convert all employee plan balances into equivalent life annuities and then test the hypothetical annuity payments for nondiscrimination. You will not need to perform this test, but you do need to understand it conceptually.

This process will benefit all older workers because any underfunding revealed through cross testing can be retroactively fixed by the company making an additional contribution. Typically, the older workers will be the HCEs, but that is not always the case. Theoretically, there could be some NHCEs that also fall into the pool of older workers.

Plan costs for a cross tested plan will be much higher than other plan types because of the extensive actuarial efforts required and the annual testing that must be done to ensure compliance.

A cross tested plan also has a 5 percent gateway, which means that at least 5 percent must be contributed for all NHCEs. In general, cross testing is a good and legal way to skew contributions in favor of older employees, but it does come with higher administrative costs.

Age Weighting

A much more complicated cousin to cross testing is called **age weighting**. In an age-weighted plan, the benefits must be structured so that everyone receives the same rate of benefit accruals. You will not need to calculate an age-weighted benefit on your own, but you will be required to understand how this works conceptually. It will be easiest to explain the concept of age weighting with an example.

Consider a plan with three participants. Jen, age 50, earns $150,000. John, age 35, earns $30,000. Stephanie, age 28, also earns $30,000. Jen is the business owner and she wants to contribute $52,000 into an age-weighted plan in 2014.

The first step is to convert all three employees to the same rate of benefit accruals. We will use a rate of 1 percent of each employee's monthly pay. So, Jen's 1 percent benefit accrual equals $125 [($150,000/ 12 months) × 1%]. Since both John and Stephanie have the same gross compensation, they will both have the same 1 percent benefit accrual of $25 [($30,000/12 months) × 1%].

The second step is for an actuary to use a government mortality table to find the current contribution equal to one dollar of benefit. Since you will not need to calculate this yourself, the table value of $95.38 will be a given. We then apply this table's value to each person's benefit accrual to determine their future dollar need. Jen will need $11,922 ($95.38 × $125), and both John and Stephanie will each need $2,384 ($95.38 × $25).

If we assume that plan assets will grow near the historical average of 8.5 percent, then we can calculate the current dollar amount required to provide the needed future dollar amount. Susan will need $3,506 of current contribution to yield $11,922 at 8.5 percent interest over 15 years (her time until retirement). This is a simple time value of money application. John will need $206 of current contribution to yield $2,384 at 8.5 percent after his 30-year expected remaining working life. Stephanie will only need $117 of current contribution because she has 37 years until reaching normal retirement age of 65.

Now, we will calculate each participant's age-weighted required percentage allocation of the planned $52,000 total contribution. Jen should receive 91.57 percent of the contribution because her current contribution needed of $3,506 is 91.57 percent of the total $3,829 ($3,506 + $206 + $117) required. John should receive 5.39 percent, while Stephanie should receive 3.04 percent. One caveat with this process (there are always caveats!) is that NHCEs must receive at least a 5 percent allocation. So, we would adjust Jen's percentage down to 89.61 percent and Stephanie's percentage up to 5.0 percent. Jen will receive a dollar contribution of 46,597.20 ($52,000 × 89.61%), while John will receive $2,802.80 and Stephanie receives $2,600.00.

That was a lot of work! Because of the level of work required to calculate such a simple three-person age-weighted plan and because someone in Stephanie's situation might be frustrated that she earns exactly the same amount as John but gets a smaller retirement plan allocation, most employers simply go with a cross tested plan if they want to skew benefits in favor of older workers.

Common Choices for Various Plan Types

You have now learned about safe harbor options, integrated options, cross testing, and age weighting. Which combinations are most widely used in the various plan types?

Profit-sharing plans and their various offshoots typically stick with a safe harbor design. They might choose a level percentage or a plan integrated with Social Security. They are able to use either a cross tested or age-weighted model, but the safe harbor is most common in practice.

All 401(k)s must apply either the actual deferral percentage (ADP) test or the actual contribution percentage (ACP) test depending on whether or not the employer offers matching contributions. Because they are profit-sharing-like plans, they can also offer the same design choices that apply to profit-sharing plans. Safe harbor is also the most common design type in practice.

MPPPs, like profit-sharing plans, have access to everything, but employers usually just stay with a safe harbor plan. If they wanted the complexity of the other plan design types, then they would instead offer a profit-sharing plan to capture the benefit of contribution flexibility.

If employer matching is involved, 403(b) plans need to apply the ACP test. However, they avoid ADP testing. They are also profit-sharing-like plans and so they can access safe harbors, integrated plans, cross tested plans, or age-weighted plans. They also typically stick with safe harbors.

The only option for a simplified employee pension (SEP) is a safe harbor. Cross testing and age weighting are not permitted. A savings incentive match plan for employees (SIMPLE) also has specific rules, which were discussed in Chapter 6.

Target benefit plans are not widely used in general. Because they are so close to a straight DB plan, it is usually the DB plan that is chosen if a company wants this type of plan. DB-type plans are being used less and less because of the unfavorable risk profile for the employer. If a target benefit plan were being chosen, then they would not want to use age weighting if there are any older NHCEs. This would not have the desired effect.

A straight DB plan has its own set of choices. A DB plan can use a safe harbor design that offers either the same dollar benefit to all employees or the same percentage of final average compensation (FAC) for all employees. These two options both assume that the employer offers a uniform retirement age. It would not be appropriate for executives to be permitted to retire at 60 while rank-and-file employees are required to work until age 65. DB plans are permitted to integrate their benefits with Social Security, but they have a complex calculation that involves a different calculation for "covered compensation" instead of the TWB.

Voluntary After-Tax Contributions

Up until now, we have focused on employees deferring a portion of their gross salary and saving it for retirement. These deferrals are known as *pre-tax savings*. Employees are also permitted to make **voluntary after-tax contributions** within all qualified plans. These after-tax contributions are similar to taking money out of their savings account and investing in a mutual fund or exchange-traded fund (ETF). Employees might do this through their employers because it is easy, it creates natural discipline, and they like the investment choices offered within their retirement plan. After-tax contributions are tracked in a separate "account" within their retirement account, although the funds are often comingled with the pre-tax funds as well. This means that the retirement account custodian will keep track of any voluntary after-tax contributions and provide a running total on all account statements.

It is most common to see after-tax contributions in a 401(k). Employees might elect to save this way because after-tax contributions can be accessed anytime without the restrictions imposed on the pretax contributions. The ACP test for nondiscrimination compliance will include all employee pretax deferrals, all employer contributions, AND all employee after-tax contributions.

Discussion Questions

1. A friend from your college days has just been told by his employer that economic conditions necessitate that they will be losing their access to an employer-sponsored retirement plan. Your friend tells you that he remembers reading somewhere that the employer cannot alter any projected benefits within their DB plan. Your friend recalls that you took a class on retirement planning and asks if you know anything about this. What would you tell them?

2. A different friend tells you that his employer offers an MPPP, which is integrated with social security. He tells you that he is planning on not participating in the integration portion of the plan because he does not want to sacrifice any money from his take-home pay as a contribution. What advice would you give him?

3. An employer contacts you to provide advice about what to do with their employer-sponsored retirement plans. They have an MPPP and they also have a profit-sharing plan to allow for contribution flexibility. They want to give their HCEs an extra incentive to stay with

the company, and so they plan to integrate both plans with Social Security. What would you need to communicate to them?

4. An employer contributes 4.25 percent of the total compensation for each employee into an MPPP that is integrated with Social Security. They use the TWB as the integration level. A certain HCE who grosses $500,000 noticed that she had an excess contribution of $6,077.50 into her account. She was expecting a much larger number. How would you explain this number to her?

5. If an employer contributes 6 percent of total compensation for each employee, then how much more could be contributed for employees who earn more than the integration level, which is set at 75 percent of the TWB?

6. How can cross testing be used to skew the employer's contributions in favor of older employees?

7. Does the inclusion of older NHCEs limit the ability of an age-weighted contribution formula to skew benefits in favor of HCEs?

8. A small business owner approaches you with an interest to integrate their SIMPLE plan with Social Security so that the company's HCEs are realizing greater value. What comments should you make?

9. A company comes to you for advice after learning that they have not passed the mandatory coverage testing in their 401(k) plan. Upon inspection of their plan, you learn that the employer offers matching contributions and that many of the executives also make voluntary after-tax contributions. What would you say to this employer?

CHAPTER 9

Plan Loans, Vesting, and Retirement Age Selection

Introduction

Sometimes unexpected events occur. Rational people are aware of this. Some of these seemingly rational people are less likely to save for their retirement using a tax-deferred vehicle, like an employer-sponsored plan, because they are concerned that this money would not be available if an unforeseen emergency presents itself. One way to minimize this inhibition to saving is to offer access to loans from their retirement assets. Certain limitations apply, and it is not recommended to take a plan loan, but its existence may help encourage higher levels of plan participation.

At one time, it would have been possible for an employer to say that they would provide their employees with a certain level of retirement benefit, but to receive the benefit, the employee would need to work for the company for 30 years. With this carrot dangling in the foreground, employees would work loyally for a single employer for their entire working career. Some employers began to see an opportunity to save money, and they would find a business reason to terminate these lifelong employees in year 28 or 29, thus resulting in no pension. If that does not make you angry, then I don't know what will. Congress was made aware of this tendency and began to work toward a solution. That solution is the Employee Retirement Income Security Act (ERISA), which mandates certain minimum vesting schedules to help correct this injustice.

Even with a vesting schedule in place for protection, employees will still want to retire eventually. The company will internally determine a given retirement age, but under certain circumstances, they may want to offer early retirement packages as part of a downsizing initiative, or they may want to defer retirement for a valuable employee to retain their key talents.

Learning Goals

- Understand the general features and rules of a plan loan
- Describe when a plan loan could be useful
- Understand why a plan loan is usually not recommended
- Explain the various vesting requirements
- Identify the differences among normal, early, and deferred retirement age

Overview of Plan Loans

The American culture is driven by the availability and use of loans. Loans can be a very useful tool that greases the wheels of capitalism. But they can also be a tool that enslaves people who spend more money than they really have to spend on items that are wants and not needs.

Within the world of retirement savings, participants are allowed to take loans from certain types of retirement savings vehicles. Loans are permitted within all *qualified* accounts and within 403(b)s. Employers with these plan types *may* offer a loan program out of each participant's account, but they are *not required* to do so. It comes down to a choice by the company's management. Plan loans are not available within simplified employee pensions (SEPs), savings incentive match plans for employees (SIMPLEs), or any other plan type, which are funded by an individual retirement account (IRA). They are most commonly offered within 401(k)s and 403(b)s. It is possible to allow them within either a straight defined benefit (DB) plan or a cash balance plan, but the exponential administrative hassles typically encourage those employers to forgo them.

The simple reason they are offered is to encourage participation. If the employees know that they could still access their retirement savings in the event of a real need, then they may be more inclined to participate.

The logic behind plan loans runs counterintuitive to the stated purpose of retirement planning. If money is withdrawn from a retirement account to create a personal loan, then that same money is not compounding within the plan. I have seen this work favorably in one situation. Imagine a poor stock market environment. Perhaps even a negative year. A certain participant's 401(k) assets are declining in value as is the general market. The participant takes a personal loan from the 401(k) to buy a car. He or she is paying 4 percent interest on his or her plan loan. To whom is he or she paying this interest? To himself or herself! As he or she makes loan payments, covering both principal and interest, they are redeposited into the 401(k) account. He or she is effectively earning 4 percent on that block of money while his or her other assets may be declining with the general market. However, this is a risky bet. For this client, the market just happened to be nearly a net zero return during the tenure of the loan. He or she was lucky, but this is a very rare circumstance.

There are three scenarios in which participants do not want to take a loan. The first scenario is when the investments within their 401(k) would earn them considerably more than the loan interest rate (opportunity cost of capital). The second and third scenarios will be explored in more detail later in this chapter. The basic concept of the second scenario relates to the participants proximity to retirement. The third scenario relates to a participant possibly not being able to repay the loan and therefore defaulting on themselves.

Plan Loan Rules and Administration

ERISA has a few rules in place to govern the use of plan loans. The first stipulation is that they must be reasonably available to all participants within a plan if they are offered at all. It would be discriminatory if plan loans were only available to executives or business owners and not available to the rank-and-file employees. The second ERISA stipulation is that the loans must be "adequately secured." This is generally interpreted to mean that any plan loans should not exceed 50 percent of the vested balance in the account. Plan loans are essentially secured by the assets that remain left in the retirement account. The third ERISA mandate is that plan loans must charge a reasonable rate of interest. This is generally thought to mean that the plan should use a current market loan rate. They cannot offer loans at 1.5 percent interest if loans everywhere else are charging 5.5 percent. This would create (1) an unfair advantage for plan participants and (2) demand for loans that may not be *needed*.

The Internal Revenue Service (IRS) has its own set of rules governing plan loans. To avoid the loan being deemed a "withdrawal," the loan cannot exceed the lesser of $50,000 or 50 percent of the vested account balance. This last sentence is VERY important to understand! This loan limit is reduced if there are other outstanding loans from the plan. The IRS also mandates that all plan loans must be paid back within five years (five-year level amortization). The one exception to the five-year payback rule is for a loan to purchase a house. The payback period is then 30 years, but this presents some other challenges. Do you really think that the available return on plan assets over a 30-year time period will be less than the current market interest rate? Taking a 30-year mortgage loan from your retirement account is unwise.

Another reason that 30-year plan loans are unwise is because of the increased risk of default over that long a time period. If an employee retires and still has an outstanding loan balance, then he or she is deemed to have defaulted on the loan. What if an employee actually defaults on a plan loan by missing a series of payments? In a default scenario, whether actual or deemed, the remaining plan loan balance is considered a withdrawal by the IRS. Withdrawals from retirement accounts are 100 percent taxable as ordinary income. Can you imagine defaulting for whatever reason on a $50,000 plan loan? If the participants could not make monthly payments, where will they come up with the money for taxes? To compound the potential severity of this situation, if the default occurs before the participants are 59½ years old, then they will also incur an additional 10 percent penalty payable to the Department of the Treasury as a penalty for taking an early withdrawal. Tread cautiously…

Companies often try to reduce the potential of plan loan defaults by requiring loan payments to be deducted from gross wages at every pay period. They may also require the loan to be paid in full upon termination of employment. This would mean that the other assets (collateral) within a participant's account might be sold to repay the loan to avoid the requisite implications of a withdrawal. Both of these policies are useful to employees, but require more administrative oversight within the plan. That means more costs for the employer.

Another component of plan administration is enforcing spousal notification before a plan loan occurs. Retirement assets are considered marital property. It would not be fair for a participant to take a loan, squander the money, and then default without their spouse even knowing about it. Unfortunately, in our modern world, marriages sometimes do not last. A plan loan would also potentially remove marital assets from divorce proceedings. For these reasons, plan loans require spousal consent. This is also another step for the company to supervise...ergo, assume more administrative expense.

One reason why plan loans are popular is that they reduce a participant's inhibitions with respect to saving money for retirement. Most people want something tangible they can touch and feel today...not 30 years from now. They know that they have less money to spend now, but the potential reward of a secure retirement in the future is sometimes difficult to conceptualize. Enabling a plan loan helps alleviate some of their anxiety.

One subgroup of participants who often find this to be a psychological teddy bear are the business owners. They sometimes want to be able to access their retirement savings in the event that a business need arises. For them, flexibility is key.

Another reason they are popular is that this category of administrative costs can be somewhat minimized by how the loans are made available. Some companies will limit plan loans to certain events like paying for a college education, purchasing a car or home, or hardship. Limiting the acceptable categories could slow loan demand and thereby reduce administrative costs. Another acceptable way to slow loan demand is to set a loan minimum at $1,000 to eliminate multiple small loans from a given participant.

Plan loans might be used as a carrot to entice participation among the nonhighly compensated employee (NHCE) population of a company. If this strategy were to be successful, then the actual deferral percentage (ADP) or actual contribution percentage (ACP) testing would be easier to pass.

Some plan types, like the money purchase plan, which do not permit hardship withdrawal could use plan loans as a way of still providing access to retirement savings and thereby legally getting around the regulatory restriction against hardship withdrawals.

Required Vesting Schedules

Recall from our previous discussions that *vesting* is the retirement planning term for complete ownership of the assets within your retirement plan. Before ERISA came along, employers could set any vesting schedule that pleased them. Often, they would say something like "All participants must work for our company for 30 years before they become vested in their retirement plan." This allowed for tons of potential abuse. What would happen if the company *decided* to lay a group of employees off in their 29th year of employment? Zero retirement benefits. A series of abuses brought this issue to light in Congress, and ERISA was born in part to address this very issue in Title II. Now, there are two mandatory combinations that could be applied. One for DB plans and one for defined contribution (DC) plans. Employers can be more generous than these minimum standards, but they must at least match them.

DB plans must offer either a five-year cliff vesting schedule (Table 9.1) or a seven-year graded vesting schedule (Table 9.2) as shown in the tables below.

Table 9.1 Defined benefit five-year cliff vesting schedule

Years of service	Percentage vested
0–4	0%
5+	100%

Table 9.2 Defined benefit seven-year graded vesting schedule

Years of service	Percentage vested
0–2	0%
3	20%
4	40%
5	60%
6	80%
7	100%

Table 9.3 Defined contribution three-year cliff vesting schedule

Years of service	Percentage vested
0–2	0%
3+	100%

Table 9.4 Defined contribution six-year graded vesting schedule

Years of service	Percentage vested
0–1	0%
2	20%
3	40%
4	60%
5	80%
6	100%

Just to keep everyone on their toes, the regulators have decided that DC plans must offer either a **three**-year cliff vesting schedule (Table 9.3) or a **six**-year graded vesting schedule (Table 9.4) as shown in the tables above.

You can see that the DC plan has the required minimum schedule, which is more accelerated than its DB plan cousins. Employers can always be more generous than these mandated minimum standards, but they must meet at least these thresholds.

General Vesting Considerations

Despite the vesting schedules you just learned about, full (100 percent) vesting is still required under certain circumstances. Full vesting is required upon the attainment of full retirement age, which currently is no younger than age 66. Full vesting is also required if a plan decides to terminate for any reason. We already learned that participants are always fully vested in their salary deferrals. There is also full and immediate vesting with SEP plans, SIMPLE plans, and 401(k) plan when a safe harbor option is in use.

What would happen to the unvested balanced if employees were to sever employment before they were fully vested? Should the money just go back to the company since they funded the contribution in the first place? This scenario is actually called a **reallocation forfeiture**. With a reallocation forfeiture, the unvested balanced of a terminated employee will be redistributed among the other employees. Only if the dollar amount of reallocation forfeitures exceeds the contribution limits plus any plan expenses, would the money revert to the sponsoring company.

Another consideration in the world of vesting is the definition of a year of service. For the purposes of vesting, a year of service is generally thought to mean at least 1,000 hours within 12 consecutive months. There are certain credited hours, which can be specifically excluded. Any years of service earned before a plan was established (prior service) can be excluded when calculating vesting tenure. Any employment before age 18 can also be excluded. Do not confuse this with the 21-year-old threshold for plan eligibility. There is a window between age 18 and 21 when an employee could be accruing years of service for vesting purposes but not yet eligible for plan inclusion (at age 21). Another exclusion for vesting purposes is called the break-in-service rule.

The **break-in-service rule** applies to any year when an employee does not complete at least 500 hours of service. The employer is free to apply this rule or disregard it if they so wish, but they must apply their standard uniformly for all employees. Under this rule, three things could happen. First, any prebreak service could be disregarded for vesting purposes until the employee is reemployed with at least 1,000 hours in a service year. The second event that could happen is *only for DC plans*. The nonvested portion of the participants' accounts could be permanently forfeited if they should incur five consecutive breaks in service. The third possibility is that the company could elect to not aggregate prebreak and postbreak service for computing vesting tenure IF the employee is 0 percent vested and there are five consecutive breaks in service. Because this last possibility is so difficult to administer and monitor, it is rarely ever applied in practice, although it could be.

Normal Retirement Age

In the context of retirement plan design, an employer has the ability to establish an internal retirement age for their participants. This is the age at which they would be entitled to full benefits through employer-sponsored plans. It has been common to see either age 62 or 65 selected as a given

Table 9.5 Normal retirement ages for social security

Year of birth	Normal retirement age
1943–54	66
1955	66 and 2 months
1956	66 and 4 months
1957	66 and 6 months
1958	66 and 8 months
1959	66 and 10 months
1960 and later	67

plan's normal retirement age (NRA). Why age 62 or age 66? Easy; age 62 is when someone could begin to apply for Social Security benefits, and age 66 is the current threshold technically defined as the NRA. The NRA is when someone could begin to collect full benefits from Social Security. The NRA will likely be a moving target as Social Security is expected to periodically adjust their relevant retirement ages to combat budgetary shortfalls. The current schedule of NRAs from the Social Security Administration is listed in Table 9.5.

The most restrictive internal retirement age is generally age 66 (or perhaps 67) with a minimum of five years of service. The five years of service caveat will prevent someone from working for an employer for only a few years to receive a retirement benefit. If someone began working at a given company at age 64, then their internal retirement age would then be 69.

Early Retirement

When persons begins their working career, their goals are often to make a difference in their company and to maximize their career potential. As they age, a new goal of retiring as soon as humanly possible begins to emerge. They must weigh numerous pros and cons in their analysis, and we will look at some of those here.

Technically, **early retirement** is any retirement date prior to the NRA. Sometimes, early retirement is thrust upon an employee due to downsizing or disability. Downsizing cannot be used as a legitimate tool to target forcing older workers out of a business. Often when a company determines that downsizing is necessary, they may offer an early retirement option and then commence with strategic layoffs to the extent that employees have not voluntarily agreed to take early retirement. Those who take early retirement in this scenario are most likely very well prepared, and their sacrifice will typically save a younger employee's job (or less prepared older employee's job). Any early retirement packages offered by the company will represent an additional retirement cost to the employer beyond what the actuaries have already estimated for the retiree. Typically, companies will impose a minimum length-of-service requirement to be available for an early retirement package. The company can set whatever internal threshold of service they prefer.

One way for an employer to encourage early retirement, which would save on the cost of both wages and benefits like health insurance, is to use a years-of-service cap in their retirement savings contribution formula. If employees know that the company will stop contributing to their plan after 30 years of service have been provided, they may have less incentive to remain with the company. However, it is important to understand that the Federal Age Discrimination in Employment Act (FADEA) does not permit termination of employment to be based upon the age of the employee. The sunsetting of an employee must be based solely upon business needs.

Deferred Retirement

Yet, some employees choose to work beyond the internal retirement threshold age. They might choose to keep working because they love what they do and feel that they can continue to make a solid contribution.

Employees might work past the NRA because they began working for the company in their mid-60s, and they have not yet fulfilled the five years of service requirement to receive full benefits. Under a less desirable scenario, the employee might simply be unprepared for retirement due to poor planning or poor market performance.

Whatever the reason for remaining employed, the company is required to continue contributing to either a DC plan or a DB plan for employees who work beyond the NRA. The only exception to this rule is if the company has imposed a service cap, at perhaps 30 years of service, and the employee has already crossed this threshold.

Discussion Questions

1. A friend of yours owns a small business, and he offers a SIMPLE plan to his employees. His restrictive cash management policy has created a short-term problem, leaving him short on cash for payroll. He is considering taking a short-term loan from his personal SIMPLE account to fix the problem. What would you tell your friend?

2. A different friend works at a company with a 401(k). His vested balance is $75,000, and he is planning on taking a loan for the whole vested balance to buy a rental property. What advice would you have for your friend?

3. A medium-sized employer is planning on offering a plan loan feature within their 401(k). They have decided that 2.5 percent is a decent interest rate to offer to their employees. What advice would you have for this employer?

4. Is this vesting schedule permitted in a DB plan?

Years of service	Percentage vested
0–2	0%
3	10%
4	30%
5	70%
6	90%
7	100%

5. Is this vesting schedule permitted in a DB plan?

Years of service	Percentage vested
0–2	0%
3	25%
4	50%
5	75%
6	100%

6. Is this vesting schedule permitted in a DC plan?

Years of service	Percentage vested
0–1	0%
2	20%
3	40%
4	60%
5	80%
6	100%

7. Is this vesting schedule permitted in a DC plan?

Years of service	Percentage vested
0–1	0%
2	10%
3	30%
4	100%

8. What is the maximum loan that can be taken by the following employees?

Employee	Vested account balance	% of ownership
Employee A	$17,000	0%
Employee B	$160,000	0%
Employee C	$200,000	50%

9. A 41-year-old employee has taken a plan loan for 50 percent of his vested balance ($20,000 loan) to buy a car. Three years into the loan repayment, he loses his job. He is single and ends up living off unemployment for over a year while looking for a new job. During this job search process, he becomes unable to repay the remainder of his 401(k) loan, and he defaults on himself. What happens?

10. Respond to an employer's statement that they "are concerned about administrative hassles of implementing the required break-in-service rules."

11. In a defined benefit plan, how can the employer legally limit the benefits for older, longer service employees without violating age discrimination laws?

CHAPTER 10

Death and Disability Planning

Introduction

In Chapter 9, you learned about the ways that plan loans can help participants and their families deal with unforeseen emergencies. But, what if that unforeseen emergency is the premature death of the participant? This chapter will describe protections for the surviving spouse in particular.

Another common death-oriented protection is life insurance. Life insurance can be purchased within certain types of employer-sponsored plans, but there are limits on the amount of the benefit. This will also be described in this chapter.

What if the participant does not die prematurely, but instead becomes disabled? Some companies elect to provide benefits to help the participant and the family.

Learning Goals

- Explain the common options for preretirement death planning
- Understand the limitations imposed by the incidental death benefit rule
- Describe why it may be beneficial to provide preretirement death benefits outside of an employer-sponsored retirement plan
- Describe common disability provisions in employer-sponsored plans

Preretirement Death Planning

What happens if you are covered under either a defined benefit (DB) plan or a defined contribution (DC) plan and die in the preretirement (before retirement) period? A preretirement death is especially a problem for married participants. The surviving spouse had been planning on the benefits for a joint retirement. Many employers offer a solution to this unexpected event.

One such solution is called a **qualified joint and survivor annuity (QJSA)**. The QJSA is an insurance overlay to a qualified plan that only applies to married participants. It is available in defined benefit plans, cash balance plans, and money purchase plans. QJSAs are also available in profit-sharing and 401(k) plans if the employer offers an annuity option in those plans. If a participant selects the QJSA option and the employer does not subsidize this benefit, then the participant's payment stream in retirement will be reduced to compensate for the longer term benefit of a QJSA. The benefit is that the participants will receive payments during their lifetime, but at their death, their surviving spouse will continue to receive payments. Benefits payable to a surviving spouse under a QJSA must be no less than 50 percent of the payments that the participants received before their death. If a married participant elects to waive the QJSA option and simply receive the higher monthly payments offered by a non-QJSA payment stream, then both the participant *and* their spouse must sign a waiver of this option.

Similar in concept to the QJSA is the **qualified preretirement survivor annuity (QPSA)**. The QPSA is basically the same thing as a QJSA with one important distinction. The QJSA is a payment stream for both the participant and surviving spouse in which the participant retired, selected the option, and then died sometime during retirement. The QPSA applies to participants who die in the preretirement phase (before they reach the point of retiring). The participants did not live long enough to retire and receive benefits themselves, so their surviving spouse will now receive benefits that match the benefits that they would have received under a QJSA arrangement (no less than 50 percent of what the now deceased participant would otherwise have received).

It is common to provide the QPSA to spouses who have been married for at least one year, although this one-year threshold can easily be waived by the employer. There is no mandatory payout for unmarried participants who die before they begin to receive benefits. Some companies are good citizens and provide a lump-sum payment to the deceased employee's estate, but they are not required to do so.

The law requires that QJSA and QPSA be made available to participants, but there is no requirement that the company pay for the additional benefit. Sometimes, the employee bears the cost and sometimes the company does so at their discretion, but they should be consistent. It would not be appropriate for the company to pay for the benefit for highly compensated employees (HCEs) and not pay for the benefit for nonhighly compensated employees (NHCEs).

It is worth mentioning that if someone has his or her own balance in a DC plan and dies in the preretirement phase, then his or her balance is still part of the estate that becomes inherited by the heirs. For example, if employee A has $250,000 in his 401(k) and he dies at age 53, then his estate will receive the $250,000 in accordance with the deceased's will and the laws of the relevant state in which he lives.

Incidental Death Benefit Rule

Sometimes, it is more convenient for a participant to own life insurance within the retirement plan rather than outside. Insurance is disallowed in any retirement vehicle funded by an individual retirement account IRA [like simplified employee pensions (SEPs) and savings incentive match plan for employees (SIMPLEs)] and in 403(b) plans, but it is permitted in all other *qualified* plans. For a qualified plan to remain qualified, any insurance-related benefits, like QJSA or actual life insurance, must provide only an incidental benefit.

The term *incidental* sounds nebulous, but it has been specifically defined. In a DC plan, the aggregate premiums paid over the lifetime of a life insurance contract cannot exceed 25 percent of aggregate employer contributions for term life insurance or 50 percent of aggregate employer contributions for whole life insurance. In a DB plan, the 25 percent and 50 percent rules can be followed OR they can follow a new rule.

The **100-1 rule** states that the death benefit from life insurance purchased within a DB plan cannot exceed 100 times the expected monthly benefit. For example, if a participant is expected to receive $1,500 per month in retirement, then his or her maximum acceptable life insurance amount on insurance held within the DB plan is $150,000.

There are only two exceptions to the incidental benefit rule. The first exception is insurance purchased with after-tax contributions. Employees can always purchase as much life insurance as they want with after-tax dollars. The only limitations are on insurance policies purchased under the umbrella of a tax-advantaged retirement plan. The second exemption is for profit-sharing plans. Profit-sharing plans can purchase whatever insurance they wish, assuming that the company permits in-service withdrawals *and* the insurance premiums do not exceed the amount of money that would have otherwise been available for an in-service withdrawal.

Before we discuss why someone would even want to own life insurance within their retirement account, we need to understand a few tax implications. The ultimate death benefit (proceeds) of life insurance purchased with after-tax dollars is tax-free. This is one of the allures of life insurance. It has tremendous potential for estate planning. However, when life insurance is purchased within a retirement account, the exact opposite of this tax scenario is true. An estimate is made of the cost of the insurance, and this is added to the respective employee's W-2 (taxable wages). The amount added to an employee's W-2 creates a cost basis within the qualified account. Then, the ultimate death benefit is paid into the retirement account, which creates a large qualified plan balance that becomes taxable income for the beneficiary when distributions are ultimately made.

Table 10.1 provides selected data from Internal Revenue Service (IRS) table 2001, which is used to determine the imputed cost of insurance for a covered participant. Consider a 50-year-old employee who is a participant in a money purchase plan. This employee has a life insurance benefit in the plan of $250,000. According to table 2001, the cost of $1,000 of benefit is estimated to be $2.30. This employee will have $575 [$2.30 × ($250,000/$1,000)] added to the annual W-2 for tax purposes. This dollar amount will compile a cost basis over the years. The amount determined from IRS table 2001 that is added to each employee's W-2

Table 10.1 Selected data from IRS table 2001

Attained age	Interpolated annual rates
40	1.10
45	1.53
50	2.30
55	4.15
60	6.51

Abbreviation: IRS, Internal Revenue Service.

accumulates a cost basis just like nondeductible IRA contributions, which you will learn about in Chapter 17. The participant's surviving spouse, who inherits the retirement account, would then deal with pro rata cost basis recovery, which you will also learn about in Chapter 17. This is done so that there is no double taxation. Most often, the premiums are paid by the employer and then imputed to the employees on their W-2 rather than literally being paid by the employee. The government uses table 2001 to estimate the cost of insurance because it is easier for the government to track that way rather than auditing everyone for the exact amount of actual premiums paid.

If the "employer" is a self-employed individual, then they will have a dilemma because self-employed persons cannot deduct insurance costs on their business returns. They must take them as a deduction on their personal returns subject to various limits.

Now for the promised discussion of why. From the employees' perspective, holding life insurance within their retirement account can build a significantly larger account balance, which would be available for their surviving spouse or other heirs. It becomes even more attractive if the employer offers to pay for it and just make it part of the package. From the employer's perspective, offering an insurance component in their retirement plan is another boost for attraction and retention of valuable employees. If they buy insurance as a group, they will have access to the greatly discounted group insurance rates. Buying as a group can also have favorable underwriting outcomes. There may be some employees who would not be able to qualify for life insurance on their own due to a medical condition, but the group status may subvert the need for medical examination to qualify for coverage.

Large- and medium-sized companies typically prefer to provide insurance outside of the umbrella of a retirement plan. This enables them to avoid the benefit limitations, and the ultimate proceeds are then tax-free. Small companies usually prefer insurance within a retirement plan. Why? In small companies, the decision makers are often the business owners. They can build a large benefit for their heirs and shift an otherwise personal expense (the actual insurance premiums) over to a business expense.

Disability Benefits

Just as companies can provide a solution to offset the untimely death of an employee, they can also offer benefits in the event of disability. The first item to be addressed by a company who is considering offering a disability benefit is to define *disability* clearly and objectively. The easiest way to do this is to assume a third-party definition. The safest path for a company is simply to adopt the definition of disability as endorsed by the Social Security Administration. If the board of directors determines a different definition, then they may be opening themselves up to potential litigation.

Some companies offer a formal disability insurance program. In such a case, they should be careful to coordinate any disability programs offered through their retirement plan with that already covered by insurance. If there is overlap, then the disability insurance the employer has already been paying for could deny the claim based upon duplicate coverage.

Typically, the first thing that a company will do when disability occurs is to declare the disabled employee fully vested. Some plans will offer a reduced benefit payable upon the occurrence of disability. Others will permit benefits to continue to accrue as if the employee were still working and not disabled! This usually occurs in the form of the years-of-service portion of a defined benefit's formula. Benefits might accrue until the employee reaches age 65 (assuming that is the employer's normal retirement age). Employers should consider adding an age or service requirement or both to limit disability benefits to long-serviced employees.

Discussion Questions

1. An employee receives a notice from his employer that because he is married, he is eligible for a QJSA. He is told that the QJSA requires that a payment to a surviving spouse must be at least 40 percent of the participant's benefit. He is also told that he can waive the QJSA option, which would lower his monthly payment in retirement by a reasonable margin, by simply signing a form himself. Is this company's disclosure correct?

2. A 55-year-old participant recently got married. While on honeymoon, there was a tragic accident and he was accidentally killed while parasailing in the Caribbean. His surviving spouse is surprised to learn that the now deceased spouse's DB plan will not pay her any benefits under a QPSA arrangement. Explain the reasoning to this bereaved and bewildered person.

3. Other than instantly creating an estate, what are the top two reasons that an employer might offer a life insurance option within their qualified retirement plan?

4. The owner of a business wants to purchase a large amount of whole life insurance with their own profit-sharing plan account. Is there any want to satisfy the incidental benefit problem?

5. What is the difference in tax treatment between whether an insurance policy is owned inside or outside a retirement savings account?

6. Assess the accuracy of this statement: "Most large employers prefer to offer life insurance benefits through their retirement savings accounts."

7. At the end of a given plan year, a company's money purchase plan had the following participants.

Employee	% ownership	Salary	Account balance
Employee A	95%	$85,000	$100,000
Employee B	3%	$170,000	$60,000
Employee C	2%	$50,000	$40,000
Employee D	0%	$45,000	$12,000
Employee E	0%	$35,000	$8,000

Which employees are "key employees," and does this company's money purchase plan have a top-heavy problem?

8. What is the minimum required top-heavy contribution if an employer has a top-heavy 401(k) plan that only contains employee salary deferrals, and at least one key employee makes a 5 percent salary deferral within the plan?

9. What two pitfalls should an employer be wary of with respect to offering disability benefits within their retirement savings plan?

CHAPTER 11

Plan Funding and Investing

Introduction

There is a sacred trust that an employer will contribute whatever they commit to contributing for the benefit of their employee's retirement. Unfortunately, there have been gross violations throughout history, and so the regulators installed rules to govern the process. This chapter will discuss those rules. This chapter will also introduce you to the funding instruments used behind the scenes to hold the assets in an employer-sponsored plan.

Having the assets safely in a specified funding vehicle is extremely important, but once there, the assets must be invested. There are many great books, like *Investments* by Bodie, Kane, and Marcus that will educate an interested learner on the specifics, but this chapter will make a few comments on the investment side of the equation. Some of those comments will introduce you to investment policy statements (IPSs) and why they are loved by fiduciaries. You will also learn, very briefly, about the risk–reward trade-off inherent in investing.

Learning Goals

- Describe the funding requirements for a defined benefit (DB) plan
- Interpret and assess the funded status of a DB plan
- Describe a fully insured plan
- Understand the funding rules for defined contribution (DC) plans
- Identify the various funding instruments
- Know what should be included in an IPS and how this information can help a fiduciary
- Describe relevant investment characteristics for an employer-sponsored plan
- Understand the risk–reward trade-off

Funding a DB Plan

The Pension Protection Act (PPA) of 2006 requires that DB plans focus on year-by-year solvency. Prior to this law's enactment, employers had the flexibility to choose among several approaches if they were behind on funding their retirement plan. PPA now mandates a specific approach. That is what we will explore in this section.

The whole process begins with the **actuarial cost method**. Basically, an actuary will use various assumptions about an employer's projected growth in wages and staffing and marry that with their own projections about investment returns and mortality rates. A great deal of estimation goes into this process. The actuary will then develop a projected schedule of costs and discount (taking the present value) the series of projected costs at the assumed investment growth rate. This discounted sum of costs is known as the **projected benefit obligation (PBO)**. For our purposes, the PBO is the estimated plan liability. If actuaries get too creative with their assumptions, then the company could have a greatly reduced initial cost only to find themselves heavily underwater with plan assets significantly below plan liabilities.

The real issue at question is the **funded status** of the plan. If the plan was just funded, then its plan assets would equal its PBO. The best scenario is to be overfunded because in this case, a company could over-contribute when times are good and then not need to contribute when times are not so good. Milliman, an actuarial consultancy, has recently reported that the 100 largest American employers now have a funded status of 91.8 percent.[1] The stock market has greatly helped these employers move closer to being fully funded. Using a 7.5 percent investment return assumption, Milliman projects that by mid-2015, these top 100 employers could be fully funded unless the market falls apart between now and then. However, data gathered from Securities and Exchange Commission (SEC) filings by consultancy Towers Watson on the top 1,000 American employers yield a 77 percent funded status.[2] Too many plans are actually underfunded.

At one time, it was acceptable for pension benefits to be a pay-as-you-go system where benefits where paid out of current cash hoards on an as-needed basis. This is no longer permitted. Plans must now be

prefunded. They must establish a pool of assets that are accessible to pay plan liabilities as they become due. This pool must be irrevocable, which means that once the company contributes money to the plan assets, they cannot raid the fund for capital expenditures, payroll, or executive retreats.

At the beginning of every plan year (some plans are not established on January 1 and therefore their plan year starts annually on their establishment date), an actuary will recompute a schedule of expected costs and subsequently the PBO. They will then compare the value of the PBO with the current balance of plan assets and declare a certain funded status. Each year's required contribution will consist of the **funding target**, which is the present value of any projected benefits that will be fully accrued by the end of the current plan year, *plus* any special contributions to correct an underfunded status.

If a fund is deemed to be under-funded, then it must follow a specific program. Instead of forcing companies to correct any actuarially calculated shortfalls all at once, the PPA of 2006 allows them to smooth their catch-up contributions over seven (7) years. They can take their calculated shortfall for every year, divide it by 7, and then use that as their catch-up contribution. This option will certainly extend the potential period of underfunding, but it will also be much friendlier to the budget of the company in question. There is one caveat; this extended option is only available to companies who are at least 80 percent funded (no more than a 20 percent shortfall between plan assets and PBO). If they are less than 80 percent funded (or more than 20 percent underfunded), then they will be forced to use a much more accelerated catch-up funding schedule, depending on how underfunded they are. Funds in this last category are known as **at-risk plans**. To avoid a potentially crippling outcome for smaller businesses, this special rule for at-risk plans does not apply to companies with 500 or fewer employees. If a company fails to meet its funding requirements, then there will be a 10 percent excise tax, which is essentially a penalty, made payable to the U.S. Treasury.

Because regulators like to encourage overfunding of DB plans, a company is permitted to deduct for tax purposes the minimum funding amount for any given year plus a **cushion amount**. The cushion amount is defined in the PPA of 2006 with a complex formula with a base dollar amount of at least 50 percent of the funding target for the given plan year. The exact dollar amount of the cushion is not important for this discussion, but the idea is that an employer can deduct an extra amount if they overcontribute to a plan. Why would they want to overcontribute? Perhaps they have a large amount of available money at present, but their future looks less certain. By overcontributing now, they may be able to reduce the need for a contribution in their uncertain future. In general, companies with a DB plan must contribute a dollar amount that falls between their minimum threshold and the maximum deduction amount determined by the cushion.

It is sometimes a temptation for deeply underfunded plans to try to correct their underfunded status by shifting their investments to a riskier mix in an attempt to let the market correct the shortfall through higher returns. The danger here is that getting riskier could be beneficial, or it could substantially worsen the underfunded status. In theory, as funds gets closer to being fully funded, they will rotate more of their investment holdings into fixed income (bonds) to protect their improving funded status. The challenge in a low interest rate environment, like the one in which America finds itself today, is that interest rates will move higher sometime in the not so distant future. When interest rates do move higher, fixed income investors will lose value, which would defeat the normal purpose of rotating into fixed income. Many pension asset managers in this market are forgoing the normal rotation into fixed income for this reason.

Fully Insured Plans

Companies with a DB plan can alleviate the uncertainty of unknown cash flow volatility by purchasing an insurance-based product. You can think of this as the sleep-at-night factor. With an insurance-based alternative, the risk gets shifted to the insurance company, and the employer could have fairly reliable cash outflows for an otherwise uncertain cash demand.

The way this alternative works is that an employer can purchase an annuity contract where the employer makes level periodic payments to an insurance company, and then the insurance company is responsible for making the ultimate payments to participants once they retire. The risk of actuarial assumptions will then reside with the insurance company and not the plan sponsor.

An employer who chooses to follow this method has selected what is called a §412(e) fully insured plan. If an employer chooses to operate a fully insured plan, they will pay fees to the insurance company for assuming the risk. The plan sponsor will then be exempt from minimum funding requirements within its DB plan because the insurance company is guaranteeing full payment of the benefits to retirees.

For this exemption from regulation to apply, the fully insured plan must include certain specific features. The first feature is that the series of payments to the insurance company must be in the form of a level annuity. They cannot make a series of balloon payments (large dollar amounts clustered at certain tie periods) because these balloon payments would look a lot like a plan that is not truly fully insured. The second feature is that all benefits paid from the insurance contract must equal the benefits due per the plan document of the DB plan. The third feature is that the plan must be expressly guaranteed by the insurance company. The next feature is that all premiums must be paid on time. Regulators do not want a company to enter into a fully insured contract and then default on the insurance company, which would be the same thing as defaulting on the DB plan outright. The final feature is that the insurance product cannot permit any loans from its balance to the employer.

Funding a DC Plan

There are only two DC plans that have a minimum funding requirement. They are both in the "pension plan" category along with DB plans. They are the money purchase pension plan (MPPP) and the target benefit plan. The other DC plan types, which are not on this list of two, do not technically have a minimum funding requirement. However, if those exempt funds fail to meet any contributions that are promised in the plan document, then those funds risk being disqualified. Recall that plan disqualification means that the all-retroactive contribution since the plan's inception is no longer tax deferred and then there is a huge tax nightmare to unwind. This is obviously a scenario to avoid at all costs.

Because the DC plans do not have a required payout in retirement, the minimum funding requirement is determined by whatever is promised in the respective plan documents. Just like with their DB cousins, a DC plan that fails to meet its minimum funding requirement will have a 10 percent excise "tax" levied against it.

Recall that the maximum contribution for all DC plans is the greater of 25 percent of aggregate compensation or $52,000 (2014 limit). This is the §415(c) limit discussed previously. There is one notable exception to this limit—the 401(k). In a 401(k), the employer can contribute up to its own maximum of $17,500 (2014 limit) PLUS they can contribute using a profit-sharing feature up to 25 percent of aggregate compensation or $52,000 (2014 limit) at the same time. With a 401(k), someone could defer up to $69,500 ($17,500 + $52,000).

Consider a sole proprietor who has decided to become incorporated (S corp.). He has no other employees, has a MPPP, and plans to have total compensation for 2014 of $100,000. This individual's maximum contribution for 2014 is $25,000 (25% × $100,000). What if his income jumped to $250,000? Now, the maximum contribution is $52,000. But if he established a 401(k), he could have $52,000 as a profit-sharing contribution and an additional $17,500 as a regular 401(k) contribution. This nuance is perhaps more complicated, but it is one of many reasons why businesses need to hire a trained financial professional.

Funding Instruments

A funding instrument is conceptually just a bucket where money is stored for later use. Qualified plans must use a trust, a custodial account, or a guaranteed insurance contract (GIC) as their funding instrument. Simplified employee pensions (SEPs) and savings incentive match plans for employees (SIMPLEs) must use an individual retirement account (IRA) as their funding instrument.

A trust is the most popular type of funding instrument. The "grantor" of the trust is the employer—the entity who deposits money into the trust. For the trust to function as a retirement asset-funding instrument, it must be **irrevocable**. This means that the employer can never alter or eliminate the purpose of the trust. It also means that the employer cannot access money for capital expenditures or other business uses once it has been deposited within the trust.

The trust document will detail several specific factors related to the trust's operation. There are four core categories in which these factors will fall. The first is the investment powers granted to the plan's administrators. The employer may maintain a high degree of control by limiting asset class or individual security choices. On the other hand, they may give the administrators tremendous discretion in selecting assets for inclusion in the plan's investment pool. The second category is a statement about **fiduciary responsibility**. We will discuss fiduciary responsibility in detail in Chapter 12, but for now it is important to understand that this is a technical legal term describing the person or group that has the authority to administer the trust fund, select investments, and manage distributions. The core thought process with fiduciaries is that they must act in the best interest of the plan beneficiaries and cannot just do whatever they want with plan assets. Some plan fiduciaries will manage the plan's investments themselves, while others will hire a series of professional asset managers to handle this task. The third category will be a discussion on how benefits will be paid out from the trust, including benefit triggers and policies. The fourth category is to disclose any rights that the beneficiaries might have in the event of a plan termination. Most of this information is just a duplication of what would be found in the plan document.

The trustees have several specific duties. They will accept and invest contributions on behalf of the plan's beneficiaries. They will pay benefits out of plan assets to the beneficiaries once they enter retirement. They will report the status of the investment pool (plan assets) to the employer on a regular basis. To help facilitate this last step, the trustee will need to maintain accurate and up-to-date records.

The trustees may elect to deposit the plan assets in a **common trust fund**, which is essentially a group of several small plans that have comingled their funds. They will each own a proportionate share in the common trust fund and benefit from its pooled investment performance. Why would they comingle funds? It is much easier for a larger pool of assets to diversify. It is also easier for the trustees to hire more reputable managers (who will, in theory, perform better) due to the large size of the investment pool.

Another option for a trustee is split funding. With split funding, the trustees will invest part of the plan assets in investments that they themselves have selected and the remainder of the investment pool in an insurance-based product like an annuity. This could happen if the plan is a DB plan, which offers life insurance for employees within their plan. The trustee will naturally be purchasing both investments and an insurance product. A trustee also may elect to purchase some form of annuity as an investment to gain a more certain cash flow stream when it is time for payment of benefits.

A plan could choose to utilize a custodial account, which is essentially a less formal version of a trust. Most fiduciaries would prefer a trust because the formality helps to protect them from legal issues. A plan could also choose a GIC, which is basically like a money market account where an insurance company is the provider and offers a higher rate of return than a straight money market. This could be used as an option to generate a more reliable stream of cash flow for the ultimate payment of benefits to retirees. The returns on a GIC, while guaranteed, are typically considerably less than could be found in a diversified selection of mutual funds. The fiduciary must balance the trade-off between stability and return potential.

Investment Guidelines, Policies, and Objectives

It is in the best interest of the plan assets if they create an **IPS**, which is a formal document that spells out everything that the plan needs to accomplish along with any risk parameters and asset classes that should be expressly excluded. The IPS has a specific benefit for the plan's fiduciary. If the fiduciary follows the IPS to the letter, then the plan's beneficiaries will have a difficult time proving that the fiduciary did not act in their best interests. It provides the fiduciary with a cushion.

Within the IPS, there should be a detailed discussion of the plan's guidelines. It is important to know what the policies are, what the goals and risk objectives are, and who is responsible for meeting these objectives. There must be a target in mind, or the plan will end up in chaotic operation.

The plan needs to have a formal, written funding policy. Basically, a description of how the employer intends to fund the promised benefits. For a DB plan, the funding policy must address any minimum funding requirements, procedures for a detailed review of the funding process, and a list of any changes implemented to address any issues encountered. A DC plan must address the timing of any specific contributions and any trigger events for discretionary contributions. Notice that a DC plan does not need to include anything relative to its funded status because it technically does not have one. Remember that employers with a DC plan must make a certain contribution, not pay a certain benefit.

As mentioned earlier, to arrive at a destination, you must first know where you are going and how you plan to get there. "Where a plan is going" is formally called its *objective*. The primary objective of a DB plan is to have enough plan assets to cover its promised benefits. This is often measured by the relationship between the plan assets and the PBO, which is also called the funded status. The secondary objectives for a DB plan are to minimize cumulative contributions and to smooth out the variability in the annual contributions. Too often, these secondary objectives take precedence in practice over the primary goal of the funded status. The funded status should always be the most prominent goal for a DB plan!

The primary objectives for a DC plan are more broadly applied since the DC plan does not have a mandatory payout in retirement, but a specified contribution during the participant's tenure of employment. One of the DC plan's primary objectives is to provide a retirement savings mechanism to encourage and help their employees. Just by offering a plan, the company has partially satisfied this goal.

Another primary goal for a DC plan is to provide a sufficiently diverse group of investment alternatives. What is sufficiently diverse? This is a very subjective goal. Typically, a company will offer between 10 and 15 investment choices. Less than 10 might not provide enough alternatives and more than 15 may just confuse employees who already do not have a clue how to allocate their retirement portfolio. Too often in practice, you will see a group of investments that is not as diverse as it appears. For example, it is not very common to see medium company mutual funds or specific sector funds like utilities, financials, or technology. DC plan assets are usually diversified with bond funds, large company funds, global funds, and perhaps a small company fund.

The last primary objective of a DC plan is employee education. As alluded to in the last paragraph, not all employees will know how to allocate their assets. They will sometimes solve this by simply investing 1/10th of their plan balance into each investment alternative if the plan offers 10 choices. Some employers will retain a financial advisor to be available to talk with their employees at certain intervals to provide both educational training sessions and help with asset allocation design.

General Investment Considerations

The plan's fiduciary must consider certain investment concepts to discharge their duty properly. These considerations apply more so to DB plans, but are useful to discuss in general. They are most likely to be subcategories in the plan's IPS.

The first consideration that needs to be understood firmly is the trade-off between risk and reward. If you become a financial professional who works with the general public, you will commonly hear clients asking for more return with less risk. This is not the right equation. Lower risk equals lower return potential! Higher return potential means that the investor must be willing to accept higher risk levels. The risk–reward trade-off is really about reducing risk to an *acceptable level*. This is key! Some form of risk will always exist when investing. The idea is to lower risk to a level that is both acceptable and that will provide enough return to satisfy an objective.

Another investment consideration is the **time horizon**. In investment terms, the time horizon is the timing of the planned cash flow needs. There may be several. Common personal retirement planning horizon events are taking a special trip, buying a specific car, actually retiring, specific gifts to various charities or universities, and leaving an estate (at death). Common business horizon events are the scheduling of planned retirements from participants, funding status milestones, and potential plan terminations.

Liquidity is also an investment consideration for plan assets. In the context of retirement planning, liquidity means having cash to pay for planned expenses when they arise. This might involve maintaining a cash reserve or having cash-producing assets (such as bonds, GICs, or an annuity product) that can provide cash precisely when it is needed.

Risk and stability are two related concepts. They are both related to downside volatility in the plan assets or participant retirement accounts. The fiduciary needs to establish stability (downside) parameters to minimize the risk to plan assets.

Imagine a scenario where a company's retirement plan is so large that it purchases the controlling interest in a partnership to capture an expected stream of cash payments over time. What would this mean for the competitive landscape for that partnership? The portion of the partnership that is owned by the retirement plan assets would generate tax-free income because the retirement fund is tax deferred. The same scenario could apply to any income-producing property such as rental real estate. If this scenario was left unchecked, then retirement plan assets would be able to create an unfair business environment. For this reason, the regulators established the **unrelated business income tax (UBIT)**. The UBIT applies when a retirement trust materially operates a business. The most likely causes of UBIT applying are investments in partnerships and income-producing properties. If this does apply, then the retirement trust will need to pay what would otherwise have been normal taxes for the business. The only exception to this rule is for an employee stock ownership plans (ESOP) that does not include a salary deferral option. It is best to avoid UBIT at all costs. If there is any doubt as to whether a certain investment might generate UBIT, the plan's fiduciary should seek legal counsel.

Switching gears to diversification, if a DC plan holds publically traded employer stock, then certain diversification requirements must be met. These rules apply to all employee contributions and to any employer contributions for participants with at least three years of service. The diversification requirement is that the plan must offer at least three investment choices other than the employer's stock. They must also permit employees to change their investment allocation at least quarterly. Recall that ESOPs have their own special diversification requirement for those aged 55 with at least 10 years of service.

There are several different types of investments that might be made available to retirement plan participants to help satisfy the diversification requirement. One option is cash (or more commonly a money market mutual fund). Another idea is bonds. Direct bond ownership could be practical for a DB plan, but a DC plan would typically offer fixed income mutual funds to enable participants to diversify volatility. Bonds are usually not included in an asset allocation for significant returns but for volatility reduction potential.

The most common diversifier is the broad category of mutual funds. These could be large company mutual funds, small company funds, fixed income funds, or global funds. These are the most common inclusions in DC plans. There are so many different types of funds that a DB plan would need an experienced financial professional to guide participants through the maze of choices.

Another option is called a **stable value fund**, which actually is a generic subcategory term for one of three assets. A GIC is technically a version of stable value fund. Recall that a GIC is an insurance contract guaranteeing a certain return to the investor. It is subject to the reliability of the insurance company. A **separate account GIC** is also a stable value fund. A separate account GIC is when an insurance company carves out a block of assets from within the insurance company's pool of assets to specifically secure the GIC contract. This option will be more costly for the employer to access because the insurance company is providing another layer of service in the securing of the GIC contract. A third type of stable value fund is a **synthetic GIC**. This is a product of creative finance where a base book value is guaranteed, and then the insurance company sets up a wrap fee account with a subadvisor to manage the investment.

Discussion Questions

1. What is the biggest concern with using the actuarial cost method to determine DB plan funding needs?
2. Is it true that DB plans are established as pay-as-you-go systems just like Social Security?
3. You read on Wikipedia that the funding target for a DB plan is equal to the present value of the accrued benefits for a given year. Is this correct?
4. You overhear the CFO of your company telling the head of HR that the PPA of 2006 permits an employer to correct any underfunded status over a seven-year period. The CFO goes on to say that your

company's plan is 25 percent underfunded, and they plan to use this smoothing effect. What would you say about this conversation?

5. You read in your local newspaper that DB plans are only allowed to make contributions up to the point of being fully funded. After this point, no more contributions (employer deductions) are permitted until more benefits accrue from employees completing another year of service. Is this concept correct?

6. What is one technique for outsourcing the responsibility for a plan's funded status?

7. We know that DB plans have required levels of funding. Is there a type of DC plan that also has required funding?

8. Is there a way to contribute more than the cap of $17,500 (2014 limit) into a 401(k)?

9. What is a common trust and why would it be used?

10. What is the purpose of an IPS?

11. You are having lunch with an employer who is a prospective client. They tell you that their primary goal with their DB plan is to minimize the unpredictability in their contributions. What would you tell them?

12. What is the most common diversification tool in the DC world?

CHAPTER 12

Fiduciary Responsibility

Introduction

As a person is growing up, he or she is always encouraged to become more responsible. In the world of employer-sponsored plans, the responsible parties are called fiduciaries and they are rightly held to a high standard to protect the participants' best interests. Fiduciaries are actually personally liable for any wrongdoings. This knowledge creates a need to be laser focused upon what can and cannot be done with plan assets. This is a good thing for plan participants, but the degree of restrictions creates a high hurdle for individuals to be willing to become plan fiduciaries. Because of this, there are some measures that can reduce the burden for a fiduciary. You will learn about some of the rules and methods of limiting fiduciary liability in this chapter.

The role of a fiduciary is being actively reexamined by both regulators and the courts. In one notable case currently before the Supreme Court, the question has been raised whether a fiduciary over an employee stock ownership plan (ESOP; where employees own employer stock specifically with their retirement assets) is violating the participant's best interests when the employer stock appears to be headed down with no immediate hope of reversal.[1] This lawsuit is questioning the viability of the ESOP plan type, but it is also questioning specifically a fiduciary's standard of prudence.

Learning Goals

- Identify the scope of fiduciary rules in retirement planning
- Describe the affirmative duties of plan fiduciaries
- Explain the individual account plan exception that limits fiduciary liability

- Identify what the prohibited transaction rules intend to accomplish
- Describe the impact of failing to satisfy the fiduciary standard, and ways to protect plan fiduciaries

Fiduciary Duty

Before we can discuss what a fiduciary does, we must first define who a fiduciary is. Entities are considered **fiduciaries** if they have discretionary authority over the plan assets, over distributions from the plan assets, or over the holistic plan administration. **Discretionary authority** means that they can take whatever action they so choose without seeking the approval of another. Someone could also be considered a fiduciary if they render investment advice about the plan for a fee.

The list of potential plan fiduciaries could include the plan sponsor (employer) itself, any plan trustees, any paid investment managers, or any officers of the company who pick either the plan trustees or paid investment managers. While the employer could be considered a fiduciary, plan establishment, or termination are not considered fiduciary acts. These are both simply business decisions.

Attorneys, accountants, external plan administrators [sometimes called third-party administrators (TPAs)], or someone who simply sells investments to the plan participants without rendering advice are not considered fiduciaries. They are simply ancillary service providers. The broker where plan assets are custodied (held) is also not considered a fiduciary. There is an ongoing debate about the role of investment managers as fiduciaries. It is generally understood that an investment manager, who only provides education and not advice to participants, will not be considered a fiduciary.

Why so much concern over whether or not an entity is considered a fiduciary? Being a fiduciary carries a tremendous amount of responsibility. On a very basic level, a plan's fiduciary is responsible for managing the plan's assets and the payment of any benefits to the participants. The fiduciary is responsible for making sure that the plan functions as it needs to. However, they are not required to do all of the physical work. If they are not an expert in an area, then they should hire a third-party expert to manage that function.

The concept of a fiduciary applies to all qualified plans and also to simplified employee pensions (SEPs), savings incentive match plans for employees (SIMPLEs), and 403(b) plans. Basically, the concept applies to all tax-advantaged retirement plans regardless of whether they are considered qualified or not. There is an exemption (why wouldn't there be) for 403(b) plans without any employer contributions, for government-sponsored plans, for church-sponsored plans, and for plans that only cover a 100 percent owner or spouse or both.

Earlier, it was mentioned that one of the fiduciary responsibilities is to manage the plan assets. While the term *plan assets* sounds intuitive, like everything in finance, it requires a unique definition. Of course, salary deferrals and any employer contributions are plan assets. It deserves mentioning that any deferrals must be transferred from the company's bank account to the plan's account by the 15th of the month following the month in which the salary was earned. Salary deferred from wages due September 30 must be deposited by October 15 of any given year. This prevents the employer from using the salary deferrals for their own gain.

What about an equity investment in another company? Do you need to include a proportionate amount of the investment's balance sheet as "plan assets"? The answer is no, if it is a publically traded company. The answer is yes, if it is privately held. If the plan assets are used to purchase an ownership interest in a privately held company, then a minority interest in the investment's balance sheet assets must be included as plan assets. It seems a bit technical, but technically it is part of the rules.

Fiduciary Conflict Mitigation

Conflicts of interest are a significant part of what regulators try to supervise with respect to the conduct of fiduciaries. The core concept is known as the **exclusive benefit rule**, which states that a fiduciary must act in the sole interest of the plan participants (sometimes also called plan beneficiaries). The regulators are laser focused on searching for any collateral benefits that the fiduciary might receive. A **collateral benefit** is any personal, secondary benefit realized by the fiduciary as a result of making a transaction with plan assets. Tangential to the exclusive benefit rule is the requirement that fees paid by the plan assets be reasonable in nature. It is in the best interest of participants if the fiduciary hires help for areas where they are not experts, but fees paid to third parties must not be excessive.

In practical application, conflicts of interest do sometimes arise. In such a scenario, the fiduciary should disclose any conceivable conflict of interest that cannot be eliminated. An example of a conflict that can easily be eliminated is gifts from investment managers. In the wide world of investment, it is common for investment managers to offer meals, golfing packages, trips, and other incentives to potential clients. Fiduciaries are obligated to avoid these enticements at all costs…no matter how tempting the carrot being dangled.

If you have already studied investments, then you will likely understand the existence of 12 B-1 fees. These are essentially an advertising and marketing fee that is rolled into the expense ratio on mutual funds. Investors pay this fee behind the scenes, before investment results are reported to them. Investment managers often receive these fees as incentive for recommending a given fund company to their clients. This trend is pervasive in the industry. It is not a conflict that can be eliminated, but it should be disclosed to plan participants.

There is also a **standard of prudence** levied upon the fiduciary. They must behave as prudent persons would be expected to behave while conducting their duties. The standard of prudence is often linked to "care, skill, and caution." Prudent fiduciaries will display care, skill, and caution as they manage plan assets and supervise distributions to participants in retirement.

The Department of Labor (DOL) has compiled a list of factors that constitute prudence from their perspective. The first prudent factor is to consider the role of an investment as a part of the larger portfolio, essentially the notion of asset allocation. The next factor is that an investment must be reasonably designed as a part of the asset mix. It would not be prudent to put 50 percent of plan assets in a biotech start-up. The next factor is that the fiduciary must balance the risk of loss with the potential for gain. You already learned about the risk–reward trade-off. Fiduciaries must be careful not to assume needless risk. Related to the factors mentioned thus far is the next factor—diversification. It is incumbent upon the fiduciary to ensure that plan assets are properly diversified. The fiduciary must also be mindful of the liquidity needs of the plan and structure plan assets so that they meet the needs of the plan. One way to accomplish this DOL mandate is to match projected returns of assets to the plan's funding objectives.

With all of this oversight and focus on only employing investments that meet plan objectives, how is a fiduciary to function in an uncertain market? The logic behind each investment is judged based on the information available at the time that the investment decision is made and not based upon the end result. This is only prudent and fair. With this key feature in mind, fiduciaries must carefully document their rationale before making an investment to protect their own liability.

Other Fiduciary Disclosures and Requirements

The requirement of diversification does not mean throwing in a bit of everything. This behavior could result in "diworsification" where the wrong assets are mixed together. First and foremost, there must be diversification among asset classes. The prudent fiduciary will look at how a benchmark, such as the Standard and Poor's 500 Index, is allocated across asset classes and use this as a guide. They do not need to simply pick the same percentages in each category that the benchmark uses; otherwise why not just purchase the index as the sole investment. The goal of the plan is probably more specific than simply tracking the benchmark, and it certainly will include less volatility than the market. The benchmark is simply one place to look for ideas on which sectors to invest in. At this point, diversification will be best thought of as minimizing beta and maximizing the Sharpe ratio. Both of these concepts are beyond the scope of this book.

Diversification within a single asset class is also key. For instance, if the fiduciary plans to include the category of healthcare, then they should be mindful to include some portion of insurance carriers, pharmaceuticals, medical device makers, and perhaps biotechnology firms. If the fiduciary does not personally have this level of expertise, then it is the fiduciary's responsibility to hire someone who does.

In general, the fiduciary must manage the plan assets in accordance with the plan document and the investment policy statement (IPS). The fiduciary must be careful not to violate any specific prohibitions against certain investments or investment types. For instance, the IPS or plan document might forbid expressly the use of derivatives or margin trading (buying assets with a loan secured by other plan assets in an attempt to amplify the investment results—riskier strategy).

Any fees, which will be paid by the participants and not by the plan sponsor *must* be disclosed to participants. This includes any administrative charges, fees for investment advice, and any charges for receiving paper statements as opposed to downloads. A schedule of fees must be presented annually, and actual fees paid must be fully and clearly, disclosed on a quarterly basis.

The Effect of Participant-Directed Investing

Just ask any fish…getting off the hook is a good thing. Section 404(c) is a mechanism to help alleviate some of the fiduciary's mandated responsibility. This rule removes the investment monitoring mandate from the fiduciary IF participants have the ability to direct their own investment selection and they exercise that ability. Section 404(c) does not exempt the fiduciary from offering prudent investment choices. This rule is employed most often in a 401(k) setting. The participants can choose their own investments and so the fiduciary's only logical investment responsibility is to select reasonable investment alternatives for the participants to choose from.

For §404(c) to apply, the participants must be offered a broad range of investment alternatives. Now, it does not sound very broad, but the rules state that participants must be offered at least three different core investment options. The options offered must have materially different risk or return characteristics. For example, a large company mutual fund, a global mutual fund, and a bond mutual fund. It is perfectly acceptable to include employer stock as an option as long as there are additional options that provide for the potential of diversification. Mutual funds are often chosen because they are by default more diversified than adding individual stocks in a few different industries.

There must also be an option for participants to change their investments at least quarterly. If §404(c) is employed by a fiduciary, then participants must be notified of this fact. They must also receive specific information on each investment to be able to choose effectively between them. The specific information requirement can be satisfied by providing the mutual fund's prospectus (their legal disclosures) and a schedule of past returns and risk measures (standard deviations, etc.).

What happens if alternative investment choices are made available, but participants simply do nothing? Should the fiduciary still be held liable for investments in this scenario? The short answer is yes. Unless, the plan employs what is known as a qualified default investment (QDI) alternative. Regulation provides that if a plan employs a **QDI**, then the fiduciary is exempt from all investment responsibility except that they still will be required to provide a reasonable blend of different investments for participants to choose from. The DOL provides a very loose definition of what a QDI is exactly. We do know that they intend for it to be easy diversification for employees who do not know what they are doing and that it cannot invest directly in an employer's stock.[2] Procedurally, the fiduciary will typically use a target date fund (like the Vanguard Target Retirement 2050 Fund: VFIFX), a lifestyle fund (like the Vanguard LifeStrategy Moderate Growth Fund: VSMGX), or a balanced fund (like Fidelity Balanced Fund: FBLAX) or they will offer an outsourced discretionary investment management service who will pick all of the participant's investment options for a fee. By establishing one of these alternatives as the default investment, if an employee fails to exercise his or her own investment selection rights, then the fiduciary is relieved of investment supervision responsibility. The QDI cannot be simply a money market fund.

Fiduciary-Prohibited Transactions

There is a long list of specific transactions that should be avoided at all costs by a plan's fiduciary. Typically those transactions occur between the plan assets and the fiduciaries themselves, the plan trustees, legal counsel for the plan, the plan sponsor (the employer), an employee organization (unions), any 10 percent owners of the plan sponsor, any employees, any relative of any previously mentioned at-risk group, or any organizations related to the plan sponsor (like a subsidiary). Transactions between the plan assets and any of these at-risk groups will raise a red flag for the regulators and generate additional scrutiny. Better to avoid that, if at all possible. Even if §404(c) is in force, the fiduciary still must be on guard against prohibited transaction types.

Regulators especially watch for **self-dealing**, which is any transaction that uses plan assets, which present a benefit for the fiduciary. Common benefits that would create a regulatory alert are any financial kickbacks (payment by someone to the fiduciary to incentivize a certain transaction), any ancillary benefits (paid trips or golf outings), personal financial gain from selling an asset to the plan (perhaps at above-market rates), or personal financial gain from buying an asset in the marketplace, which drives up the price for the fiduciary to sell a personal holding in the open market (large purchases can impact market price on stocks with lower trading volume).

The regulators have also compiled a list of prohibited transactions to help a fiduciary know exactly what to stay away from. Any sale, exchange, or leasing of property between the plan assets and an interested party (like the plan sponsor or the relative of an owner) is expressly prohibited. The plan should not lend money or furnish any goods or services to any of the at-risk groups previously described. It is also a big red flag if any more than 10 percent of the plan assets are used to purchase the stock of the plan sponsor. Regulators are trying to guard against the employee seeking to use the plan assets to control a valuable voting block of the outstanding shares of the company. It is very common for small businesses to unintentionally violate the prohibited transactions list. This is usually a mistake and not a willful violation. If fiduciaries have any question about a given transaction, they should seek legal counsel before placing the trade.

There is a very broad series of exemptions to the prohibited transactions list. Without a sequence of exemptions, fiduciaries would not be able to pay for basic needs like third-party service providers or external investment managers. There are three categories of exemptions. The first category is called *statutory exemptions*. Statutory exemptions cover transactions like plan loans, ESOP loans, reasonable compensation to plan service providers, and a special clause for bank or insurance company employees who want to purchase a proprietary investment that is assembled and sold by their employer (the bank or insurance company). Without these statutory exemptions, you can see how some basic functions of the plan would not be legitimate. The second category of exemptions is called *administrative exemptions* and they come specifically from the DOL. The administrative exemptions are too numerous to list, but know that a fiduciary may have access to a certain transaction if there is an administrative exemption on a file with the DOL. The final type of exemption is called an *individual exemption*. These individual exemptions are similar to private letter rulings previously discussed…they only come into play if no other exemption exists for the transaction. A fiduciary can petition the DOL for a one-time exemption if they can prove that the exemption is administratively feasible, in the best interests of the plan's participants, and ultimately protects the rights of the plan's participants.

Some common transactions that will always get a regulator salivating are loans from the plan assets to the company, the company's owners, or relatives of the company's owners. Another huge red flag is a contribution of anything other than cash. If the company wants to contribute an ownership interest in an income-producing real estate property, not only would the fiduciary need to contend with the potential for unrelated business income tax (UBIT), but will need to be concerned with valuation issues. This type or transaction should just be avoided. Another common trouble spot is if the plan sponsor uses plan assets to purchase property or voting shares of another company and then uses the plan's ownership for the plan sponsor's ultimate benefit.

One final exemption exists for investment advisors. Because they provide investment advice to a plan or directly to the plan's participants, investment advisors are typically deemed to hold a fiduciary status. Recall that fiduciaries are prohibited from self-dealing, and charging a fee to the plan is self-dealing. So, how do they get paid? Investment advisors are permitted to charge fees if certain criteria are met. First, the fees must be static (they cannot vary depending upon the investment options selected). However, they can charge a different level of fees if computer models are involved in the financial advice because computer models (algorithmic trading) are very specialized and very costly. Second, the fees must be specifically authorized by the plan's fiduciary and monitored by the fiduciary on an on-going basis. Third, the fees must be audited annually to ensure compliance with these other criteria.

Limiting Fiduciary Liability

Fiduciaries are *personally liable* for any losses that result from a breach in their fiduciary duty.[3] There is also a provision to claw back (take back) any profits that the fiduciary earns illicitly from personal transactions with the plan assets. Fiduciaries are also personally liable for breaches of duty committed by other plan fiduciaries! They could be on the hook if they knowingly participated in illicit activity with a cofiduciary or helped to conceal a violation. This includes deleting emails or shredding paperwork. They could also be liable if they failed to put in place controls to prevent another fiduciary's breach of duty. If the regulators do rule that a transaction was a breach of duty, not only will they go after the fiduciary in question, but they can also charge the party on the other end of the transaction a 15 percent excise tax penalty!

If a fiduciary's role were viewed as an investment, one would certainly be fair to say that it is an investment with limited, moderate return potential, and unlimited risk. Not really a great deal for the plan fiduciary. But some must fill the role.

With all of these limitations and the risk of regulatory oversight, why would anyone willingly agree to become a plan fiduciary? There is a mechanism to place a cap on the risk taken by the fiduciary. The first step in this risk-limiting process is to document every action taken with respect to the plan. If every action taken is documented and it fits within the limits of the law and the plan document, then there is nothing to fear. It is also important that the various roles of plan administration and investment supervision be allocated specifically to specific people so that it is clear who makes which decisions. In real estate, there is a phrase that the most important component of a piece of property's value is location, location, and location. In the world of fiduciary duty, a vital component is delegation, delegation, and delegation. If the fiduciary does not have expertise in an area, then they are obligated to delegate the function to a paid professional who is an expert. The icing on the cake of risk limitation is that either the fiduciaries themselves or more likely their employer can purchase a **fiduciary bond**, which is an insurance contract that will pay benefits if the fiduciaries breach their duty. This series of protective mechanisms transforms the fiduciary relationship into a moderate-return investment now with limited risk. With this risk profile, professionals are typically willing to accept the role of a plan's fiduciary.

Discussion Questions

1. The CFO of a large company only has discretion over the assets of the employer's retirement plan. Is this individual a fiduciary?

2. An attorney, who only recently passed his bar exam (allowing him to become an attorney), for a given employer-sponsored plan is under the impression that he is free of fiduciary obligation for the retirement plan. Is he correct?

3. You overhear a legitimate plan fiduciary saying that she is able to be a bit more liberal with her judgments because she has no personal consequences if something goes wrong. What would you tell her?

4. A legitimate fiduciary uses the same brokerage company personally that he uses for plan assets. Due to the size of the business relationship, the brokerage company has given the fiduciary a 50 percent reduction in trading costs for both plan assets and personal assets. Is this an issue?

5. Is the prudence of a fiduciary's investment decisions based upon the ultimate investment outcome?

6. There are many required duties of a fiduciary. However, diversification of the pool of investments is a voluntary duty. Is this understanding correct?

7. In an attempt to access the reduced responsibilities offered by §404(c), a fiduciary decides to alter operations to allow each participant to exercise investment authority. Those who do not exercise discretion will automatically be placed in a well-diversified large company mutual fund. The fiduciary simply makes the change and provides a notice to all participants stating that they "will now have the opportunity to exercise investment discretion. Anyone who does not exercise this discretion will be automatically allocated into XYZ

Large Core Mutual Fund." What issues, if any, do you see in this scenario?

8. A plan's fiduciary receives notification of what they perceive to be a fantastic investment opportunity. It meets all of the requirements for prudence...it truly is a good investment. This would be an investment in a privately held business, which is part-owned by the cousin of one of the owners of the plan sponsor. Is there any issue?

9. A loan from an employer-sponsored retirement plan to an employee is a violation of the prohibited transactions rules. Is this statement correct?

10. You are an investment advisor working for XYZ Capital Management. You have been hired to educate participants in ABC Manufacturing's 401(k) plan. Are you considered to be a fiduciary?

11. How could the inherent personal liability associated with being a fiduciary be limited or removed?

PART III

Retirement Plan Administration

CHAPTER 13

Plan Installation and Administration

Introduction

There is a formal process that must be followed if an employer does not already sponsor a plan. They will need to jump through certain metaphorical hoops and perform certain administrative tasks. A prospective client who is interested in offering a retirement benefit for their employees needs to be aware of the issue presented in this chapter. They should also be aware of certain protections in the event that an employee divorces while covered by an employer-sponsored plan.

Have you ever made an unintentional mistake? If you are honest, the answer is a resounding yes. Mistakes within the employer-sponsored plan environment need not become a disqualifying problem for the plan. The regulators have provided a path to self-report issues and subsequently received an easier path to correction. This is very important to understand properly.

Learning Goals

- Describe the steps to install an employer-sponsored plan
- Understand the purpose of a summary plan description (SPD)
- Identify the ongoing duties of plan administration
- Understand how a qualified domestic relations order (QDRO) interacts with an employer-sponsored plan
- Describe the implications of the defeat of the Defense of Marriage Act (DOMA) on employer-sponsored plans
- Identify what should be done if a compliance discrepancy is discovered

Installing a New Plan

Some employers wake up one morning and realize that their lack of retirement plan benefits might be impairing their ability to attract and retain valuable employees. The only solution is to install a new plan.

The first step to installing a new retirement plan is for the employer's board of directors to pass a resolution formally "adopting" a retirement plan. This means that they agree to assume whatever responsibilities correspond with the plan type that they have selected. If they are a smaller company and do not have a board of directors, then the business owners can assume the role. Once adopted, the board will approve a funding instrument (like a trust). Then the employer needs to notify all employees (not just eligible ones) that the plan is being initiated.

After notifying the employees of the new plan being offered, they will conduct an *enrollment meeting*. Enrollment meetings are most necessary for plans that will involve employee salary deferrals. They are also one way that companies can encourage more rank-and-file employees [nonhighly compensated employees (NHCEs)] to participate, which will help out with compliance testing!

All contributions must be physically made into the plan by the tax-filing deadline (April 15) for the company to receive a tax deduction. But, if the employer is initiating a new plan, when in the year would they most likely be to do so? The employees in a plan offering salary deferrals would prefer that the plan be initiated in the beginning of the year so they can make contributions all year long. However, employers tend to prefer the end of the year. They are still able to make retroactive employer contributions up to the beginning of the year, but by waiting to the end of the year to initiate a plan, the employer will have a better understanding if they can afford to make the contributions in one year of the plan.

Where does the advance determination letter (ADL) fit into this process? Before employers submit an application for approval, they must first send notification to all employees that they are seeking Internal Revenue Service (IRS) approval to offer a certain plan type. Once they have provided notice, they must make certain that the required forms to receive an ADL are submitted before the due date for a corporate tax return. If they miss this deadline, then the IRS could deny them the ability to correct the application if errors occurred or something was missing. They could just be forced to wait another 12 months before reapplying for an ADL, which is ultimately issued by the IRS. Recall that this is a strictly voluntary step that is highly recommended but not required.

The SPD

Have you ever tried to research a topic contained in a piece of legislation. Try Googling the Pension Protection Act of 2006 to see just how jumbled things can get with various concepts, rules, and exceptions.

The full plan document can read in the same way for an employee who is not familiar with reading in *legalese*. In an attempt to bridge the gap between legalese and common language and thought patterns, the regulators have mandated that participants be provided with an **SPD**, which is a summary of all pertinent terms of the plan in clear and simple language.

The SPD must provide all relevant information on eligibility, vesting schedules, benefit calculation formulas, withdrawal availability, and the Employee Retirement Income Security Act (ERISA)-endowed rights. The SPD must not be used as an advertisement for participation in the plan. It is simply an easy way of communicating what is being offered. The employer must also disclose any event (such as vesting or plan termination) that could result in a loss of benefits.

The SPD must be distributed within 120 days (basically four months) after the plan has been adopted. The employer will typically wait until after it has received an ADL, assuming that they applied for one, before they will contribute to the plan, but everything else can and should be done while waiting for the ADL to arrive.

Employers need to be extremely careful what they put in the SPD. What if there is a typo or a blatant error? Their employees could be confused and lose confidence in the retirement plan concept. In recent years, some employees have actually sued their employers because errors in the SPD promised more generous benefits than the employer had originally intended.

Plan Administration Requirements

Plan administration has many, many duties. All of the duties are important, but perhaps the most important is to file paperwork with the regulators. The IRS requires Form 5500 annually. For large plans, this is a big deal because there are numerous schedules that need to be prepared. A small company, with fewer than 100 employees, can file the abbreviated 5500-SF form. This simplified form is only available if they do not use employer stock in their retirement plan. An even more special option is available for retirement plans with only one participant. If the single-participant plan has less than $250,000 in it, they do not need to file any forms. If the single-participant plan has more than $250,000, they can use the extremely basic 5500-EZ form. All versions of Form 5500 are due on the last day of the seventh month after the plan year ends (July 31 for a calendar-year plan).

What about defined benefit (DB) plans? They not only report to the IRS, but also to the Pension Benefit Guaranty Corporation (PBGC). They must file an annual report with the PBGC and, of course, pay the fee of $35 per participant per year. In addition, participants in a DB plan must be notified of the current funded status of the plan along with any steps that the employer has taken, since the last such report, to correct any underfunding. This funded status notice must be presented to the participants within two months of the Form 5500 due date.

In the previous section, you learned about the SPD. Part of the administrative responsibility is to make sure that all new employees receive a copy of the SPD. The fiduciary must also make sure that a new SPD is provided to everyone every 10 years or every 5 years if material changes have occurred from the previous version. Speaking of material changes... whenever a material change to the plan does occur, the fiduciary must also provide a **summary of material modifications (SMM)** report to everyone. The IRS has stipulated that a *material* change is anything related to an address or name change of either the plan sponsor (employer) or the plan's fiduciary, any change in vesting schedules, any changes in eligibility requirements imposed by the plan sponsor, any circumstances that could result either in a plan disqualification or a general loss of benefits, or any changes in the benefit claim procedures.

The fiduciary must also provide for participant education. Plan participants need to be educated on what benefits are available to them and perhaps also about investment selection when they need to choose their own options.

Another administrative duty is to process timely distributions from the plan. Distributions could be in the form of a rollover to an IRA when the participant leaves the company or they could be the direct payment of monthly benefits during retirement. Whatever the form of distribution, all retirement account distributions are reported to both the IRS and the taxpayer (participant) on IRS Form 1099-R. This is a very basic form. The distribution code (box 7) will tell the IRS if the distribution was premature and therefore subject to the early distribution 10 percent penalty, if it was a normal distribution, or if it was a qualified rollover.

The fiduciary will also need to supervise any plan loans and the repayment procedures for any outstanding loans.

Their last significant duty is to amend the plan documents, which ripples all the way down to the SPD, if the plan sponsor elects to materially amend or terminate the plan. A termination does not need to mean that the employer is no longer offering a retirement plan. It may simply mean that they have decided to close the current plan type and offer a new plan type for whatever business reason. If the plan does amend the plan document, it may require applying for a new ADL from the IRS if the change is big enough.

Common Errors and the QDRO

I don't know about you, but I never make mistakes…really, just ask my wife. Sometimes inadvertent mistakes do happen. This is one reason why plan administrators need to provide the SPD and the SMM to participants, who should always be able to cross-check the actual benefits with the promised benefits.

One common mistake is that not all compensation gets factored when calculating benefits. By now, you already know that every employer must have a consistent definition for *compensation* that must be uniformly applied to all employees. Occasionally, a company will provide one definition, but calculate benefits based on something else.

Another common mistake is for the benefits formula to either include the wrong percentage multiplier (the unit benefit formula) or not factor all years of service.

Sometimes basic personal information is wrong. Information like birth dates, addresses, or beneficiary designations (whomever the participants would like to inherit any assets in the event of their death). Other times, participants will fail to notify their Human Resources department about a marriage or divorce. This information can affect benefits greatly.

Another concept is analogous to our discussion of a participant's marital status. Under normal circumstances, the only person who can receive a distribution out of a participant's retirement account is the participants themselves. The one exception is if the court issues a **QDRO**. In the event of a divorce, the ex-spouse may be due a portion of the participant's retirement account balance. A portion of the retirement account can be transferred to the ex-spouse (or other court-appointed alternate payee) only with a valid court order that specifies three vital pieces of information: the parties involved, the exact amount to be paid, and the number of payments (it could be only one or sometimes more).

Another spousal issue has recently come to the forefront. On June 26, 2013, the Supreme Court declared the DOMA to be unconstitutional.[1] Setting both your opinions and mine to the side, this ruling is now the law. At issue is whether a same-gender partner should receive comparable rights as a spouse. The defeat of DOMA means that until further laws are issued to clarify legal rights, any state, like Massachusetts, which recognizes same-gender marriages should also extend QDRO rights to a same-gender partner. This same logic also extends to the qualified joint and survivor annuity (QJSA) and qualified preretirement survivor annuity (QPSA) concepts that were discussed in Chapter 10.

Dealing with Compliance Issues

By now, you should have some perspective that there are a whole host of regulations and rules in the world of retirement planning. The best-case scenario is that the company, its fiduciaries, and its paid retirement plan consultants will institute a series of policies and procedures that will ensure regulatory compliance. But, what should a company do if they happen to discover a compliance violation themselves before the regulators uncover it? The first step is always to correct the problem as soon as it is discovered. Period. The next step requires a high degree of integrity. The company should contact the regulators and inform them that the company discovered an issue, which was promptly fixed. If a company elects not to inform the regulators and the issue is discovered during an audit, then significant fines could be levied.

The IRS has a program called the **employee plans compliance resolution system (EPCRS)**. The Department of Labor also has a similar program for voluntary compliance infraction reporting. The concept is the same in both circumstances. If a company self-reports a violation that has been promptly corrected, then there is a chance that the regulators will not levy any fine whatsoever. The company will also build goodwill and a reputation with the regulators as an entity who is trying to do the right thing for its employees. If a fine is levied following a self-reported compliance infraction, then the fines are generally greatly reduced from a scenario where a regulator discovers something themselves during a routine audit. A regulator discovering an issue during an audit will also trigger more frequent audits, which are time-consuming and therefore costly.

The key is to correct any compliance shortfalls immediately and then report them to the relevant regulator to minimize the potential negative implications of a compliance breach.

Discussion Questions

1. A medium-sized company has decided to begin offering a DB plan. Do they need to host an enrollment meeting?
2. Why is the SPD frequently used as a means of fulfilling the employer's obligation to explain the plan to participants?
3. Who is typically appointed to be the plan administrator?
4. Is it correct that the only tax-related form that an employer-sponsored plan needs to file is a Form 1099-R in the event of a distribution?
5. From the perspective of employee disclosure, what happens when a significant change is made within the structure of an

employer-sponsored tax-advantaged plan (i.e., change in eligibility or vesting schedules)?

6. If there have not been any significant changes to the plan, then the employer only needs to provide an SPD when the participant enrolls in the plan for the first time. Is this statement correct?

7. A plan administrator receives a valid court order instructing that a portion of a participant's account should be paid to his ex-spouse. This qualified domestic relations order (QDRO) specifies the parties involved and the amount to be paid. How should the plan administrator proceed?

8. A plan administrator finds an accidental compliance infringement while performing a routine review of the plan operations. What should they do?

CHAPTER 14

Plan Terminations

Introduction

Have you ever said yes to something only to realize that with changing circumstances, you really need to back out? Sometimes this happens with employer-sponsored plans too. Business conditions are always changing, and sometimes the best of intentions are rendered toxic to the health of a company's finances. There are mechanisms to terminate a plan. There are also alternatives to simply deconstructing a plan. But if the plan is too far gone, the regulators might not permit these alternatives and just simply shut the plan down by operation of law. Before you say yes to a new plan, be sure to understand how to unwind it if conditions change.

Learning Goals

- Identify commonly cited reasons for a plan termination
- Describe a few alternatives to a plan termination
- Identify the steps for terminating a defined contribution (DC) plan
- Identify the steps for terminating a defined benefit (DB) plan
- Understand the available options when a DB plan has excess assets
- Describe when a plan could be terminated by the operation of law

Commonly Cited Reasons for a Plan Termination

When an employer establishes a retirement plan, their intention is for the new plan to be a lasting legacy for all plan participants. Their initial quest for the attraction and retention enhancement that a retirement plan offers is noble indeed. But, sometimes business conditions change, and what was once feasible is now not.

Technically, a **termination** is equal to a complete dissolution of the retirement plan being offered. This is very different from *freezing a plan*, which will be discussed later in this chapter.

As you might easily guess, the typical reason for a plan change is that the plan sponsor can no longer afford the contributions and ongoing administrative costs. Although it could be that the company simply wants to offer a different, and perhaps better, benefit. Maybe they are doing very well, and they want to increase participant benefits. The stigma of a weak company needing to terminate its plan is not always the case. Another common cause of needing to dissolve a retirement plan is the merger or sale of a company. When one company buys another, typically only one company's retirement plan survives. The other must be, in some way, adjusted.

Alternatives to Plan Terminations

The most common alternative to the outright termination of a plan, where everything comes to a grinding halt, is freezing a plan. When a plan is *frozen*, all benefit accruals stop. This means that any service provided beyond the point of freezing a plan will not accrue any additional retirement contributions or benefits from the employer. This option requires that participants be notified 15 days in advance of the freezing point.

For a DB plan, any benefits earned, based on the formula specified in the plan document, must remain intact. Those benefits were already earned and must now be provided. If the employer has not made contributions to fund accruals based on past service, then they must still do so in a frozen plan. A frozen plan will still incur ongoing administrative costs including Pension Benefit Guaranty Corporation (PBGC) coverage expenses.

If the employer offered a DC plan, then they must make any contributions required for services already provided. Then they can stop making further contributions. This employer will still have ongoing administrative costs as well, but since they are not a DB plan, they do not have the added expense of the PBGC coverage.

Another alternative to full-on termination is to amend the plan. It is possible to *amend* (convert) one plan type into another plan type. For instance, an employer could change their 401(k) into a profit-sharing retirement plan. An employer can amend any DB plan into another DB plan. They can also amend any DC plan into another DC plan. However, a DB plan cannot be *amended* into a DC plan. This transaction requires a full termination and then a new plan installation.

Limits on Plan Termination

Since retirement plans are intended to be facilitators of long-term retirement savings, the Internal Revenue Service (IRS) especially watches for terminations that appear to suggest that the employer was actually scheming a temporary tax shelter instead. In particular, the IRS gives great scrutiny to any plan that is terminated within 10 years of its installation. If the plan is deemed a temporary tax shelter, then the IRS will disqualify the plan, and the retroactive tax nightmare will commence.

What if business conditions change in the first 10 years, and the company simply has no choice but to terminate its plan? If an employer, who desires to terminate their retirement plan within the first 10 years, they can show to the IRS that the termination is the result of a legitimate change in business conditions that is beyond their control, and then the IRS will often not disqualify the plan.

Would a DC plan ever terminate due to insufficient funding? In an extreme case, it could. The employer might not have enough money to make their current year contribution and hence the motivation either to freeze or terminate their plan.

Would a DB plan ever terminate due to insufficient funds? The answer to this question is a resounding yes! DB plans most often terminate due to insufficient funds. When the plan assets dip too low (due to missed contributions in the past or poor market performance), the plan's temptation to freeze or terminate becomes substantial.

It is important to note that a plan cannot use a plan termination to avoid a compliance issue. When a plan goes through the formal termination process, the IRS will look extremely closely at any possible regulatory infraction. The employer will be held financially responsible if one is found.

Steps to Terminate a DC Plan

Terminating a DC plan is relatively easy compared to terminating a DB plan. The first step in the process is for the company's board of directors to formally pass a resolution to terminate the plan. At this point, benefit accruals will cease, and all participants must become 100 percent vested. The actual termination will take effect 15 days after the plan participants have received notice of the intended termination.

Once notice has been delivered, is the employer now free of retirement plan expense? No, under normal circumstances (excluding bankruptcy), the employer must be current on any retirement contributions. After the retirement contributions are current, the employer can consider plan asset liquidation options. Sometimes, the company will sell (liquidate) everything within the plan and proceed to distribute the proceeds to the various plan participants. The alternative is called an in-kind distribution. With an **in-kind distribution**, all assets are transferred to a different plan type as is. The assets are not sold in the process. The other plan type could be another DB plan, another DC plan, or a direct rollover to an individual retirement account (IRA).

The employer will then begin to process the various paperwork needed to physically distribute the plan assets. One such form is their annual Form 5500, which must be labeled as a final form. Another piece of paperwork is entirely optional, but 100 percent recommended. Just based on this description, you might be thinking of the IRS's advanced determination letter (ADL), and you would be right. Why would an employer need an ADL to terminate? Isn't that an installation step? It is actually used both for installation and termination. Submitting for an ADL during the termination phase allows the IRS to, in essence, rubber-stamp the process. There is no guarantee that the IRS will not audit a plan after an ADL has been issued, but if they are subsequently audited, the audit will typically be a much smoother process. If an employer chooses to neglect filing for an ADL, then it is almost always a guaranteed audit trigger for the IRS.

Steps to a DB Plan Termination

What about a DB plan? How easily are they able to be terminated? For the employer to initiate a plan termination, it must fall into one of two categories. The first category is called a standard termination. In a **standard termination**, the plan assets are equal to or greater than the projected benefit obligation (PBO), which is the estimate of the plan's liabilities. This plan is fully funded and may even be overfunded. Good for them! Perhaps they simply want to switch to a different type of retirement plan for whatever legitimate business reason. The second category is called a distress termination. In a **distress termination**, the employer's plan is usually underfunded. The employer must demonstrate that their ability to stay in business is substantially in question if their plan remains intact. Think of General Motors. These are the two allowable, company-initiated plan terminations if the plan is covered by the PBGC.

After the board of directors passes a resolution to implement a standard terminate in a DB plan, which is covered by the PBGC, the employer must then notify all participants. For a DB plan, the *notice of intent to terminate* must be sent 60 to 90 days before the proposed plan termination. This is substantially different from the 15-day notice given to DC participants. The employer will also need to notify all participants that PBGC coverage over their retirement benefits will cease as soon as the plan is terminated formally.

Often in a DB termination, the employer will transfer all plan assets to an insurance company who will then provide a retirement annuity to the participants. You will learn about the annuity-based option later in Chapter 24. The participants must be given the name and contact information of the insurance company, and all relevant benefits must be thoroughly explained.

Because the DB plan is covered by PBGC "insurance," the employer must promptly notify the PBGC of their intent to terminate. This step is applied uniquely to DB plans. The notice to the PBGC must contain a statement that the plan is fully funded. This essentially indemnifies the PBGC. At this point, the company is free to physically distribute plan assets to the insurance company or through some other instrument if that alternative is chosen.

Distressed terminations are managed by the PBGC. This process involves notifying the employees and then turning over all plan assets to the PBGC, who subsequently assumes the role of plan administrator.

Reversion of Excess Plan Assets

Sometimes, in a standard termination, the plan assets will exceed the PBO. This means either that the company contributed too much into the plan or that the investments provided returns that exceeded the actuarial expectations. Either way, the company has a good problem!

The employer has two options to resolve this "problem." The first option is to give each participant a proportional allocation of the excess assets. The second option is for the excess assets to revert to the employer. This second option is only available if the plan document specifically permits such an arrangement.

There is a taxation effect to reversion of plan assets because the employer already received a tax deduction for any contributions in the year in which they were made. The IRS charges a 50 percent excise tax (code word for a nonviolation penalty) on any plan assets that revert to the employer. Wow, that seems a bit excessive! The IRS is really trying to encourage the plan to allocate at least a portion of the plan's excess assets to the participants themselves. The excise tax is lowered to 20 percent if either 20 percent of the excess assets are allocated to the participant's accounts or 25 percent of the excess assets are transferred to a qualified replacement plan. A *qualified replacement plan* is just what it sounds like...an authorized secondary plan for the participant's benefit. These plans are often under the care of an insurance company.

Termination Distribution Options

Depending upon the stipulations of each plan, the employer may offer ultimate distributions either in the form of an annuity (which you will earn about in this section) or in a single lump sum. The employer can always elect at the time of termination to add a single lump-sum payment option, but they cannot remove the lump-sum option if the plan document formally establishes it. Participants usually choose the single lump-sum option if it is offered. They may withdraw all of the money at once and pay a huge tax liability, or they may roll the lump sum into an IRA (most common choice).

Plan administrators will need to provide participants with a benefit election form and notices of any spousal protections like a qualified joint and survivor annuity (QJSA). They also need to provide participants with a notice of their right to roll their single lump sum into an IRA. This topic will be discussed thoroughly in Chapter 23.

When plans do not offer a single lump sum, they are typically offering an annuity through an insurance company. Specifically, they will offer a **single premium annuity contract (SPAC)**, which means that the employer will use the money in the retirement plan for each participant to purchase a group annuity contract. One stipulation is that the stream of annuity payments must be equal to the benefit promised to the participant by the plan.

This effectively shifts the risk from the employer to the insurance company. Great for the company…risky for the insurance company, who now has the burden of making actuarial assumptions to determine exactly what to charge the employer for assuming the risk of making the promised benefit payments. The insurance company is well compensated for taking this risk.

Even when the plan is shifted to an SPAC, the plan's fiduciary still has risk exposure. The choice of the insurance carrier is considered a fiduciary responsibility with the full liability of any other fiduciary obligation. The biggest concern is: What happens if the insurance company goes out of business while they are still paying benefits to the plan's retirees?

To handle this risk, fiduciaries must solicit several different bids for the insurance premiums to purchase an SPAC. They should then thoroughly review each insurance company's ratings from several different ratings providers. The fiduciary should be careful to thoroughly document this search process. They should also not pick the lowest insurance quote. Because a lawsuit could follow an insurers collapse. Especially if the fiduciary chose the cheapest option.

Terminations by Operation of Law

There are a few different situations where the company may not have chosen to initiate a termination, but it is forced upon them by operation of the law. One such circumstance is when the IRS will deem an event to be a **partial termination**. This rule is designed to protect employees during a massive layoff. If at least 20 percent of the employees are subject to a layoff, then the company is deemed to be in partial termination, and all terminated employees must be 100 percent vested immediately. This can hurt a small business more than a larger business. If there are only four employees and one is fired, then technically they have crossed the threshold of 20 percent.

The company can rebut an IRS ruling of partial termination with facts and circumstances. If they can prove that this size of a layoff is a normal part of their business cycle, then typically, there will not be an issue for them. To avoid potentially being labeled as a *partial termination*, the employer could simply fully vest all participants at the time of the layoff. This option may not prove very costly because vesting schedules are already very advanced, and the participants may not have much plan balance in which they were not vested at the time of the layoff. This option also is no different than what the IRS would impose, but it carries the benefit of having a less confrontational relationship with the IRS.

Profit-sharing type plans, like the 401(k), the stock bonus plan, the employee stock ownership plan (ESOP), and the profit-sharing retirement plan, have a different set of rules. The IRS will require full vesting if the plan makes discretionary contributions and then abruptly stops for whatever reason. This rule will apply if the discretionary profit-sharing contributions have been recurring and substantial. This last clause sounds a bit vague, but the IRS will explore the specifics because they routinely audit plans when they terminate.

The nasty side of plan terminations is when the PBGC needs to step in and take over plans because they are so deeply underfunded that the PBGC's risk is simply too high and not expected to be reversed. This scenario is known as an **involuntary termination**. The PBGC will confiscate all assets of the plan and then figure out what portion of the benefits can be paid to the participants. Sometimes the PBGC will go after other assets of the company if they are able to. The logic behind this is that the company needed to fund the plan, but did not choose to do so. If there are other corporate assets that could be attached with a lien, then this may occur as the company is either struggling financially or in the process of filing for bankruptcy. Each situation is unique.

When someone abandons a pet, if they are lucky, the pet will find their way to the animal shelter and then be adopted into a new home where they are wanted and will be loved. What happens to a retirement plan that is abandoned? Yes, it is possible for this to happen. Sometimes, when companies merge or are acquired, the retirement plan just sort of gets lost in the process. The old owners are gone, and the new owners don't always know where everything is located. The basic question is: How can the financial institution who is holding the plan assets distribute them to the participants when the named fiduciary is gone? The only solution is for a court to appoint a **qualified termination administrator** who will then file reports with the Department of Labor (DOL) and distribute plan assets according to the DOL rules for such occurrences.

Discussion Questions

1. What are the common reasons for initiating a plan termination?
2. What are common alternatives to a plan termination?
3. An employer with a DB plan approaches you about amending their plan into a 410(k). How would you advise them?
4. At your 10-year college reunion, an old friend tells you that he started a business five years ago and installed a 401(k) at the time. He has rethought offering an employer-sponsored plan and has decided that it is too cumbersome and costly to retain the plan. He is planning on terminating the plan. What advice would you give him?
5. A client comes to you with information that they have discovered a major, yet accidental, compliance violation within their prof-it-sharing plan. They have decided to terminate the plan rather than fix the problem with additional contributions. What advice would you give this client?
6. Is the only time that a voluntary ADL is recommended to be used at the installation of a plan?

7. What differences exist between the process of terminating a DC plan and a DB plan, assuming that the DB plan termination is a standard termination?

8. A large employer has been a very good steward of their DB plan. They have a PBO (plan liability) of $100 million, but they have accumulated $125 million in plan assets through contributions and market performance. They have decided to amend the DB plan into a cash balance plan with frozen accruals, and then they plan to install a 401(k). The company is planning to take back the $25 million in excess plan assets. Is there a way to avoid paying $12.5 million in fines to the government?

9. A plan administrator is in the process of terminating their DB plan. They have chosen to use an SPAC for all participants. What issues does the plan administrator need to be aware of?

10. A small bicycle repair shop has established a 401(k). They have a total of four employees including the business owner. One employee, who has a reasonable unvested balance, has been with the company for two years when his employment is terminated. From the perspective of regulatory oversight, what issues might this scenario present?

11. What is an involuntary termination? Why does it occur? What happens when this does occur?

PART IV

Special Plan Types

CHAPTER 15

Nonqualified Deferred Compensation Plans

Introduction

So far you have primarily received the message that employer-sponsored plans cannot disadvantage rank-and-file employees. There have been a few notable exceptions with plans that are integrated with Social Security, cross tested, or age weighted. Another significant exception is the opportunity for executives to defer some of their otherwise current compensation into a nonqualified deferred compensation plan.

The goal of these plans is to shift income from the current period down the participant's timeline and perhaps all the way until retirement. There are certain actions that could be taken that would completely destroy this goal and render all benefits taxable in the current period. This is very important to understand if either you or a potential client has access to a nonqualified deferred compensation plan.

Employers also have a few life insurance-based options either for minimizing their own risks or for creating additional value for their top-ranking executives. All of these concepts need to be explored and understood thoroughly.

Learning Goals

- Compare nonqualified plans with qualified plans
- Understand the tax treatment of nonqualified plans
- Identify the key nonqualified plan design considerations
- Describe how a plan can be designed to protect somewhat the interests of the participants
- Identify the different types of §457 plans
- Understand the possible application of an executive bonus life insurance plan

Nonqualified Versus Qualified Plans

By now, you are already familiar with the tax structure of a qualified plan. The business receives a tax deduction at the time that the contribution is made, and the participants do not pay any tax until they eventually withdraw the funds from the retirement account. For the participants, this is known as tax deferral.

At its very simplest level, nonqualified compensation is viable compensation that a worker has earned in one year but does not receive until another. Nonqualified plans follow the accounting matching rule. The employer receives a deduction for wages when an employee receives the taxable income. If the wages are deferred, then the employer does not get the deduction, and the employee does not have "taxable income" until certain tests have been met. In this chapter, you will learn all about this process.

Consider company A and employee B. Employee B earns a certain wage from company A, but not all of it is received in the current year (2014). For now, let us assume that employee B defers the money for three years (2017). While the money is deferred, it is sitting somewhere. It is most likely in a bank account or some other very liquid asset. It is earning some rate of interest during the deferral period. Are the earnings tax deferred? Or does someone have a tax consequence in each year where the deferred assets have earnings? The answer is that company A will pay taxes on the earnings during the deferral period. When the deferred wages PLUS earnings are paid to employee B in 2017, the company will receive a tax deduction for the full amount paid to the employee, and the employee will recognize all compensation as taxable income in the year in which it is received (2017).

In terms of design features, nonqualified plans are more flexible than qualified plans. They can structure almost any combination that they want and often outside the purview of the Employee Retirement Income Security Act (ERISA). Because of the reduced regulatory oversight and the requisite compliance testing, nonqualified plans are also less costly to administer. Nonqualified plans can be used to legitimately favor highly compensated employees (HCEs). As such, they are a great recruitment tool!

Consider another company called Johnson Fabricators. They are a very small company with only 10 employees in total. Two of the employees are also the owners, and they each earn $100,000 per year. The other eight employees earn a total of $240,000 (an average salary of $30,000) per year. If Johnson Fabricators decided to implement a profit-sharing plan with the maximum 25 percent contribution, then the cost to the employer would be $110,000 [25% × ($100,000 + $100,000 + $240,000)]. However, if the company decided to offer instead a 25 percent nonqualified deferred compensation plan to only the two owners, which is completely legal, their total cost would be $50,000 [25% × ($100,000 + $100,000)]. The company will also have an incremental loss from not having a current tax deduction and the opportunity cost of any investment gains on the money that would have been saved as a result of the tax deduction. They would still receive a corporate tax deduction when the funds were ultimately taxed to the employees or owners. Even if we estimate the combined tax and opportunity cost expense to be $25,000 then the total cost of offering the nonqualified plan is still only $75,000 compared to $110,000 with the other alternative. This example ignores the administrative costs, but they will be lower in a nonqualified plan, and this will further amplify the cost savings.

The nonqualified plan is certainly the lower cost option, but it will still cost more than one dollar to provide one dollar's worth of benefit. The loss of a tax deduction and any administrative costs will still push the total cost above one dollar for each dollar of benefits received.

Economic Benefit Rule

From a tax perspective, the employer will only receive a tax deduction when the income is taxable for the employee. Income is not considered taxable as long as there remains a **substantial risk of forfeiture**, which means that the employee might lose the money under certain circumstances. To maintain a substantial risk of forfeiture, the employer could use longer vesting schedules, performance thresholds, or provisions that the money will revert to the employer if the employee does not consult with the employer during retirement or chooses to work for a competitor of the employer.

If there is no lingering substantial risk of forfeiture, then the compensation will automatically be taxed…unless the deferred compensation plan does not violate two rules. If these rules are not violated, then the deferred compensation will remain deferred and untaxed. The first rule is called the *economic benefit rule*, which you will learn about in this section, and the second is called the *constructive receipt rule*, which you will learn about in the next section.

The **economic benefit rule** (§83) states that any economic benefit must be included in taxable income if it has a value that is both ascertainable and current. If the exact dollar amount is known and there is no risk of forfeiture, then it is currently taxed to the employee, and the employer receives a deduction. The idea is that if the employee has no risk of forfeiture and the company transfers the dollar amount to a trust where distributions can only be paid to the participant, then there is an ascertainable economic benefit, and the compensation should be taxed to the employee.

If the benefit is taxed in the current year, then the whole purpose of deferring the compensation has been negated. The purpose to defer income is to shift it from being taxed in a time period when there is substantial income (higher tax bracket in a progressive tax structure) to a period when there is less income (theoretically a lower tax bracket).

To not violate the economic benefit rule, the assets in a nonqualified plan must remain assets of the employer until they are actually paid to the employee. You will see later in this chapter what issue this may create.

Constructive Receipt Rule

Another rule that may impact the tax deferral of nonqualified deferred compensation plans is known as the **constructive receipt rule** (§409A). The essence of the constructive receipt rule is whether participants have the ability to choose to receive compensation now or later. If they have ad hoc authority to choose the timing of their compensation on a month-by-month basis, then they will violate this rule and the compensation will be taxable in the current period.

One common example of this scenario is a schoolteacher. Technically, they only work during the physical school year, although they do work on enhancing courses and research during the summer months. Most teachers receive a paycheck every month. The Internal Revenue Service (IRS) would say that they are deferring a portion of their salary, which is then spread evenly over the months so that they receive paychecks during the months when they are not actually teaching a class. Another example could be an executive who receives a bonus, but decides when to receive that bonus based upon his tax-planning strategies. The doctrine of constructive receipt does not require physical possession of the funds to deem them as having been received and therefore taxable in the current period.

The IRS does not want people choosing when they receive a portion of their compensation on an event-by-event basis. If someone is found "managing" when they receive compensation, then not only will have current taxable income but also a 20 percent penalty.

It is perfectly legal for an employee to decide to receive a portion of their compensation at a later time…they just cannot defer a bonus at the point in time when they find out that they will receive a bonus. They must make the election to defer a portion of their income for a given calendar year *before* the end of the previous calendar year.

The constructive receipt rule does not apply if the compensation is received within the first 2½ months following the year in which the participant becomes vested in the compensation.

If deferred compensation does not violate either the economic benefit rule or the constructive receipt rule, then the compensation is tax deferred until it is distributed. The employer will not receive a tax deduction until the participant has taxable income, and the employer will pay taxes on any investment gains earned by the deferred compensation while it is waiting to be distributed.

Distribution from a nonqualified deferred compensation plan could occur at a specific date, at the point of separation of service, at death or disability, at a change in corporate ownership, or at the point of an unforeseen emergency.

What about Wage-Based Taxes?

If you look on your paycheck stub, you will notice a subtraction from your gross pay for FICA. This stands for the Federal Insurance Contributions

Act, which is a glorified term for social security taxes. The taxes are based upon earned income. What happens when some of that income is deferred using a nonqualified deferred compensation program? The income is applied to FICA taxes not when it is distributed but at the later of (1) the date services were performed to earn the money or (2) when there is no longer any substantial risk of forfeiture.

Consider participant A who defers 10 percent of his or her wages every year into a nonqualified deferred compensation plan. This particular plan is set up such that all funds in the plan are fully vested after participant A has completed five years of service. After five years have passed, the entire account balance is included in taxable income for the purpose of calculating FICA (social security) taxes because substantial risk of forfeiture has been removed. For FICA taxes, it does not matter if the participant has been careful not to violate the economic benefit rule or the constructive receipt rule or both. Social security taxes are a completely different animal.

For any given year, income earned above a certain threshold does not apply to social security taxes anyway. In 2014, that income threshold is $117,000. To the extent that normal income plus deferred compensation exceeds this number, it will not be taxed for FICA whether the income is from normal wages or deferred compensation.

There is also a concept known as the *nonduplication rule*, which applies to the FICA tax. Income may be taxed for FICA purposes that is still tax deferred for regular income taxes because the participant has not violated either the economic benefit rule or the constructive receipt rule. In such a case, the deferred compensation will eventually be recognized as taxable income. When this happens, the deferred compensation is not taxed, for Social Security purposes, a second time.

Objectives of Nonqualified Deferred Compensation

The obvious objective of a nonqualified deferred compensation plan is to attract and retain key executive talent. If an employer wants the best people, then they must be willing to pay for it. In essence, the nonqualified plan is a supplemental layer of benefits. Think of it as the top tier on a two-tiered cake. An employer's qualified plan provides a nice base on which to build. The nonqualified plan is the upper layer where most of the decorations are displayed.

How could a nonqualified deferred compensation plan uniquely benefit start-up companies? Start-ups are not known for being cash rich. In fact, they are usually levered (in debt) as much as possible. They can use nonqualified deferred compensation plans to attract key people necessary for success and then pay them once their business has taken off and has plenty of cash. There is more risk on the table for the participants in this case because the start-up might not take off. It might actually flop big time, and the participants would lose all deferred compensation. To adjust for this increased level of risk, start-ups will often offer very generous nonqualified plans.

The employer might use nonqualified deferred compensation as a dangling carrot to incentivize participants to reach certain performance targets. In this case, economic benefit may be more linked to performance than attainment of a certain tenure of employment.

There are also three golden incentives involved with nonqualified deferred compensation plans. The first golden is the **golden handshake**, which is an incentive to retire. This might be a deferred compensation program that will pay the participant a certain sum only after retiring from the employer. This incentive will soften the impact of retirement for the employee. The second golden is the **golden handcuffs**, which is an incentive to stay. This might take the form of a very long vesting schedule or a consulting stipulation where benefits are only payable to the participants if they consult for the employer for a specific time period after formal retirement. The third golden is the **golden parachute**, which is an incentive to permit a takeover. In this scenario, an executive will receive additional deferred compensation if the company is sold or in some way merged with another company. This incentive might remove an executive's personal incentives to block a potential suitor.

Specific Types of Nonqualified Deferred Compensation

Up to this point, nonqualified deferred compensation plans have been presented as a general category. This larger group can be subdivided into two smaller categories to help you understand exactly how these plans function.

The first subcategory of nonqualified plans is called **salary reduction plans**. You can probably guess from the name how this group functions. It works very much like a 401(k) plan where the employer takes a portion of the participant's gross salary and defers it into the nonqualified plan. There is no dollar limit on the deferrals. Sometimes, executives will elect to receive certain types of bonuses in the current period and other types of bonuses as deferred compensation.

The second subcategory of nonqualified plans is called a **supplemental executive retirement plan (SERP)**. The SERP provides additional income beyond the participant's normal gross salary. It is not a reduction from salary, but an addition to it. This is a way to raise the executive's compensation package up to a competitive level outside the purview of nondiscrimination testing! The SERP essentially provides the missing piece of the compensation puzzle.

There is also a subcomponent of the SERP, which is called an **offset SERP**. An offset SERP will use the nonqualified deferred compensation plan to offset the employer's qualified plan to provide for a certain income replacement ratio in retirement. The replacement ratio is the amount of preretirement income, which is replaced by income-generating assets during retirement.

Forfeiture Provisions

A **forfeiture provision** is designed to create the inherent uncertainty necessary for the IRS to not tax the deferred compensation in the current period. Forfeiture provisions are very common in SERPs, but they are much less common in salary reduction plans. The four most common types of forfeiture provisions are vesting schedules, performance conditions, postretirement consulting clauses, and noncompete agreements.

Because ERISA does not apply to nonqualified deferred compensation plans, companies can establish a vesting schedule that serves their own purposes. They might set a vesting schedule of 5 years, 10 years, or even 15 years! There is no limit beyond the plan administrator's creative design ideas and what the participants are willing to accept.

A company might set certain performance benchmarks to encourage specific goals. This forfeiture provision would help to mitigate the agency conflict, which is when the goals of management can differ from the goals of the owners. A company could say that the balance in a nonqualified plan is subject to complete forfeiture unless the participants' division reaches a specific growth target in sales or margin improvement. It is imperative that the participants should have the ability to influence whatever performance metric is chosen. It would be unfair to set the benchmark as a target that they will only hit by chance.

Sometimes, an employee's contribution to the company is so incredibly valuable (and virtually irreplaceable) that the employer just does not want to let him or her go. They can place a clause in the nonqualified deferred compensation plan that provides a benefit only if the participant completes a certain amount of consulting work post retirement. This can be an effective way to lock in key talents for a longer window of time and allow the participant more time to locate and train a replacement.

Another potential forfeiture clause is a noncompete agreement. This would state that the participants would lose all benefits if they work for a competitor within a certain window of time. One caveat is that the window of time must be reasonable, such as a few years. It would not be legal to say that they could never again work for a competitor, period. The noncompete clause will also only work within a specific geographic region. For example, a senior executive at a regional bank could be prohibited, through the nonqualified deferred compensation plan, from working for a competitor within a two-year period of time in the same region covered by the former employer. However, it would be perfectly legitimate for the executive to work for a different regional bank in another part of the country.

Remember that after a substantial risk of forfeiture is removed, the balance in a nonqualified deferred compensation plan is fully taxable for the participants unless they also do not violate the economic benefit rule and the constructive receipt rule.

To offset the effect of these forfeiture clauses, it is common for companies to offer some level of protection for plan participants. The most common is the golden parachute that we already discussed. In the event of a takeover, the participants could be given additional benefits, full vesting, and an immediate payout. Another protective mechanism is that participants have access to hardship withdrawals. In the event of a hardship withdrawal, the portion of the account that is withdrawn is taxed in the current period, but the remainder of the account is not deemed to have violated the constructive receipt rule and thus trigger taxation of the entire account. The amount of the hardship withdrawal is limited to the dollar amount of the unforeseen immediate financial need. A new flat screen TV for the Superbowl does not qualify as an immediate financial need.

In the event of a legal dispute over the way the plan is functioning or options are applied, there is typically a clause that all grievances will be handled through arbitration. Arbitration is a legal process where a panel of lawyers will assess any legal breaches and impose any requisite financial remedies. This is more cost-effective than going to court.

Design Considerations

From a design perspective, is a nonqualified deferred compensation plan a defined contribution (DC)-type plan or a defined benefit (DB)-type plan? The answer is, it depends. A salary deferral plan can be thought of as a DC-type plan because it involves participant contributions much like a 401(k) might. On the other hand, a SERP is more like a DB-type plan because the burden of making contributions rests entirely with the employer.

Who can be eligible for a nonqualified deferred compensation plan? Technically, anyone *could* be included. For reasons discussed later in this chapter, nonqualified plans are usually reserved for only the HCEs like executives and other key employees.

A nonqualified deferred compensation plan can offer a benefit in the event of either a preretirement death or a documented disability. Typically, the company would remove any forfeiture overlay remaining for the participant.

Offering a benefit for disability can present a tricky challenge if the employer also offers disability insurance. The insurance company providing the disability insurance for employees could see this as duplicate coverage and deny paying the full benefit that the insurance otherwise would have provided. The employer should check with their insurance provider before offering a disability benefit within their nonqualified plan if the potential for duplicate coverage exists.

Funding Issues

A nonqualified deferred compensation plan can be funded, unfunded, or **informally funded**, which means that funds are reserved on the employer's balance sheet for the intention of paying benefits in the future.

If the plan is funded, then the employer will have established a trust and contributed all funds into that trust for the sole purpose of making payments to participants when the time comes. This method has the highest level of certainty for the plan participants. They know that the money is available to pay them off when they need it. *This funding method would violate the economic benefit rule.* This means that as soon as the substantial risk of forfeiture (vesting, etc.) is removed, money is then fully taxable for the employee. This could result in the receipt of additional taxable income during their working years when their tax rate is still quite high, thus defeating the whole purpose of the nonqualified plan.

An unfunded plan is easy to understand...the employer simply does not set aside any current funds to pay the nonqualified deferred compensation. This method does not violate the economic benefit rule, but it also does not provide the participant any measure of safety. They will be paid only if the company can make the payments at some future date. The lowest probability of current taxation with the highest risk of not being paid.

Informal funding is the middle ground. This is essentially creating a reserve account, which is still accessible by the creditors of the company. The funds in the reserve account can be used to pay benefits if the company does not get sued and does not go out of business. This method will also avoid violating the economic benefit rule.

Company-Owned Life Insurance

Corporate-owned life insurance (COLI) is one popular way to fund a nonqualified deferred compensation plan. *The company must be the owner*

NOT the participant! Companies will often use a whole life product, which will accumulate a cash value, rather than a term life insurance product, which is pure insurance that becomes worthless unless the covered individual dies. The whole point of a COLI is to fund the nonqualified plan in the event of the premature death of a participant.

As described earlier in this chapter, if the plan is funded and the assets increase in value due to investment performance before they are distributed to the participant, then the employer will owe taxes on the growth. Not so with a COLI. Life insurance contracts offer **tax-free inside buildup**, which means that the earnings are tax-free until a life insurance contract is paid out either due to death or the company canceling the policy. The ultimate proceeds from the life insurance contract are tax-free to the company if certain conditions are met. First, the insured individual must be notified that the company is insuring their life, *and* the participant must consent to the insurance. The second condition is actually a three-way test, and one of the tests must be passed. The tests are (1) that the insured participant must be employed when the insurance is initiated, (2) that the insured was an employee within 12 months of death, or (3) that the death benefits are paid directly to the participant's heirs or used to buy out the deceased participant's ownership interest in the employer.

The company "ownership" portion of the COLI enables the company to borrow against the policy if cash flow were ever to become an issue.

Both the economic benefit rule and the constructive receipt rule can be sidestepped if the life insurance is owned by the company, the premiums are paid by the employer, *and* the employer is the sole beneficiary. The previous rule about the participant's heirs being the beneficiary is related to the taxation of the insurance proceeds after death. The economic benefit rule and the constructive receipt rule apply when the participant is still alive.

Benefit Security

How safe are the benefits in a nonqualified deferred compensation plan? The answer is, it depends. If the plan is funded, it provides the maximum amount of safety for the participants, but it will create a current taxation problem by violating the economic benefit rule. If the plan is unfunded, then there is very low risk of creating a taxation event, but the participant is at the mercy of the long-term financial strength of the employer. There are three creative funding instruments that can be used to increase the level of security offered to plan participants. They are rabbi trusts, secular trusts, and surety bonds.

The **rabbi trust** received its name because it was first used to offer protection to a rabbi's nonqualified deferred compensation plan in 1981. With this creative funding instrument, the employer will establish an *irrevocable trust*, which is a trust that cannot be altered after it is created. The catch is that the assets in a rabbi trust must remain available to the creditors of the company. This is accomplished through a special clause in the *trust agreement* (the actual legal document known as *the trust*). This clause enables the rabbi trust to avoid violating the constructive receipt rule. This instrument does set money aside to ease the participants' minds, but this only works if the company does not get sued or go bankrupt. From a benefit security perspective, this is better than being unfunded, but not as good as being funded.

Another funding instrument is a **secular trust**, which is a full-on irrevocable trust. The employer will create a trust and then contribute funds to it that would satisfy the payments due to participants through a nonqualified plan. In this type of trust, the trust's assets are not available to the creditors of the firm. This offers great benefit security for participants. The security comes at a cost…immediate taxation as soon as any risk of forfeiture is removed. By now, you know that this is opposite to the original intent of the nonqualified plan. For this reason, secular trusts are hardly ever used in practice.

The third creative security instrument is called a security bond, which is a form of insurance against the risk of the participants receiving their payments. A bonding company will sell insurance to the participant. If the company does not make good for whatever reason, then the bonding company will step in and make the required payment. The participants must pay for this protection themselves. For a bonding company to be willing to offer insurance, the employer will need to have a strong balance sheet, and the bonding company will review annually whether or not they will renew the insurance policy.

The Top-Hat Exemption

ERISA-mandated compliance is a big factor in the cost structure of a company's retirement plan offerings. Anything that can be done to minimize the oversight is a cost-saving must.

There is an option to avoid the ERISA requirements for vesting, participation testing, funding requirements, and the fiduciary standard! It is known as the **top-hat exemption**. This exemption basically states that if the plan is unfunded (not formally funded) *and* is only available to a "select group of management and/or highly compensated employees," then the above ERISA mandates can legally be avoided.

What if the company said that they wanted to offer their nonqualified deferred compensation plan to all employees? In this case, they have not limited the plan to only a select group, and therefore ERISA will apply. This is a BIG issue! Just consider the impact of applying ERISA funding requirements. If the plan is required to be funded, then the economic benefit rule has been violated and current taxation of benefits is mandated. Not the intended effect!

The top-hat exemption is one reason why nonqualified deferred compensation plans are primarily offered to only the HCEs.

§457 Plans

The term *nonqualified deferred compensation* is sometimes psychologically synonymous with a §457 plan. In reality, §457 plans are only a subset of the nonqualified marketplace. A §457 plan is simply a nonqualified plan available only to nonprofit companies. Any nonqualified plan that is not a §457 plan is used by a for-profit company.

The reason that a separate category was created is that nonprofit organizations (as companies) do not care about the tax deductions that result when a for-profit company makes a retirement contribution. The employees still care, but it is the businesses that offer the plans and make the decisions. *The reality is that nonprofit organizations are, in practice, more likely to use nonqualified deferred compensation plans than their for-profit counterparts.*

The first type of a §457 plan is called a **457(b) plan**, which is also known as an *eligible* plan. This plan type is only available to those who physically provide a service to a nonprofit organization. The salary deferral limit for 2014 is $17,500 or 100 percent of compensation, whichever is lower. Unaffected by qualified contributions made to a 403(b) of 401(k) plan. Earlier we discussed the constructive receipt rule, which basically says that to defer funds from a given year, the employee must elect to do so before the end of the previous year. With a 457(b) plan, employees can make the election month by month. To defer any money for a given month, they must elect to do so before the end of the previous **month**. Distributions from a 457(b) plan are only permitted, while the participants are still employed by the company, in the event of an unforeseen emergency (hardship withdrawal) or after they reach age 70½, should they decide to keep working that long. Just like their for-profit counterparts, to avoid ERISA, the top-hat exemption will apply.

The second type of §457 plan is called a **457(f) plan**, which is also known as an ineligible plan. Think of the "f" plan as having failed a test of some kind. In reality, they have not failed anything (this is just a memory cue). They have chosen not to adhere to the contribution limit applicable to the 457(b) plan. By ignoring the contribution limit, they have now created a taxation event as soon as a substantial risk of forfeiture is removed. This is more of a bonus deferral program than a retirement planning tool.

Executive Bonus Life Insurance

Executive bonus life insurance plans (§162) are another way in which it is perfectly legal for a company to discriminate in favor of HCEs. Basically, the company decides to offer the employee a life insurance policy, and unlike the COLI, the company does not own the policy. The employees own their own policy. This is a way for the company to help employees build cash value in a whole life insurance product and add another layer to their estate plan. The employer will simply pay the employee a "bonus," which is used to pay a life insurance premium. The employer will receive a tax deduction for the bonus, and the employee will receive taxable income.

The employer could elect to pay the actual premium directly to the insurance company or they could elect to pay the employee who then is responsible for relaying the payment to the life insurance company. If the company chooses this last option, then typically they will gross up the bonus so that the employer is also paying the taxes due by the employee for receiving the bonus. This creates a *double bonus* feature because the company is paying the actual life insurance premiums and they are also paying the taxes associated with the transaction.

Discussion Questions

1. What are the differences between a qualified and a nonqualified plan?
2. An employee will not pay taxes on the full value of a nonqualified deferred compensation plan until certain requirements have been met. However, he must pay taxes on the earnings during the deferral period. Is this a correct understanding of how nonqualified deferred compensation works?
3. Why is the notion of a substantial risk of forfeiture such a major issue for nonqualified deferred compensation?
4. Describe the economic benefit rule and its importance.
5. What is a "constructive receipt" and how can it be avoided?
6. What are the objectives of a nonqualified deferred compensation plan?
7. What is the difference between a SERP and an offset SERP?
8. What roadblocks can cause a substantial risk of forfeiture?
9. What must exist for a noncompete clause to be enforceable?
10. What is the difference between a COLI and executive bonus life insurance?
11. A company has one employee whose industry contacts have been extremely valuable to the business. The employee is now nearing normal retirement age, and the company is concerned that she might leave the company either through retirement or attrition. How can a nonqualified deferred compensation plan help the company manage this risk?
12. Explain the function and purpose of a rabbi trust.
13. What is the "top-hat" rule and why is it important?
14. What is the difference in the two types of nonqualified deferred compensation plans that are available to nonprofit organizations?

CHAPTER 16

Equity-Based Compensation

Introduction

There is a mechanism for providing employees (usually executives) with a substantial monetary benefit and also aligning their interests with shareholder interests. Equity-based compensation programs transform employees into shareholders. There are numerous different options to create this transformation. The company could use one of several strategies to transfer actual shares to employees, or they could create an asset that gives them stockholder incentives without having the requisite voting rights. Each strategy has different pros and cons, and each different taxation. If you are either an executive or a professional who might advise someone who is, then this chapter will provide you with valuable information on equity-based compensation plans.

Learning Goals

- Understand how equity-based compensation can be useful
- Identify what unique considerations apply to a closely held business that offers equity-based compensation
- Understand the differences between nonqualified stock options (NQSOs) and incentive stock options (ISOs)
- Identify the usefulness of employee stock purchase plans (ESPPs)
- Identify how a smaller business might use phantom stock or stock appreciation rights to offer a meaningful benefit to their employees

Overview of Equity-Based Compensation

Up to this point in the book, the retirement planning focus has been on either qualified or nonqualified retirement savings plans. We will now broaden our view to include **equity-based compensation**, which could include NQSOs, ISOs, ESPPs, restricted stock, phantom stock, and stock appreciation rights (SARs).

The common trait among all of these different plan types, which will be explained thoroughly in this chapter, is that they all help to resolve agency conflict by giving the employees an incentive for the company's stock to do well. You may recall, from a previous class, that **agency conflict** is the tension that exists when the firm's owners are not also the managers. The managers might not make decisions that are in the best interest of the owners. This is the essence of agency conflict, and employee stock ownership is one way to help manage this risk for the owners.

Equity-based compensation is very common with start-up companies. They are rich in ideas and (hopefully) potential, but poor in cash. They can reward valuable employees with shares of stock with the unwritten promise that the employee owners will benefit handsomely when the market realizes the full potential of the company.

This category of compensation can also be used to encourage specific business goals. The award of shares could be contingent upon the executive or even the company meeting a certain performance threshold.

What About Closely Held Business?

As you can imagine, equity-based compensation receives its value from the value of the underlying company's stock. But, closely held companies do not have publicly traded stock; so the value is not as simple to measure. Typically, when we think about a closely held business, we think of small companies. This is usually true, but not always so. Consider Mars (the candy company) and Koch Industries (a large private company engaged in many industries) as examples of some very large closely held companies.

The key to applying an equity-based compensation plan to a closely held business is that the company must apply a consistent valuation concept across both time and divisions. They must use the same valuation multiple over various time periods. They also cannot use a different valuation multiple for different divisions of the same closely held business. Companies might apply an industry standard multiple on book value per share or earnings per share or even revenue per share. Different industries have different standards, but revenue per share is a very common choice because it is subject to the least amount of accounting manipulation.

From the perspective of the employee, one might wonder: How will the employee realize value if the shares are not publicly traded? There is typically an internal market for the shares in which either other owners or the company itself will repurchase the shares issued through an equity-based compensation program.

The existing owners of the closely held business may be concerned about having their ownership interest diluted by the inclusion of new owners. The shares to cover equity-based compensation will typically come from Treasury stock, but the inclusion of new owners will lower the percentage of ownership (and therefore the division of profits) of existing shareholders.

One nuance that must be monitored is the percentage ownership that an employee is assigned if the company is an S corporation. You might be thinking, "Great, what is an S corporation?" An S corporation is a domestic company with fewer than 100 shareholders that elects to have all corporate profits taxed as income directly by the owners and not at the corporate level.[1] They are usually smaller businesses. In an S corporation, anyone who owns more than 2 percent of the business will have some odd personal taxation issues dealing with the cost of medical insurance and life insurance premiums, which are paid for by the employer. If the employee crosses the 2 percent threshold, then they might lose certain tax-free benefits.

Other Preliminary Concerns

One concern that will face a company that desires to establish an equity-based compensation plan is how formal to make the "plan." The board of directors could establish a formal plan with a compensation committee to award equity-based compensation to employees. In this scenario, the board will typically permit awards up to a certain aggregate dollar amount, at which point the board would need to approve more funding if further awards became necessary. The alternative to this approach is for the board of directors to approve equity awards on a case-by-case basis. This second option is much more time consuming for the board.

Another concern is the method of accounting used to reflect equity-based compensation on the company's income statement. In years past, companies had discretion on when to report an expense for this category. Now, the rules are clear. The company must record an expense based on an options pricing model for any equity-based compensation that is fully vested, but the mechanics of this approach are beyond the scope of this book. Publicly traded companies are limited to $1 million of stock awards except when performance-based thresholds are used, in which case there is no limitation. Any amounts awarded under an equity-based compensation plan must be disclosed on regulatory filings called an annual proxy statement to shareholders.

The mandatory expense of equity-based compensation in the current period has made companies a little less willing to use it. However, the tool is still used in many large companies.

Does equity-based compensation have any effect on the company's existing shareholders? It may dilute ownership interests if there are a small number of shares outstanding.

Companies also need to be careful about using equity-based compensation because it may be deemed a public offering, which will require costly Securities and Exchange Commission (SEC) filings and approvals. The potential costly application of public offering rules can be avoided if the company applies the top-hat exemption. If the plan is restricted to only a select group of employees [like highly compensated employees (HCEs)], then the share awards are considered a private offering and do not require additional regulatory hurdles.

Nonqualified Stock Options

The whole idea behind equity-based compensation is to encourage executives to be focused on increasing the stock price through whatever legitimate and legal business means they can come up with.

An **NQSO** gives executives the right to purchase shares of their employer at a specified price (called either the *exercise price* or the *strike price*) within a certain window of time. Executives will only exercise their option (actually use the option to purchase shares) if the option is *in the money*, which means that the current market price is higher than their option price. It would be foolish for executives to exercise an option with a strike price of $50 per share when the stock is trading at $40. They could buy the shares much more cheaply in the open market and just let their option expire worthless.

The strike price on an NQSO must be at least 100 percent of the current market price, which is also called the fair market value (FMV). It is very common for the option to expire after 10 years. This is a huge window of time in which the executive can earn a substantial profit if the stock appreciates in value. Companies can use either a cliff vesting or a graded vesting schedule. There is no mandated vesting requirement like an Employee Retirement Income Security Act (ERISA) plan will have.

Per the constructive receipt doctrine, all equity-based compensation is taxable once the executive is fully vested unless the company chooses from a series of specific distribution dates. The company can choose to set the distribution date at termination, at death, at disability, or at a specific date, which is longer than the vesting time period.

NQSOs have a unique tax treatment. They are taxed at ordinary tax rates when the option is exercised. The ordinary tax rate applies to the difference between the FMV and the strike price. Social Security taxes are due at the same time, and the employer will receive a tax deduction equal to the same amount that the executive realizes as taxable income. Assuming that the executives do not immediately sell their shares after exercising the options, any additional gain (or loss) is treated as a capital gain. If the shares are held longer than one year, then the executives will receive the more favorable long-term capital gains tax rate.

Consider an executive who receives an NQSO to purchase 500 shares of the employer's publicly traded stock at the current market price of $25 any time over the next 10 years. After four years, the stock has risen to $65 and the executive decides to exercise his option in which he is fully vested. He holds the shares for an additional two years and then ultimately sells them at $90. Tremendous deal for the executive!

What is the tax effect for such executives? They will pay $12,500 ($25 × 500 shares) to purchase the stock. They will receive $20,000 [($65 − $25) × 500 shares] of taxable income, and the employer will therefore receive a $20,000 tax deduction in year 4 when the option was exercised. When the executives eventually sell their shares, they will have a long-term capital gain of $12,500 [($90 – $65) × 500 shares]. Had the shares declined below $65, then the executives would have realized a taxable loss instead of a gain.

Incentive Stock Options

An **ISO** is very similar to an NQSO. Like its nonqualified counterpart, an ISO must have a strike price, which is at least 100 percent of the FMV at the time that the option is granted, but an ISO must be approved by shareholders. The time window on an ISO is limited to 10 years, while an NQSO does not have a strict limit. While an NQSO does not have any specific dollar limit, an ISO is limited to $100,000 annually. This limit is based upon the number of shares multiplied by the strike price. There is an additional limitation if the executive is already at least a 10 percent owner. In this case, the strike price must be at least 110 percent of FMV at the time of the option award and the time window is also limited to only five years. While an NQSO can be awarded to anyone the board wishes (consultants, contractors, etc.), an ISO can only be awarded to employees of the company.

You can see that the ISO has less flexibility than the NQSO. Why would anyone want to use an ISO? The answer is the tax treatment…

At the time that an executive chooses to exercise an ISO contract, there is no tax consequence! However, there may be an issue with alternative minimum taxes (AMT) rules. The nuances of AMT rules are beyond the scope of this book, but understand that under certain special circumstances, an executive could still owe AMTs when no ordinary income taxes are due.[2] They should consult with their tax professional before exercising their options.

With an ISO, the real taxes are due when the stock is ultimately sold. If the stock has been held for at least two years from the grant date *and* at least one year from the exercise date, then all gains are considered long-term capital gains. Table 16.1 shows the various income tax brackets and the associated long-term capital gains tax rates. Notice that the long-term capital gains rates are always lower than ordinary income. If

Table 16.1 Capital gains tax rates

Tax bracket (ordinary income)	Income range	Long-term capital gains rate
10–15%	$0–$36,900	0%
25–35%	$36,901–$406,750	15%
39.6%	$406,751+	20%

the earnings are all considered capital gains, then the employer will not receive a deduction. They only receive a deduction when the employee has ordinary taxable income. If the two-year or one-year holding require-ment is not met, then the ISO will be taxed the same way that an NQSO is taxed…ordinary income on the difference between the strike price and the exercise price and capital gains based on the actual holding period (could be either long term or short term).

Consider an executive who receives an ISO for 1,000 shares of com-pany stock with a strike price of $10. One year later, the employee exer-cises his or her ISO and holds the shares for exactly one year before selling at $15. In this scenario, all $5,000 [($15 – $10) × 1,000 shares] of the gain is taxed at long-term capital gains rates, and the employer will not receive any tax deduction.

What if this same executive exercised the option one year after the grant date (at a price of $12), and then saw the stock jump up to $15 within the first six months and sold at that point? Because the executive did not adhere to the two-year or one-year rule, he or she will have ordi-nary income of $2,000 [($12 – $10) × 1,000 shares] and a short-term capital gain of $3,000 [($15 – $12) × 1,000 shares]. The employer will receive a tax deduction for the $2,000 of ordinary income.

What if this same executive exercised the option six months after the grant date (at a price of $12), and then held for one year and two days before selling? In this scenario, the executive has also violated the two-year or one-year rule. He or she will have ordinary income of $2,000 [($12 – $10) × 1,000 shares], but now, the $3,000 [($15 – $12) × 1,000 shares] capital gain is a long-term gain because it was held for at least one year after being exercised. The employer will receive a tax deduction for the $2,000 of ordinary income.

Another very important distinction between an ISO and an NQSO is gifting. An ISO must be nontransferable, which means that only the executive who received the grant can exercise it. On the other hand, an NQSO can be gifted, subject to gift tax rules. This means that executives could give their NQSOs to a child or grandchild to help with a financial need. Gifting an NQSO will remove an asset from the participant's broader estate and target to money toward one specific beneficiary.

Employee Stock Purchase Plans

An **ESPP** is nothing more than a discount stock-purchasing program for employees, and it is only available for employees. An ESPP must be approved by shareholders before it is implemented. This benefit is only available to full-time employees of the company (no subcontractors) who have at least two years of completed service, but anyone who already owns 5 percent of the company cannot participate in an ESPP. The plan is limited to $25,000 in actual purchases for any given year.

One special feature of an ESPP is that this plan must have broad participation. This means that the employer cannot offer the plan to only the HCE population...every employee must be included that has at least two years of full-time service to the company. Every employee except those who own more than 5 percent of the company. The idea is that the executives might be offered stock options, while the rank-and-file employees could be offered an ESPP to provide incentives for employees of all income ranges.

ESPPs have what is called an *offering period*, which is simply the window of time in which the employee can purchase shares at the stated percentage discount. The percentage discount could be based upon the price at the beginning of the offering period or at the end of the offering period. It is not a situation where the employee gets to pick any day in between. Some companies will apply the **look back rule**, which states that employees can retroactively choose whether they want the price at the beginning of the offering period or the ending price. If this extra benefit is applied, then the offering period is limited to 27 months.

Functionally, employees who choose to participate in an ESPP will have money withheld from their *net* pay (after-tax) to purchase shares of the company at a discount. This gives all employees a tremendous incentive to purchase shares and therefore have a vested interest in how the company performs.

If an employee holds the stock for at least two years from the beginning of the offering period and at least one year after the shares are purchased, then the employee will receive special tax treatment. The dollar discount received will be taxed as ordinary income, while any subsequent growth (or loss) in value is a capital gains issue.

Consider an employee whose employer has a publicly traded stock currently priced at $10 per share. If the company offers a 15 percent discount, then the employer will withhold money from the employee's after-tax paycheck and use the money to purchase shares at $8.50. This is all after tax; so there are no complex tax rules to understand. The employee simply will have a capital gain (or loss) whenever he or she should choose to sell. If this employee, who purchased shares at $8.50, sold the shares immediately, then he or she would realize a 17.6 percent [($10 – $8.50/$8.5] instant return! Note that a 15 percent discount will produce an immediate benefit greater than 15 percent. In this case, the investor would pay taxes at the higher short-term capital gains rate, but at least they locked in a profit...

Special Equity-Based Plan Types

Another way to structure employee stock ownership without forcing employees to pay out of pocket is called phantom stock. **Phantom stock** is nothing more than a *unit* of ownership, which is tied to the movement of the company's actual stock. The phantom stock units will have a fixed term (maturity period). Employees will receive a payout based on the appreciation in the units, which is actually the appreciation in the underlying stock. The employer establishes, in advance, when the phantom stock is redeemed.

One neat feature is that employee accounts can be credited with dividends based upon any dividends paid to the actual underlying company stock. The value of any phantom stock received is considered ordinary income for the employee and therefore a tax deduction for the employer. The company should be clear on any additional payment triggers such as retirement, death, or disability.

Consider an employer who grants an executive 10,000 shares of phantom stock when the company's stock is trading at $50. The phantom stock matures in five years and at that time, the company's stock has grown to $75. The executive will receive a check for $250,000 [($75 - $50) × 10,000 shares], which is all ordinary income and therefore tax deductible for the employer and fully taxable for the employee.

Can you image a birthday where you are given a brand new iPhone with the understanding that if you fail to meet a specific behavior target, then you will lose the iPhone? That is essentially how restricted stock works. A **restricted stock** is a gift of shares from the employer to an employee, but the gift contains a caveat that all shares are forfeited if the employee leaves the company within a certain window of time. This is a great way to retain key talent!

While the restricted shares are owned by employees, they will collect any dividends paid to those shares. This form of equity-based compensation is a great way to encourage employment loyalty and to marry the employee to the performance of the company. From the employee's perspective, this method of compensation is more secure than a traditional nonqualified deferred compensation plan because the stock is registered in the employee's name and is therefore not subject to the creditors of the employer.

Once the substantial risk of forfeiture has been removed, the shares will become taxable for the employee. At this point in time, the value in the company's stock is treated as ordinary income, and the employer will therefore receive a tax deduction. There is one special tax advantage available to recipients of restricted stock. This is derived from §83. Employees with restricted stock can elect to be taxed on the value of the stock within 30 days of the day when the shares are granted to them. This is very risky for employees. If they elect to be taxed, but then they breach the restriction and the shares are forfeited back to the employer, then the employees have paid tax needlessly. It is also risky because the stock might decline in value during the ownership period. If the shares decline, then the participants could have paid tax on a smaller value if they had waited.

SARs are very similar to phantom stock. They are an ownership interest not in the employer's stock directly but in the appreciation potential over a certain period of time. Just like with the phantom stock counterpart, any gains from a SAR are taxed as ordinary income. A key difference is that SARs can be exercised at any point during the offering period!

Consider an employee who has a SAR for 1,000 shares of their employer's stock with a strike price of $100 per share. Because the employee has a short-term financial need, he or she watches the stock closely and notices it jump upward to $110. He or she decides to exercise 100 shares of the SAR. He or she will receive a check for $1,000 [($110 – $100) × 100 shares] and be taxed on that amount. The employer will receive a tax deduction for the $1,000 of ordinary income recognized by the employee. Because they do not need any more short-term money, they let the other SARs ride. Just before the remaining 900 shares in the SAR expire, the employer's stock has risen to $200 per share. The employee will exercise the remaining 900 shares and realize $90,000 [($200 – $100) × 900 shares] of taxable income. The employer will also receive a tax deduction for $90,000.

Discussion Questions

1. Identify two reasons why equity-based compensation might be used in practice today.
2. How could equity-based compensation be used to mitigate the agency conflict?
3. What are some of the key considerations for a closely held company that wants to offer equity-based compensation?
4. What is one reason why some companies have become less willing to use equity-based compensation in recent years?
5. Why would current shareholders not like equity-based compensation?
6. How does a new offering of equity-based compensation avoid the costly process of filing as a new public offering with the SEC?
7. What is the mandatory vesting requirement for NQSOs?
8. What are the tax consequences of NQSOs?
9. Describe the limitations inherent with an ISO plan. Why would an executive be willing to accept these limitations?

10. What are the differences in coverage eligibility between an NQSO and an ISO?

11. An impatient executive who has been granted an ISO waits one year from the grant date to exercise and subsequently sells his or her options. What is the tax implication of this transaction?

12. A different executive has been granted an ISO; he or she waits two years from the grant date to exercise his or her options and an additional two years before selling his or her shares. What is the tax implication of his or her timing choices?

13. Describe the limitations and tax consequences of an ESPP if the participant has satisfied the two-year/one-year threshold.

14. Why is phantom stock attractive to a small business?

15. How is phantom stock taxed?

16. Why is a §83 election a risky bet for an employee with restricted stock?

17. What is the difference between phantom stock and SAR?

CHAPTER 17

Introduction to IRAs

Introduction

When most people think about planning for retirement, they think of a pension [which is really a defined benefit (DB) plan], a 401(k), or an individual retirement account (IRA). The IRA is probably the most widely used retirement plan type other than a 401(k). If an employer does not sponsor a retirement savings plan, then the employees' best option is to open an IRA and begin contributing themselves. This takes initiative and personal motivation, but it is entirely necessary. For many taxpayers, their IRA was once a 401(k) that was rolled over into an IRA when they left their job. This is a very big and growing submarket within retirement planning, and it deserves your undivided attention in this chapter.

Learning Goals

- Understand the difference between the two types: a traditional IRA and a Roth IRA
- Understand the significance of being deemed an active participant
- Identify the Internal Revenue Service (IRS)-imposed income thresholds that apply to IRAs and Roth IRAs
- Determine if a taxpayer is eligible to make deductible or nondeductible IRA contributions
- Determine who is eligible to make Roth IRA contributions
- Understand how a Roth IRA conversion functions
- Understand what creates an excess IRA contribution and how it is handled

Overview of IRAs

It is vital for a financial professional to understand fully all aspects of **IRAs**. There are two types of IRAs that you will need to be familiar with: the traditional IRA and the Roth IRA.

Traditional IRAs (commonly called just *IRA*) offer retirement savers the ability to make both tax-deductible and nondeductible contributions. The tax-deductible contributions are easy to understand. The retirement savers will deposit a certain sum into a traditional IRA and then receive a tax deduction. Whatever dollar amount is deposited is subtracted from taxable income in much the same way that employer-sponsored plans offer. The funds then grow *tax deferred*, which means that there are no taxes as the assets grow. The taxation occurs when money is withdrawn from a traditional IRA. This process is intuitive.

Why would someone want to make a nondeductible contribution to an IRA? A nondeductible contribution will typically be used by someone whose income is above the limit for traditional IRA contributions. This individual would be disallowed from making a deductible contribution, but may still want the benefit of tax deferral. With a nondeductible contribution, retirement savers will not receive any tax deduction up-front. They will receive tax deferral on investment gains until they are eventually distributed. At distribution, the nondeductible contributions will be compiled into a cost basis, which is an amount that can be withdrawn without paying taxes. This cost basis feature prevents the retirement saver from paying taxes twice on the same money. Nondeductible contributions can also be converted into a Roth IRA very easily. You will learn about Roth IRAs and Roth conversions later in this chapter.

Roth IRAs (commonly called just *Roth*) offer only nondeductible contributions. If that were all that you knew, you might think that they are a bad idea. Quite the contrary! With a Roth IRA, investors will contribute money without receiving an immediate tax deduction. Another way to say this is that they are making an after-tax contribution. This money will not grow tax deferred; it grows tax-free. The investor will not pay taxes on investment gains during their *accumulation years* (the period of saving), and when the money is withdrawn in retirement, they will not pay any taxes then either. This is a great piece to include in every retirement puzzle!

Traditional IRAs in Greater Detail

With a traditional IRA, taxpayers have no contribution limit based upon their income unless they are also covered by a retirement plan at work. You will learn more about this nuance later in this chapter. While there is no income limit, there is a limit to the dollar amount of the contribution. For 2014, the dollar limit is the lesser of $5,500 or 100 percent of compensation. For this purpose, compensation is wages paid for providing service to an employer or self-employed income. Compensation does not include investment earnings, pension payments, or annuity payments received by the taxpayer. If the taxpayer is divorced, then it will also include any alimony. However, child support is not included in compensation. This fine detail is usually discussed in divorce proceedings. Passive income, which could be an investment made in a partnership where the taxpayer is not an employee but an investor, does not count. Income-producing real estate is also a passive income source that is not included.

This contribution availability means that anyone with earned income is eligible to contribute to a traditional IRA. Once teenagers get their first job, it is a good idea to encourage them to begin making contributions. They might fight their parents on the idea of delaying current consumption, but it can be a great way to teach them about the power of compounded interest over very long time periods. They will be grateful later in life… Contributions for any given tax year must be deposited into the traditional IRA by the tax-filing deadline for that year. In almost all circumstances, that is April 15. In the event that April 15 is on a weekend, the IRS generally extends the deadline to the following Monday, but they will prominently publish this fact in advance. Another detail related to contributions is that they must be made in cash. An investor cannot contribute shares of stock into their IRA, but they can contribute cash and then purchase shares of stock once the money has settled in their IRA account.

There is a concept known as a **spousal IRA**, which is really nothing more than the nonworking spouse of a working taxpayer being eligible to establish a traditional IRA. There is no third category of IRAs called a spousal IRA; it is just a special privilege that escapes the normal requirement of the contribution being limited to 100 percent of compensation. In this scenario, the nonworking spouse of a working taxpayer can contribute up to the contribution limit if he or she files a joint tax return with the spouse, and the joint income at least equals double the contribution limit. Double the contribution limit in 2014 means $11,000 ($5,500 × 2).

There is one proviso that the IRS has made available to help retirement savers as they age. They have made available a catch-up contribution, which is an additional $1,000 in 2014. Catch-up contributions are available for those over age 50. This means that the contribution limit for someone aged 49 is $5,500 and $6,500 for someone aged 50. This benefit is based on the notion that most people are more focused on paying off student loans, buying houses, and living life until they reach about age 50, which is when psychologically they begin to realize that retirement is imminent. The IRS helps them make up for lost time by permitting the catch-up contribution. Of course, it is just a saving benefit for those who have planned well and are already in good shape.

Legislation enacted in 2005 has sheltered IRA assets from personal bankruptcy proceedings.[1] This protection, which only extends to bankruptcy and not to civil lawsuits, presents a great additional incentive to save money using a tax advantage plan like an IRA or a 401(k). One gray area is inherited IRA assets, which were once owned by a taxpayer but have now become inherited by an heir. The courts are still weighing whether or not an inherited IRA should receive the same bankruptcy protection. One planning solution is use a trust to hold the inherited IRA.[2] If the proper language is in place, then the asset could be protected from all forms of creditors.

Who Is an Active Participant?

Taxpayers who are covered by a retirement savings plan with their employer are known as **active participants**. This term does not apply to those covered by nonqualified plans. Within a DB plan, someone is deemed to be an active participant if he or she is eligible to receive a contribution. Within a defined contribution (DC) plan, the employee must actually receive an allocation of the aggregate contribution to be considered an active participant. For this purpose, simplified employee pensions (SEPs), savings incentive match plans for employees (SIMPLEs), and 403(b)s are considered to be DC plans.

Contributions at any level will qualify taxpayers as active participants. Even contributions as low as one dollar will earn them the title. Consider an employee who makes regular contributions into their 401(k) at work. He or she terminates employment, for whatever reason, in early February, which is just after the January contribution was made. This taxpayer accepts a new job at a small business that does not offer a retirement plan. Is this person an active participant? The answer is yes! Because he or she contributed one month's worth of salary deferral, he or she is considered an active participant.

For the purposes of determining active participation, contributions are credited in the calendar year in which the plan ends. Consider an employee who first becomes eligible for participation in the employer's 401(k) on July 1, 2014. The plan year runs from July 1, 2014 to June 30, 2015. Is this taxpayer an active participant in 2014? The answer is no! The plan year ends in 2015. He or she will be an active participant in 2015 but not in 2014.

There is a special rule for profit-sharing plans. They offer discretionary contributions, which the employee cannot control. An employee is considered an active participant in a profit-sharing plan for any year where a discretionary contribution is made. The contribution is counted for active participation purposes for the year in which the contribution is actually received. One event that could disrupt this concept is if there were to be a reallocation of forfeitures from a nonvested departing employee. The forfeiture contribution would trigger active participation status even if the employer did not directly make another contribution in the tax year. Consider an employee who is subject to a discretionary profit-sharing plan. The employer makes a contribution for plan year 2014, but the contribution is not made until June of 2015. The employee is not an active participant in 2014, but is an active participant in 2015. This rule was implemented so that employees could plan their own IRA contributions, which are due by April 15th.

For anyone to be eligible to make a contribution into a traditional IRA, they must be younger than 70½ years old. They must also have

Table 17.1 Schedule of IRS phaseouts for active participants (2014)

If your filing status is...	And your modified AGI is...	Then you can take...
Single or head of household	$60,000 or less	A full deduction up to the amount of your contribution limit
	More than $60,000 but less than $70,000	A partial deduction
	$70,000 or more	No deduction
Married filing jointly or qualifying widow(er)	$96,000 or less	A full deduction up to the amount of your contribution limit
	More than $96,000 but less than $116,000	A partial deduction
	$116,000 or more	No deduction
Married filing separately	Less than $10,000	A partial deduction
	$10,000 or more	No deduction
If you file separately and did not live with your spouse at any time during the year, your IRA deduction is determined under the "single" filing status		

Source: Internal Revenue Service.
Abbreviations: AGI, Adjusted gross income; IRA, Individual retirement account; IRS, Internal Revenue Service.

earned income. Consider a taxpayer who is self-employed, and their business loses money in a given year. If the taxpayer also maintains a second job to make ends meet, then he or she would technically be eligible for an IRA contribution because he or she now has earned income.

Table 17.1 provides the various income limits if a taxpayer is considered an active participant. Taxpayers who are married and file a joint tax return with their spouse will be able to make a full deductible contribution of $5,500 if their income is $96,000 or less (2014 limit). They will not be able to make a deductible contribute if they earn above $116,000. When taxpayers cross the lower bound of the income threshold ($96,000), they begin to have access to a reduced deductible contribution. This is called a **phaseout** scenario. What happens when a taxpayer's income falls within this phaseout range, between $96,000 and $116,000?

$$\text{Deductible \$} = \text{Max Contrib.} - \left[\text{Max Contrib.} \times \frac{(\text{AGI} - \text{Filling Status Floor})}{\text{Total Phaseout Range}} \right]$$

(17.1)

Formula 17.1 is used to calculate the amount of the available deductible contribution if a taxpayer falls within the phaseout range. Consider a married couple. They are both in their 40s, and they are both active participants. They have a combined *adjusted gross income (AGI)* of $106,000 in 2014. What deductible contribution is available to them?

$$\$2,750 = \$5,500 - \$5,500 \times \left[\frac{(\$106,000 - \$96,000)}{(116,000 - 96,000)}\right]$$

Applying Formula 17.1, you will find that each of them has an available deductible contribution of $2,750. They could each contribute this dollar amount for a combined $5,500 between them.

What if the couple in the previous example had an AGI of $165,000, but only the husband was employed? The wife stayed at home to raise two young children. They fall into a special loophole for couples when only one person is an active participant. In this scenario, the nonworking spouse of an active participant has available the full deductible contribution of $5,500 if their AGI is below $181,000 (2014 limit). This is the same phaseout limit in place for Roth IRA contributions. Phaseout begins at $181,000 and all deductible contribution is phased out at $191,000. This is a narrower window of opportunity ($10,000 instead of the $20,000 window) than if both people are active participants, but the lower bound is now $181,000 instead of $96,000.

Of course, taxpayers are always able to make nondeductible contributions if they do not meet the AGI limits for deductible contributions.

Roth IRAs in Greater Detail

In contrast to a traditional IRA, Roth IRAs do permit taxpayers to contribute after they are 70½ years old. To contribute, a taxpayer will need to have earned income. The spousal IRA concept previously discussed with traditional IRAs will also apply to Roth IRAs.

Unlike the traditional IRA where AGI limits only apply if the taxpayer is also an active participant, Roth IRA contribution eligibility is based strictly upon AGI limits even for those who are not active participants.

Table 17.2 Schedule of IRS phaseouts for a Roth IRA (2014)

If your filing status is...	And your modified AGI is...	Then you can contribute...
Married filing jointly or qualifying widow(er)	<$181,000	Up to the limit
	>$181,000 but <$191,000	A reduced amount
	>$191,000	Zero
Married filing separately and you lived with your spouse at any time during the year	<$10,000	A reduced amount
	>$10,000	Zero
Single, head of household, or married filing separately and you did not live with your spouse at any time during the year	<$114,000	Up to the limit
	>$114,000 but <$129,000	A reduced amount
	>$129,000	Zero

Source: Internal Revenue Service.
Abbreviations: AGI, Adjusted gross income; IRA, Individual retirement account; IRS, Internal Revenue Service.

Table 17.2 shows the IRS-mandated AGI limits (2014) for various classes of taxpayers. Those who are married and filing a joint tax return can contribute the full $5,500 if their income is below $181,000, and the phaseout range ends if they earn above $191,000. Notice that this is the same range that we discussed in the last section for someone who is a non-working spouse of an active participant. You can calculate the allowable deductible contribution in the same way that you already learned for the traditional IRAs in the last section.

In Chapter 24, you will learn about specific distribution rules for traditional IRAs, but the short version is that a certain amount of distribution is mandatory from a traditional IRA. One benefit of the Roth IRA is that there is no mandatory distribution amount. Taxpayers can deposit money into a Roth IRA and never touch it until it is inherited by their heirs. When a Roth IRA becomes a *Beneficiary Roth IRA*, the story changes. The owner through inheritance will need to withdraw the money out of the Roth IRA (no longer receiving the favorable tax-free compounding) either within five years or they can establish a life expectancy-based plan to withdraw the account balance over the inherited owner's life expectancy based upon government tables.

The one caveat to this rule about Beneficiary Roth IRAs is that surviving spouses do not have a mandated distribution schedule. From the IRS's perspective, they are deemed to step into the shoes of their now deceased spouse.

Distributions from a Roth IRA are completely tax-free. The only hitch is that the funds are not now growing tax-free as well. It is also important to note that qualified education expenses are not considered an early withdrawal.

Rollovers and Roth Conversions

A rollover is when a retirement savings instrument is transferred into an IRA. This commonly occurs when an employee either retires or otherwise leaves a company. If an employee elects for a lump-sum distribution, but they do not want to incur a substantial amount of taxable income, then they can roll the lump sum into an IRA. Roth 401(k)s, Roth 403(b)s, and nondeductible IRA contributions can all be rolled into a Roth IRA. All other retirement plan types (401(k)s, profit-sharing plans, money purchase plans, etc.) must be rolled into a traditional IRA.

A direct rollover is the best way to conduct this transfer. With a **direct rollover**, the assets are transferred from the custodian of the 401(k) (or other retirement savings instrument) directly to the custodian of the IRA. The taxpayer could roll into an existing IRA, or he or she could create a new IRA. If a direct rollover is chosen, the money must be deposited into the new custodian's IRA account no longer than 60 days after the funds leave the 401(k) custodian. This is generally not a problem in a world with electronic money transfers. The IRS imposes this restriction to prevent any funny business.

An indirect rollover is a hassle and is done generally only by those who do not know any better. With an **indirect rollover**, the taxpayer acts as a middleman in the transfer. The 401(k) custodian sends a check to the taxpayer who then sends a check to the new IRA custodian. If the check is made payable to the new IRA custodian and the taxpayer merely forwards the check, then this is really just a very inefficient direct rollover. The problem occurs when the check is made payable to the taxpayers themselves. In this case, the 401(k) custodian is required to withhold

20 percent from the amount of the taxpayer's account and send it to the government for income tax withholding. The assumption here is that the taxpayer is receiving a lump sum and not rolling over into a tax-sheltered IRA. The taxpayers will get the money back from the government when they fill their taxes (assuming they did forward the other money to the new IRA). The real problem is that to avoid taxation and possibly early withdrawal penalties, the taxpayer must come up with whatever amount was forwarded to the government out of pocket.

Consider two taxpayers, both of who are in their 40s. Taxpayer A elects a direct rollover of his $100,000 401(k) into his traditional IRA when he switches jobs. The 401(k) custodian will send the money electronically to the new IRA custodian and send the taxpayer a 1099-R form with a distribution code that shows the amount was a direct rollover. The new IRA will send the taxpayer a 5498 form as a tax receipt of the contribution received. Easy. However, taxpayer B mistakenly elects an indirect rollover in his $100,000 401(k). His 401(k) company will mail him a check made payable directly to him for $80,000. They will also send $20,000 to the federal government. Taxpayer B will send the $80,000 to his new IRA custodian and file a tax return the following April to get a refund of the $20,000 which was withheld by the 401(k) custodian. But, to not be deemed to have taken a premature withdrawal, which is subject to penalties and more taxation, taxpayer B will be required to deposit $20,000 from another source (savings account) into his IRA. This will bring the new IRA up to the proper balance. Taxpayer B will then refresh his savings account when the income tax refund arrives. This process is very cumbersome and could be very problematic if taxpayer B did not have $20,000 available to use as a buffer.

The IRS has recently ruled that beginning January 1, 2015, taxpayers are only permitted one rollover per year.[3] This new rule pertains to indirect rollovers, but taxpayers can still conduct direct custodian-to-custodian transfer throughout the year. Imagine a scenario where a retiree has multiple IRAs at multiple banks that all hold certificates of deposit (CDs). Some retirees have gotten into the habit of searching for the best CD rate, and when one matures at bank A, they simply cash it out and take the check to bank B, which offers a higher interest rate, to open a new IRA with a CD. The taxpayer has 60 days to get the money from bank A to bank B before it is deemed a withdrawal. The new rule will limit this action to only once every 365 days. The best option is always a direct rollover from custodian to custodian.

Related to the rollover concept is conversions. In a **Roth conversion**, a traditional IRA (or anything that must be rolled into a traditional IRA) is converted into a Roth IRA. Why would someone do this? They engage in a Roth conversion because distributions from a Roth IRA are tax-free. Sounds great? What is the catch? The catch is that whatever dollar amount is converted from a traditional IRA into a Roth IRA must be taxed at the point of conversion. If a taxpayer were to convert $25,000 of his or her $150,000 traditional IRA into a Roth IRA in a given tax year, then he or she would have $25,000 of additional taxable income in that tax year. Unlike contributions, which can be contributed up to the tax filing dead-line, conversions must take place before December 31 of the tax year in question. The conversion can be undone anytime up to the October 15 following the actual conversion. This clause provides taxpayers a chance to rethink their conversion after their annual taxable income is more cer-tain. There is also one caveat…the **five-year rule**, which states that there will be a 10 percent penalty if amounts converted are withdrawn within five years of the conversion. The government is trying to discourage tax-payers from converting just after they retire (lower tax rate) and then trying to distribute money tax-free.

Handling Excess Contributions

What happens if taxpayers contribute to a Roth IRA, but then later in the year receive a substantial jump in compensation that puts them over the limit to be eligible to contribute? This scenario is known as an **excess contribution**. Any excess contributions will receive a 6 percent excise tax (penalty by another name) from the IRS. The taxpayer has two potential choices to avoid the 6 percent excise tax.

The first choice is to withdraw any excess contributions plus any growth generated by them during the time they were in the account. If a taxpayer deposits $5,500 in January and the whole account earns 10 percent before the taxpayer discovers that they made an excess con-tribution, then the taxpayer will need to withdraw the $5,500 plus an additional $550 (based on the 10 percent growth of the account). Penalty avoided. Sometimes, the taxpayer makes multiple contributions, and the calculations can become very complex. Roth IRA custodians usually help with the calculation.

The second way to avoid a 6 percent excise tax is known as a **recharacterization**, which is a long word that means the taxpayer transfers the Roth IRA contribution into a traditional IRA. Excess contributions can be recharacterized as a deductible traditional IRA contribution only if the taxpayers are not active participants because the threshold is much lower for a traditional IRA for an active participant than for a Roth IRA. If they are active participants, they could always recharacterize the excess contribution as a nondeductible traditional IRA contribution. Penalty avoided. In either path that is chosen, the excess contribution must be out of the account it was placed in before the tax due date.

Discussion Questions

1. Compare traditional IRAs to qualified plans.
2. How is a Roth IRA different from a traditional IRA?
3. What is the difference between *tax-deferred* growth and *tax-free* growth?
4. When should someone begin making contributions to an IRA?
5. Is it true that catch-up contributions are available to taxpayers after they reach age 55?
6. You are married and also covered by a SIMPLE plan at the small company where you earn a salary of $150,000. You would like to save more and heard from someone on MSNBC that if you are not an active participant you can contribute to an IRA. What are your options?
7. A married couple, who files a joint tax return, has combined AGI in 2014 of $135,000. The husband is an active participant in his employer's 401(k), but the wife stays at home to raise their two-year-old daughter. Her only source of income is a rental property that she inherited from her grandfather. What deductible contributions can be made to a traditional IRA for both taxpayers?

8. A friend tells you that he thinks that you are not able to make non-deductible traditional IRA contributions because you earn $500,000 per year. Is this correct?

9. Why should someone prefer a direct rollover to an indirect rollover?

10. What is the process for a Roth conversion?

11. What is the five-year rule as it pertains to Roth IRAs?

12. What is the most common event that could create an excess contribution, and how is the problem remedied?

CHAPTER 18

IRAs in Depth

Introduction

Since individual revenue accounts (IRAs) are commonly used to supplement savings through employer-sponsored plans, it is very important to understand them in detail. Some assets, like stocks, can be owned without any problem, but other assets, like real estate, become a bit trickier. Sometimes investors will resort to publically traded real estate investment trusts (REITs), but other investors are desperate for direct real estate ownership with retirement assets. The self-directed IRA can help meet this need, but it has many serious potential pitfalls that should be fully understood.

The potential usefulness of traditional IRAs, Roth IRAs, and Roth IRA conversions will depend upon taxpayer's unique financial situation. You will be introduced to these issues in this chapter.

Learning Goals

- Describe the two instruments that can be used to fund an IRA
- Understand the uses and pitfalls of a self-directed IRA
- Identify prohibited investments within an IRA
- Discuss when a traditional IRA or a Roth IRA might be a better choice for a taxpayer
- Describe the Roth IRA conversion process and its usefulness

IRA Funding Instruments

In general, an IRA is a non-employer-sponsored retirement savings plan. There are two different methods for funding an IRA. Both involve the same rules and limits. Both also involve taking a contribution and depositing it into a "container." The two different methods are really just a question of packaging and not so much about function or purpose. One of the selling features for an IRA is that, unlike employer-sponsored plans, the IRA owner always has access to withdrawals at any time and for any reason. As you will learn in Chapter 24, the catch is that most withdrawals taken before the IRA owner has reached age 59½ will be subject not only to ordinary income tax rates but also to a 10 percent early withdrawal penalty. It is also important to understand that whichever funding "container" is used, the actual IRA account must be operated for the exclusive benefit of the IRA owners or their ultimate beneficiaries, or both. The beneficiaries come into play if the IRA owner indicates to their advisor that they do not need the IRA for their own living expenses, and the IRA should be managed with the beneficiaries in mind. This could have the effect of increasing the risk level of the investments in an IRA being managed for the beneficiaries.

The first method is the **individual retirement account (hereinafter IRA)**. This is the type of account that most people think of when they hear the term *IRA*. In this method, a trustee (or custodian) will physically hold the investments in the IRA and manage the account within the rules and provisions that the Internal Revenue Service (IRS) stipulates for the IRA category. The custodian could be a bank (like Bank of America), a mutual fund company (like Vanguard or Fidelity), a brokerage house (like Merrill Lynch), or a discount broker (like TD Ameritrade or Charles Schwab). It is expressly forbidden for individuals to act as their own IRA custodian.

IRAs can hold numerous types of investments. An IRA owner could hold certificates of deposit (CDs), individual stocks, individual bonds, open-end mutual funds, closed-end mutual funds, exchange traded funds, and listed options contracts. There are also other assets that could be owned within an IRA, but it will be easier to describe what cannot be held in an IRA. You will learn about prohibited assets later in this chapter.

The second method is called an **individual retirement annuity**. The individual retirement annuity must meet all of the regular rules and limitations as a straight IRA, with the primary difference being what it invests in. Instead of investing in stocks, bonds, and mutual funds, an individual retirement annuity invests only in an annuity. It could be either a fixed or a variable annuity contract, but either way, the premiums cannot exceed the annual contribution limit for a straight IRA. For 2014, the annual contribution limit is $5,500. One attractive feature of the individual retirement annuity is that the owner is not required to select any investment options. All they need to do is make contributions, and the insurance company that holds the individual retirement annuity will make all of the investment selections. This is a hands-free option, but it provides very little flexibility in terms of investment management. This method is best for someone who does not know what he or she is doing and does not want to hire a manger for help.

Self-Directed IRAs

In modern markets, investors are searching for alternative investment opportunities. Investors can own hedge funds, commodities, and REITs within their IRA, but if they want more direct alternative assets, they will not be able to hold those investments within a traditional (or Roth) IRA. For those opportunities, investors will need to consider self-directed IRAs. A **self-directed IRA** is a unique type of IRA, which may hold investments whose valuation is not easy to ascertain. Traditional IRA custodians only want to hold assets for which a fair market value is easily discernable.

You already learned in Chapter 17 that investors cannot be their own custodians or trustees. With a self-directed IRA, investors will need to find an IRA custodian who will allow them to hold nonstandard investments. There are little-known custodians who specialize in self-directed IRAs, and these special custodians typically charge more for their special service.

The most common nonstandard investment that is typically held within a self-directed IRA is investment real estate. Some investors might also hold self-storage facilities and investments in franchises within a self-directed IRA. The catch is that all costs must be paid for using IRA assets. That includes any down payments, any monthly mortgage payments, any maintenance costs, or any property taxes. Investors must be careful to not comingle self-directed IRA assets with non-IRA assets. Or they could end up with an IRS problem on their hands.

This can be a great way of diversifying investment exposure into alternative asset classes. The investor will run into regulatory problems under two circumstances. First, if any expenses or investments are made in an asset held within a self-directed IRA, the investor will encounter problems with the IRS. The second area of issue is known as **self-dealing**, which is using the self-directed assets for personal gain and not retirement account gain. You might be thinking that investors should be able to benefit personally from their own retirement account. While this logic is correct, the IRS is trying to prevent abuses like a wealthy investor with a substantial IRA balance using a self-directed IRA to purchase a primary residence with tax-deferred money and then being able to sell the primary residence and escaping the applicable capital gains rules for selling a primary residence. This is an example of a violation of the self-dealing rule associated with a self-directed IRA. Because of all of the inherent conflict possibilities involved with self-directed IRAs, the regulators are beginning to scrutinize self-directed IRAs with greater regularity and vigor.[1]

Prohibited Investments and Emerging IRA Opportunities

In general, an IRA provides the investor with a great deal of choice in investment selection. Whereas an employer-sponsored plan will typically limit the investment selection pool to no more than 10 to 15 options to choose from (usually mutual funds), the IRA provides access to any mutual fund, exchange-traded fund (ETF), individual stock, or individual bond that the investor is interested in.

There are, however, certain types of investments that are expressly prohibited within an IRA environment. The first prohibited investment is life insurance. Investors can still purchase an annuity (in an individual retirement annuity), which is only offered by an insurance company, but life insurance, such as term life or whole life insurance, is not allowed like it is in many employer-sponsored plans. Another prohibited investment category is collectibles. *Collectibles* specifically refers to investments in artwork, stamps, rare coins, fine wines, antiques, sports memorabilia, and many other types of tangible collectibles. There is an exception to the collectible prohibition for precious metals (gold, silver, platinum, etc.) and for certain government-issued gold and silver coins.

There are also certain types of transactions that are specifically prohibited within an IRA. An investor cannot borrow any money from an IRA (no plan loans). If the custodians were to permit a plan loan, then the entire IRA would cease to be a tax-qualified account retroactive to the beginning of the calendar year. This would create a potentially large tax liability. For this reason, IRA custodians do not permit plan loans.

It is also prohibited to sell property to an IRA. All contributions must be in the form of cash. The IRS is trying to eliminate a potential dispute between the IRS and a taxpayer on the valuation of an asset contributed in kind to an IRA. To avoid haggling over how to value assets to ensure compliance with the annual contribution limits, the IRS simply mandates that all contributions must be in cash.

Another prohibition relates to paying investment management fees for managing an IRA. If a professional manages an IRA, then the fees for such management can be paid out of the IRA account. Normally, a distribution from an IRA is taxable for the IRA owner and it may even generate a 10 percent penalty if it occurs before age 59½. Payment of investment management fees is not taxable for the IRA owner. Some IRA owners have tried to pay themselves for managing their own IRA. The IRS says "Nice try, but no." IRA owners are not permitted to pay themselves a fee to manage their own account.

An IRA also cannot be used as collateral for a loan. Some IRA owners have tried to use their IRA as collateral for either a business loan or even a personal loan for a mortgage or other personal assets. This is expressly prohibited. Any form of self-dealing is also prohibited.

Despite the prohibitions, there are several recent opportunities within the world of IRA planning. The contribution limits have been rising steadily and are expected to continue to rise further in the future. Another recent opportunity is the availability of a spousal IRA. They were available as recently as 1981, but with a greatly reduced contribution limit relative to a normal IRA contribution limit. The Taxpayer Relief Act of 1997 extended the full contribution limit to spousal IRAs and they have been increasing the limit whenever the normal IRA contribution limit is increased.

Another advance in IRA planning is the high income threshold for Roth IRAs. This higher limit puts IRA savings within reach of almost all Americans. However, as you learned in Chapter 17, a married couple filing a joint tax return cannot contribute to a Roth IRA after their income rises above $191,000. Those who fall into this very high earning range can still make a nondeductible traditional IRA contribution and then convert that money into a Roth IRA. This little twist is known as a **backdoor Roth conversion** and is a very interesting planning tool for wealthy clients.

If an employee has a traditional IRA, perhaps resulting a rollover from a previous employer's 401(k), and they now work for an employer who sponsors a SEP plan, then they have a special relatively new benefit. Normally, a traditional IRA has a contribution limit of $5,500 (2014 limit) with potentially an additional $1,000 if the IRA-owner is over at least 50 years old. However, if the employee is covered by a SEP plan through their employer, then the employer can now contribute the SEP contribution into the participant's traditional IRA. This works because a SEP is funded with an IRA. Why is this a benefit? The participant can now contribute up to the significantly higher SEP contribution limit into their traditional IRA. This will enable them to consolidate their holdings into one account and trade with relatively few restrictions within their traditional IRA.

Roth IRA Versus Nondeductible Traditional IRA Contributions

How should an investor pick between making a Roth IRA contribution and a nondeductible traditional IRA contribution? They both sound conceptually similar, but they are not. With a nondeductible traditional IRA contribution, the actual contribution amount is never taxed again, just like a Roth IRA. However, the earnings (growth) on the contributions in a Roth IRA are also never taxed while the earnings on a nondeductible traditional IRA contribution are taxed at ordinary tax rates. There is a complicated formula for determining how a nondeductible traditional IRA factors into the taxable picture for the larger traditional IRA when there are also deductible contributions involved. You will learn about this calculation in Chapter 23, but for now, understand that it is not as straightforward as a Roth IRA.

At the end of the day, a Roth IRA has better tax treatment than a non-deductible traditional IRA contribution. However, this assumes that a taxpayer falls below the income limit that will enable him or her to make a Roth IRA contribution.

There is a back door to making a Roth IRA contribution for an investor who is above the income limit. There is no telling how long Congress will leave this loophole open, but a wealthy client can make a nondeductible contribution to a traditional IRA and then immediately (before there is a chance for any earnings to accrue) convert the nondeductible traditional IRA into a Roth IRA without any tax liability. This only works if there are no deductible contributions made to the traditional IRA, and the conversion occurs before any earnings amass on the nondeductible traditional IRA.

If a wealthy investor is not planning on converting to a Roth IRA, then he or she is better off investing in a non-IRA, non-tax-deferred account known as a nonqualified (individual, joint, or trust) account. Within this type of account, there is no tax-favored status, but all gains are now capital gains instead of ordinary income. The investor will also have the right to choose when to realize any gains and receive tax deductions for any losses. At death, any holdings in a taxable (non-tax-deferred account) will receive a stepped-up basis. This is a very important benefit that may outweigh the tax deferral available to wealthy investors in an IRA.

Stepped-up basis means that if an investor dies while holding an asset in a nonqualified account, their actual purchase price will no longer be applied for calculating capital gains taxes. The person who inherits the asset will have a new basis equal to the value of the asset on the date of the death of the previous owner. An exception exists for accounts that are jointly owned. The new basis equals 50 percent of the original cost and 50 percent of the value on the date of death. This planning tool may benefit wealthy clients with substantial assets and no need for income out of their retirement accounts.

Consider an example where a taxpayer dies with $200,000 in a non-IRA account. His or her cost basis is $50,000 and he or she is the sole owner of the account. The stepped-up basis rules will mandate that this person's heir will receive a cost basis of $200,000 for the inherited assets if they are in a taxable (non-IRA) account. Notice that 100 percent of the otherwise capital gains taxes are forgiven. This is a tremendous benefit! What if the account had been registered in a joint name with the decedent's spouse? In this case, 50 percent of the capital gain would be forgiven instead of 100 percent. The joint owner's new basis would be $125,000 [(50% × $50,000) + (50% × $200,000)].

Roth IRA Versus Deductible Traditional IRA Contributions

The question of whether a client should make a Roth IRA contribution or a deductible traditional IRA contribution comes down to an estimate of both current tax rates and applicable tax rates in retirement. If tax rates for a client are expected to be higher in retirement, then the Roth IRA is clearly better. If tax rates are expected to be lower in retirement, then a traditional IRA is clearly better. Retirement savers will want either the tax deduction or the tax-free income in the period in which taxes are expected to be the highest.

Figure 18.1 comes from the retirement calculators on Bankrate.com. You can see the various assumptions made, and that in this instance, a traditional IRA may be a better choice. The result is entirely dependent on the accuracy of the assumptions made, and real-world decisions should be made with all of these variables carefully considered.

In general, a Roth IRA is better than a traditional IRA in terms of mandatory distributions. If a taxpayer has no need for distributions out of their retirement savings account to fund their retirement lifestyle, then the Roth IRA presents an advantage. Unlike traditional IRAs, they have no mandatory distributions. You will learn all about this process in Chapter 24.

Even though the traditional IRAs may be more appropriate for a taxpayer, based upon the calculators shown, the Roth IRA may still have a place in planning. It is advisable to diversify the sources of income in retirement. Some sources from taxable accounts and some from nontaxable accounts. This will provide those with the ability to plan the greatest level of flexibility.

Age, income and retirement information:					[-]
Current age:	30	1	24	47	70
Age of retirement:	65	10	30	50	70
Adjusted gross income:	$120,000	$0	$10k	$100k	$1m
Annual contribution:	$5,500	$0	$10k	$100k	$1m
Total contributions:	$192,500				

Maximize contributions: ☐ Increase future contributions to the maximum allowed

Investment return, taxes, employment and marital status:					[-]
Expected rate of return:	7%	0%	4%	8%	12%
Current tax rate:	12%	0%	16%	33%	50%
Retirement tax rate:	4%	0%	16%	33%	50%

Married: ☑ If you are married, check here

Employer plan: ☐ If you have an employer retirement plan, Check here

Figure 18.1 An Internet calculator to pick between a traditional IRA and a Roth IRA

Source: Bankrate.com
Abbreviation: IRA, Individual retirement account.

Roth IRA Conversions in Greater Detail

Before an investor can consider whether a Roth IRA conversion makes sense for them, they must consider both current and projected future tax rates. There is an easy online calculator available in the retirement section on money.msn.com.

When someone decides to convert a traditional IRA into a Roth IRA, he or she will be taxed in the current year for the full amount of the conversion. This is because the traditional IRA originally generated a tax deduction and Roth IRA contributions must come from after-tax money. The calculator on money.msn.com is very good because it factors in how long someone has before he or she plans to retire and how long he or she plans to be in retirement. It is important to understand if the investor will have time to let the investment growth make up for the taxes paid up-front.

One key to a conversion working effectively is that all conversion taxes must be paid from sources other than the IRA assets. It would be counterproductive for the conversion taxes to be withheld as the assets are transferred from the traditional IRA to the Roth IRA. This would result in a much smaller investable amount in the new Roth IRA, which would need to be invested more aggressively to make up for the taxes withheld. By paying the taxes from assets outside of the Roth IRA, the taxpayer is theoretically reducing the taxable estate. The reduction comes from the money paid to the government for taxes.

Who might be an ideal candidate for a Roth IRA conversion? Those taxpayers who are in the top tax bracket and expect rates to rise might be good candidates for Roth IRA conversions in the current year. The other end of the tax rate extreme also has good potential. Those in temporarily low tax brackets could take advantage of a Roth IRA conversion. I had a client who was the comptroller of a company and had significant income and a substantial traditional IRA. Due to business conditions, her employer began to struggle and sold itself to another firm. Through the process, my client lost her job and found herself on extended unemployment. Her tax rate suddenly dropped from a high range to the lowest bracket. She had substantial savings and was able to survive just fine for roughly two years until she was able to find gainful employment once again. During the period of unemployment, she elected to convert sections of her traditional IRA into her Roth IRA. She made the temporary decrease in tax rate work in her favor from a retirement planning perspective. *Converting a Roth IRA is not an all-or-nothing proposition...it is possible to strategically convert the traditional IRA in sections, and you can convert shares (in kind), there is no requirement that conversions must be in cash like contributions must be in cash.*

Another individual who might be a good candidate for a Roth conversion is someone who does not need to take withdrawals from their IRA for retirement income. Obviously either this person has planned VERY well or has significant resources outside of the IRA on which he or she plans to live. The Roth conversion could meet this individual's needs because there are no mandatory distributions from a Roth IRA, which would allow the money to remain tax deferred until his or her heir eventually inherits the account. This investor sees the Roth IRA not as a retirement funding instrument but as an estate asset. As you learned in Chapter 17, those seeking to diversify the taxability of their retirement income sources might also consider converting to a Roth IRA.

Who would not be a good candidate for a Roth IRA conversion? Those for whom a Roth conversion is not the best idea include investors with little financial means. If someone does not have enough cash available outside of the Roth conversion process with which to pay the conversion taxes, they should not attempt a conversion. There are also some taxpayers who will use a Roth conversion calculator and based on their unique situation decide that it just is not best for them. A Roth conversion can be a great tool, but it is not right for everyone.

Discussion Questions

1. There are two different types of accounts that are both known as an IRA. Discuss their differences.
2. Why would an investor choose to invest in an individual retirement annuity?
3. Is it true that individual retirement annuities enable a retirement saver to save more money than using an individual retirement account?
4. Why would a retirement saver want to go through the hassle of using a self-directed IRA?
5. A 49-year-old retirement saver has decided to use a self-directed IRA to purchase a self-storage unit. There are 100 units in the facility, and the owner uses one unit to store rental unit supplies and one to store the owner's Porsche during the winter months. They deposited their entire IRA balance into the asset. A tree falls on one corner of the unit and does $10,000 worth of damage. The owner does not want to file an insurance claim, which would raise their insurance rates, so they simply write a check out of a personal checking account. Are there any issues with this scenario?
6. A 35-year-old taxpayer is planning on contributing the maximum amount to her IRA this year. Assume that she is eligible to do so. She is planning on contributing shares of a technology company that she owns in a taxable (non-IRA) account because she thinks that this company will appreciate substantially and within the IRA, the appreciation will be tax deferred. Are there any issues with this scenario?

7. A client of yours has spoken to their long-time bank about receiving a loan to start a small business. Their only collateral that is large enough to secure the loan is their IRA. The bank is not willing to use their IRA as collateral. Your client is very frustrated and is planning on changing banks. What counsel would you give your client?

8. What choice should investors make if they are given the option of choosing a Roth IRA contribution or a nondeductible traditional IRA contribution?

9. What is one advantage of using a taxable account as a repository for savings?

10. A married taxpayer recently died, leaving his surviving spouse with a taxable account balance of $424,000. The original cost basis was $78,000. What is the surviving spouse's new cost basis in this account?

11. A taxpayer is expecting the tax rate to increase during retirement due to an expected inheritance. Should he be saving with a Roth IRA or a traditional IRA?

12. What type of client might be a good candidate for a Roth conversion?

13. A client of yours has a taxable account, a 401(k), and a traditional IRA, which was the result of a rollover from a previous employer's profit sharing plan. They are thinking about converting their traditional IRA into a Roth IRA. They are concerned about realizing a substantial amount of additional taxable income in one tax year. What would you tell them?

14. A different client approaches you about converting $30,000 from their traditional IRA into their Roth IRA. They have a 15 percent effective tax rate. They only have $1,500 in savings that could be used to pay the conversion taxes. They are planning on withholding the remainder of the taxes from the assets that are being transferred. How would you advise them?

PART V

Comprehensive Retirement Planning

CHAPTER 19

A Holistic View of Retirement Planning

Introduction

Retirement is typically a very vibrant and meaningful time in life for many Americans, but the information discussed so far in this book is just a collection of data until you begin to organize it into a useful plan. If the proper plan is in place, and being monitored, then retirees stand a much greater chance of enjoying the retirement of their dreams. It is important to understand what tools will be available to most employees and what special awareness needs to be applied to planning for female clients.

Sometimes the best way to understand how an item works is to take it apart and understand what could make it not work. Likewise, it is also very important to understand what could quickly derail a retirement plan. If you understand some common roadblocks to retirement success, then you will be more likely to avoid those potential pitfalls.

Learning Goals

- Understand how the retirement lifestyle has changed over time
- Identify the general role of the retirement planner
- Understand the key steps in the retirement planning process
- Identify the general availability of defined benefit (DB) and defined contribution (DC) plans
- Be aware of the "traditional" interaction of females in the retirement planning process
- Discuss common roadblocks to retirement planning success

A Holistic View of Retirement Planning

In early twentieth-century America, the notion of retirement meant that someone would stop working in the fields and transition to household chores, while the younger generations carried the burden of working in the fields. The Revenue Act of 1921 clarified that employers could deduct their contributions for corporate income tax purposes, and the retirement scenario began to take on a whole new shape. In 1930, roughly 10 percent of the workforce was covered by an employer-sponsored pension plan.[1] Social Security did not begin issuing regular monthly checks for nearly another decade. Retirement in the early part of the twentieth century was not about fancy vacations. It was more about subsistence and living a frugal lifestyle to be able to care for oneself during the later years and hopefully not be too reliant upon the younger generations.

Today, retirement for most people is no longer a descent from a desk job to a rocking chair. Most retirees are maintaining very active lifestyles. Some become active volunteers, some travel, some buy items that they have only been dreaming of up to this point, some focus their free time on family, and others just focus on subsistence. Most people, if they are honest, cannot conceptualize the true retirement scenario. There are many who simply do not have the cash flow to be able to provide for significant retirement savings. Others do have the cash flow, but they do not perceive *money* correctly. Those almost treat their finances as if they had a money tree in the backyard where they can just go get more when needed. It is best for all taxpayers to build a personal budget and then plan where savings can fit into their monthly finances.

Most taxpayers would rather not talk about their financial life. It is almost like little kids who close their eyes and assume that if they can't see anyone else, then they must be invisible. Avoidance does not equal solution…instead it equals a big problem in retirement. Establishing a personal budget and creating a plan to arrive at a desired retirement income level are essential for everyone who desires a reasonable retirement.

In Part 1 of this book, you learned about employer-sponsored plans and how to help a corporate client determine what is best for them. You also learned about various individual planning opportunities like individual retirement accounts (IRAs) and Social Security benefits. One thing that every financial professional will learn about helping clients in a real world setting is that they all have very unique goals that are very meaningful to them. Financial planning involves uncovering those unique desires and then determining if there is a feasible path to achieving those goals. Sometimes the financial professional's job is to communicate that a certain desire is just not prudent, given the client's financial assets.

Certain skills that you have been learning up to this point will be vital in considering a holistic view of a client's financial life. Certainly, an understanding of the various plan types will be helpful as the professional needs to advise clients on how to work with what they have and perhaps what they could add to the mix to accomplish their goals better. Understanding how to dovetail an IRA into a situation where a client has an employer-sponsored plan is required. The financial professional will also need to understand fully all tax ramifications *before* providing any advice. It is easy to get caught up in a given transaction and forget to consider the tax implications. Social Security and Medicare planning are also very important, and those topics will be covered in Chapters 20 and 22, respectively.

The Role of the Financial Professional

Sometimes the biggest role of a financial professional is to help clients think clearly and in an organized manner about their own retirement. One of the best tools to do this is to create a formal financial plan, which is a document that details current investments, assumptions about savings plans, investment growth rates, the rate of inflation, and the desired retirement date. A financial plan will roll all of these items together to provide an idea of the likelihood of a client achieving their goals. The financial plan can also be thought of as a strategic plan to get from the present to a future-oriented goal. It is imperative to understand that the strategy will need to be dynamic, which means that outside forces will act upon the plan, and the plan will then need to adjust.

Another significant area of concern is **long-term care**, which relates to end-of-life care in either assisted living or skilled nursing facilities. The deep details are beyond the scope of this book, but for now understand that healthcare, in general, will play a bigger role in retirement planning than most retirees know.

A financial professional may also help clients rationalize various housing options. It may be best to remain in a house that is paid off, but it may be necessary to sell the house and use the home sale proceeds to fund other retirement needs. Some taxpayers will also need help with estate-planning needs. This topic also is too broad for this book.

The role of the financial planner is one that will evolve and change over time. No two retirees have the exact same scenario…that challenge is part of what makes the career fun and engaging.

It is also extremely important for a financial professional to coordinate efforts with a client's other advisors, like attorneys and accountants. It would not be good for a financial professional to recommend a series of transactions that would create a tax liability for a taxpayer who has a very sensitive tax situation. Communication can prevent problems.

The Steps in the Retirement Planning Process

From the perspective of a financial professional, the first step in the retirement planning process is to establish a relationship with the client. *This cannot be stressed enough.* Too much of the personal finance industry is focused on viewing clients as an opportunity to make a commission. Clients should only be viewed as human beings who needs help making sense of an area of life about which they do not know as much as a financial professional. Yes, the financial professionals will be compensated, but they should never recommend a product or strategy because of their own personal financial gain. The client's needs should always be the highest priority. Whether or not the financial professional technically has a fiduciary duty, they should behave as if they do. While this is not the most important step in the process, it is extremely important for the financial professional view of their client as a human being and not just a sale.

The next step in the retirement planning process is to determine the client's goals. Every client will have a unique set of objectives. Common objectives include funding a comfortable retirement, leaving an estate for their heirs, funding a specific bequest (such as a charitable endeavor), taking a certain trip, or buying a certain asset.

The third step is to analyze and evaluate the client's current financial status. In an ideal scenario, younger clients will already be planning a path to being debt-free, and they will be saving at least 10 percent of their annual earnings. The best case for someone approaching retirement is for them to be debt-free (especially mortgage debt) and have a meaningful retirement account accumulated. A client in retirement should be focused on staying debt-free and living within the boundaries of a reasonable withdrawal rate from their assets.

A recent article makes the case that the conventional four percent withdrawal rate, which has been an industry standard for some time, could be a challenge to achieve in a low-interest rate environment. This article is partly grounded on the notion that many retirees shift their portfolio into a high percentage of bonds in retirement to have more stability, and therefore, they should use something closer to a 2.5 percent withdrawal rate in low-interest rate environments.[2] Too often, retired clients want to follow a riskier strategy, with equities, in an attempt to increase their withdrawal rate above the four percent standard. This could work in their favor, but if it backfires, then they have little chance of meaningfully recuperating their losses.

The fourth step is to develop a plan. To arrive at a desired retirement lifestyle, a plan is necessary. Sadly, a recent survey revealed that only 36 percent of surveyed preretirees have a formal retirement plan, but this number jumps to 67 percent for those who have already retired.[3] Clearly those who have already retired recognize the need for a plan. There are certainly postretirement benefits to be gained from a plan, but the greatest planning advantage is to develop a plan long before retiring to know how much to save.

The plan itself will involve assumptions about investment growth rates, income replacement rates, inflation, mortality, and various other aspects. An investor's retirement plan should be their guide. Many investors use either the S&P 500 Index or the Dow Jones Industrial Average as the benchmark for their investment's performance. It might be wiser to use the return budgeted for in the retirement plan. As long as an investor is at least meeting this assumed rate, the plan is meaningful and actionable. If the investments do not at least meet up with this minimum level, clients will have a much more difficult time reaching their financial goal of a comfortable retirement lifestyle.

The fifth and sixth steps are interrelated. They involve implementing the plan and then monitoring the plan. Too often what happens in practice is that a financial professional will be compensated to create a plan and then to implement it, and then the process stops there. Sometimes, clients become frustrated either with their advisor or with market conditions in general, and then they change advisors. Whether or not a change of advisor is involved, a lack of monitoring in a common occurrence. If the plan is not monitored actively, then there is a reasonable chance that failure becomes an option. *For this reason, monitoring the retirement plan for deviations from expectations is perhaps the most important of these six steps.*

Availability of Employer-Sponsored Plans

One key piece in the retirement planning puzzle is the presence of an employer-sponsored retirement plan. Figure 19.1 is the result of a study by the Bureau of Labor Statistics from 2012 detailing employee access to a DB plan.

In Figure 19.1, you can see that workers at companies with more than 500 employees are almost twice as likely to have a DB plan available to them than are companies with 100 to 499 employees. Large companies are almost five times as likely to offer a DB plan as a small business. The average access is roughly the same as the availability for small employers by themselves. According to a 2012 study by the U.S. Small

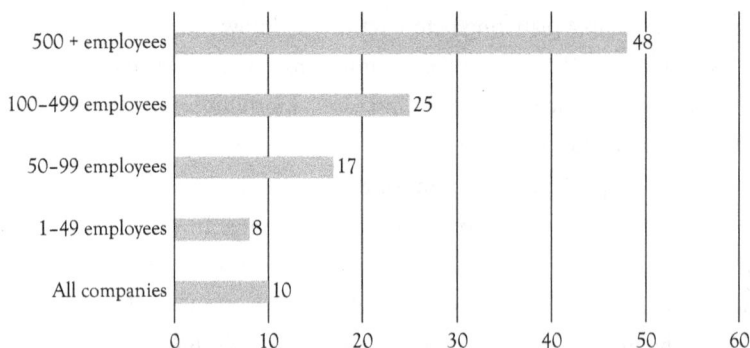

Figure 19.1 Percentage of employees covered with a defined benefit plan

Source: Bureau of Labor Statistics.

Table 19.1 Defined contribution plan access and participation rates

	Private industry		State & local governments	
1–99 employees	47%	31%	26%	19%
100+ employees	72%	54%	30%	16%
Full-time workers	68%	50%	33%	19%
Part-time workers	33%	15%	9%	5%
Union workers	55%	44%	26%	13%
Nonunion workers	59%	41%	32%	20%

Source: Bureau of Labor Statistics.

Business Administration, small businesses comprise 99.7 percent of U.S. employers, 64 percent of new private sector jobs, 49.2 percent of private sector employment, and 42.9 percent of private sector payroll.[4] There is therefore about a 50 percent chance that a college graduate may end up working for a small business.

Table 19.1 is from a 2010 study by the Bureau of Labor Statistics related to employee access to DC plans at work. It is not surprising that employees of larger firms enjoy greater access and participation rates than do smaller companies. Also of note is the fact that full-time workers are considerably more likely to have a DC plan available. What is perhaps a little surprising is that union and nonunion workers have almost equal access. There is a perception that union workers will have better access… they do but only marginally so.

Don't Forget the Ladies

In the world of retirement planning, female clients are regrettably sometimes overlooked. Women are less likely to be covered by employer-sponsored retirement plans. According to the Institute for Women's Policy Research, women's average pay is 76.5 percent of men's average pay.[5] Low pay means lower ability to save for retirement unless they are married, in which case they may have increased ability due to the factor of combined incomes.

There is also a difference in gender-based life expectancy that impacts retirement planning. Women on average live to age 81 while men currently only live, on average, until age 76.[6] In the United States, the gap between male and female life expectancy was 7.0 years in 1985, but it decreased to only 4.6 years in 2010.[7] The discrepancy may reverse, given enough time, but for now, it is more likely that the male client will die before their female spouse. And spousal issues must be considered at every stage of retirement planning if the participant is married. It is for this reason that the qualified joint and survivor annuity (QJSA) and qualified preretirement survivor annuity (QPSA) rules were developed.

Women are also more likely to need to take time off work to be a caregiver to an aging parent.[8] This trend will impact their retirement savings potential. Female clients also tend to be more risk-averse investors than their male counterparts.[9] It is very common for a husband to have a risk tolerance score many percentage points higher than his wife. A financial planner needs to help bring the married couple to consensus on a risk tolerance level to be able to assess a reasonable investment growth expectation that can be used in retirement planning projections.

Women also tend to have lower levels of investment literacy.[10] This is actually an advantage! Because of this lower level of general understanding, women are often more open to receive investment advice from a financial professional.[11] Most of the men think that they can handle it. They bring their own preformed ideas and philosophies to the investment strategy process, but female clients are much more open to learn and process new information.

Roadblocks to Success

One of the biggest roadblocks to a comfortable retirement lifestyle is poor planning, and its close cousin is poor execution of the plan if one does exist. The U.S. Census Bureau recently reported that the average 50-year-old only has $43,797 saved for retirement.[12] This should be an eye-opener that much of America will not experience the comfortable retirement as seen on TV.

Table 19.2 highlights an increasing roadblock to success…carrying a mortgage into retirement. There has been a substantial increase in those who are either approaching retirement or those who are already retired who have a loan against their house. This is very troubling because a retiree should be mortgage debt-free to have the greatest amount of flexibility

Table 19.2 Those either entering or currently in retirement with a mortgage

	1989	2010
Ages 55–64	37%	54%
Ages 65–74	22%	41%
Ages 75+	6%	24%

Source: National Center for Policy Analysis

during retirement. This means that if the taxpayer assumes a typical 30-year mortgage on their terminal house, then they should plan to begin that process no later than age 30 to 35. This step is often overlooked in the retirement planning process. Avoid this roadblock if at all possible.

The Bureau of Labor Statistics found that 18.5 percent of Americans older than age 65 remain in the workforce in 2012 and they project the number to be 23.0 percent by 2022.[13] Some of this is skewed by people like Warren Buffet who certainly do not need to continue working, but do so because they want to remain engaged and productive in a job that they love. The reality is that most of those working in their otherwise retirement years are working because they did not plan adequately during their preretirement careers. This lack of planning could be due to a lower general level of wages, which did not leave room for meaningful savings.

One should feel compassion for those in this category. They will have access to Social Security (assuming that they accrued 40 credited quarters) and government-sponsored medical care. However, some find themselves in this precarious position due to choosing too high a standard of living during their working careers, which results in a very low savings rate. Blame it on the TV and movie industries or just keeping up with the neighbor across the street, but the reality is that those who plan more effectively will have a greater likelihood of achieving the comfortable retirement lifestyle that everyone is searching for.

Another roadblock to retirement success is unexpected expenses. One caveat to life is that you should always expect the unexpected. There is a very good reason that the Boy Scout motto is "Be Prepared." Homeowners should expect that at some point they will need to replace a roof or a furnace or a refrigerator. Vehicle owners should expect to encounter maintenance issues in increasing regularity as the age of the vehicle increases. The best way to plan for these unexpected events is to build up a reserve account for such unforeseen events. There is much less stress in being prepared than in further reducing a potential retirement by taking a hardship withdrawal.

Poor insurance coverage is also a significant roadblock to a successful retirement. Retirees (and those saving for retirement) need to consider several different types of insurance needs. They should be aware of medical insurance, car insurance, and homeowner's insurance, but what about renter's insurance? It is possible to purchase insurance when someone rents a dwelling rather than owns it. The renter's insurance will not cover the physical building, but rather the personal contents stored within. This can really help create a safety net for someone, should their rented property encounter an unforeseen disaster. Especially from an estate-planning perspective, retirees should also consider long-term care and life insurance products.

For many, the biggest roadblock is a lack of available income to save. If a taxpayer is earning $250,000 per year and just can't seem to find the money to save, then I have little sympathy for them. It is the person who earns very low wages that I feel compassion for. They do not have the ability to save because there simply is not enough to provide for saving and basic subsistence needs. Retirement planning, as taught in this book, is primarily focused on those who have enough income to provide a reasonable lifestyle and still be able to budget 10 to 20 percent of their earnings for retirement savings.

Those in the subsistence category are not without hope. The replacement ratios within the Social Security system are skewed in their favor. There are also countless stories of people who were children in the Great Depression that had very little discretionary income throughout their working careers, but were still able to retire well because they somehow made saving a priority. Younger generations have lost this discipline in a world focused on lattes and iPhones. Don't let this be you!

Discussion Questions

1. What has been described in this chapter as perhaps the most important step in the financial planning process, which is sadly sometimes missed?

2. Two financial planning students are discussing their career intentions. One says to the other that he is considering a career in personal financial planning because he likes the fact that it is a relatively precise science that involves applying a formula to a client and coming up with a savings goal. He likes the certainty and predictability of this process that can simply be reapplied to multiple clients fairly easily. What would your comments be if you overheard this conversation?

3. Some retirees have been sold the notion that a 6 to 7 percent withdrawal rate from their savings is sustainable. Is this wise? Why or why not?

4. A 55-year-old decides to pay a professional to develop a financial plan. Once the plan is designed and implemented, the taxpayer feels that there is no need to pay further fees to a financial professional because the plan is now in place and on autopilot. Is this thinking correct?

5. What one retirement planning issue should all college students know about if they plan to work for a small business upon graduation?

6. What retirement planning issues are more prone to affect female clients?

7. What are some of the common roadblocks to retirement?

8. Is a comfortable retirement guaranteed for those who have an employer-sponsored plan and save privately using a customized financial plan?

CHAPTER 20

Social Security

Introduction

Almost every retiree in America is touched by the Social Security system. For some, it is an extra source of income that enables them to touch their individual retirement account (IRA) in unusual circumstances only. For others, Social Security is their primary means of subsistence. It is therefore imperative to understand properly how this system works, who is eligible for benefits, how the benefits are calculated, and if someone should file for early benefits or not.

Learning Goals

- Identify who is and who is not covered by Social Security
- Understand the differences between being fully insured and currently insured for Social Security purposes
- Understand the different coverage programs offered by Social Security
- Identify what coverage is available for a surviving spouse
- Understand how Social Security benefits are calculated
- Identify the implications of taking benefits either early or late
- Explain how to apply for Social Security benefits
- Calculate the portion of Social Security benefits that is subject to income taxes
- Determine when it might be appropriate to file for early Social Security benefits

The Inherent Importance of Social Security

Retirement is intended to be a well-deserved break for those who have spent a lifetime hard at work. Up to this point in this book, you have been learning about all of the various ways that an employer and an employee can save for retirement. This is certainly the ideal scenario, but there is another option that is arguably the most important and most widely used retirement income program in the United States. This, of course, is the Social Security system.

Roughly 90 percent of retired Americans receive some form of benefit from the Social Security Administration (SSA).[1] The other 10 percent of workers that are excluded from coverage typically fall into one of four exclusion groups. The first group excluded from Social Security is railroad workers. They are excluded because they have their own special program. Employees of state and local governments are typically excluded from Social Security unless their government body opts into Social Security will a special arrangement directly with the SSA. The third group of excluded workers includes a subset of expatriates. An expatriate is an American citizen who works oversees rather than domestically within the United States. They will be covered by Social Security only if they are working directly for a U.S. company and not for a foreign affiliate. Expatriates will not be covered by Social Security if they are working for the foreign affiliate of a U.S. company unless the U.S. company owns at least 10 percent of the foreign affiliate, and the parent company has a special arrangement with the U.S. Treasury Department. The fourth group of excluded workers is clergy who have opted out of the system. Most clergy earn much lesser salary than their private sector congregants. To help the clergy make ends meet, the government allows them to increase their take-home pay by not withholding any funds for the Federal Insurance Contributions Act (FICA) (Social Security) taxes. This can be a very short-sighted decision for the clergy unless their denomination has some form of retirement income replacement program in place.

In 2014, the SSA will pay almost $863 billion to over 59 million Americans.[2] On average, the monthly check from Social Security represents 38 percent of all retirement income for the elderly. The SSA has revealed that 52 percent of married couples and 74 percent of unmarried persons receive at least 50 percent of their retirement income from Social Security. They have also revealed that 22 percent of married couples and 47 percent of unmarried persons receive at least 90 percent of their retirement income from Social Security. The moral of the story...get married! Just kidding…but the data is sobering. Is this healthy? I will let you decide that, but it certainly is a concern if nothing else.

Does the presence of the Social Security safety net create moral hazard for Americans? **Moral hazard** is an insurance term, which basically means that if someone has insurance to catch them if they fall, then they are more likely to engage in risky behavior. From a retirement planning perspective, I wonder if Americans' understanding of a Social Security safety net has encouraged and enabled them to spend more money during the years when they should be actively saving for retirement simply because they know that they will at least have Social Security, which itself is questionable in terms of long-term sustainability under its current iteration.

Social Security Funding

Social Security is funded through taxes paid by both the employee and the employer. The taxes will appear on an employee's wage statement as FICA. The employee's portion of the tax is 6.2 percent multiplied by the employee's gross (pretax) income up to a maximum of the taxable wage base, which is $117,000 in 2014. The employer must match the employee's tax dollar for dollar by paying 6.2 percent as well. Consider an employee who receives a gross salary of $150,000 per year. This employee will have $7,254 (6.2% × $117,000) withheld from their salary and the employer will also pay the same $7,254. The earnings above $117,000 will not be taxes for Social Security purposes. This money must be sent to the federal government periodically to keep funds flowing into the Social Security system.

If the "employee" happens to be self-employed, then the relevant law is SECA, which stands for Self Employed Contributions Act. Because there is no separate employer to make the employer's contribution, the self-employed person must make both the employee's 6.2 percent contribution and the employer's 6.2 percent contribution.

It is important to understand that Social Security tax is withheld from gross wages whenever there is earned income. It does not matter if the worker is retired and receiving Social Security benefits or not. If workers of any age have a positive gross wage, then they will be paying Social Security taxes up to the taxable wage base limit. It is also important to understand that the taxes withheld for Medicare (1.45 percent for the employee and the employer each) do not have a taxable wage base limit. Employees pay Medicare taxes on whatever amount they earn, and self-employed individuals will also pay a double Medicare tax following the same logic as SECA.

To receive Social Security benefits, workers must have accrued a certain number of "credited quarters of coverage." An employee will receive one credited *quarter* for each $1,200 of earnings in a year (2014 rule). Credited quarters are subject to a maximum of four per year.

Why do the *credits* matter? To be considered **fully insured**, a worker must accrue 40 credited quarters. This is essentially 10 years of at least part-time work. Fully insured is a valuable status because it means that not only will the worker qualify for benefits in retirement, but their survivors will be able to apply for full survivor benefits with the SSA, should the fully insured worker die before the spouse.

What would happen for a young lady who enters the workforce and decides after a few years to put her career on hold to start a family? For someone who has worked less than the required 40 credited quarters, there is another status called *currently insured*. To qualify as being **currently insured**, a worker would need to have at least 6 credited quarters out of the most recent 13 quarters available. When workers are at least currently insured, their survivors will receive at least a partial benefit, should the worker pass away.

A third classification is known as *disability insured*, but it is only available if someone meets the SSA's requirements to be considered disabled. You will learn about this in the section on Survivor Benefits in this chapter.

Initial Benefit Issues

Full retirement age (also called the normal retirement age) had been age 65 for years. Now the SSA has set the age at 66 for those born between 1943 and 1954 and age 67 for those born after 1960. There will likely be further adjustments over time, but these are the current rules. Benefits are available for early retirement as early as age 62, but they are offered with a requisite reduction, which you will learn about in the Early Retirement section in this chapter.

The normal retirement age was established to be a certain number of years below the average life expectancy. In 1940, the normal retirement age was roughly 12.7 years below the average life expectancy.[3] Using actuarial data from 2009, the normal retirement age is now a little over 17.5 years below the average life expectancy.[4] This creates a challenge for the long-term solvency of the Social Security system because the duration of benefits payment has declined at the same time that the number of workers per retiree has declined. In 1945, there were 41.9 workers per retiree, and in 2010 there are only 2.9.[5] There will likely be a continued trend of gradually raising the normal retirement age to link the retirement age more accurately with average life expectancy.

Any person who is fully insured and at or above the normal retirement age can retire and receive full benefits from the SSA. According to the SSA, 72 percent of all benefits paid are to retired workers.[6]

Benefits are also available for the spouse of someone who is fully insured and has reached the normal retirement age. The caveat is that the spouse must be at least 62 to qualify for benefits. A strategy that is often employed by financial professionals is to have fully insured workers who have attained the normal retirement age file for their own benefits and then have their spouses test if benefits would be higher taking a spousal benefit or higher waiting until their own normal retirement age with payments based upon their own lifetime earnings.

What about benefits for someone who is divorced? A divorced person is entitled to spousal benefits from Social Security if the marriage lasted at least 10 years and they remained unmarried, they are at least 62 years old, the ex-spouse is fully insured and entitled to benefits, and the divorced spouse's own benefits would be lower than the calculated spousal benefit.

There are also certain benefits for survivors of a deceased person who was covered by Social Security. According to the SSA's March 2014 Monthly Statistical Snapshot, survivor benefits comprise 13 percent of all benefits paid. You will learn the details of survivor benefits in the next section in this chapter. One other category of available benefits from the SSA is for disabled persons. You will learn about this category in the next section. According to the SSA's March 2014 Monthly Statistical Snapshot, 15 percent of all Social Security benefits are paid to the disabled.

Survivor Benefits

There are some specific benefits that are available to the survivor of a deceased *fully* insured worker. The spouse of a deceased worker who is only *currently* insured will have reduced benefits available to them.

The first benefit available to the surviving spouse of a fully insured worker is a whopping $255 one-time lump-sum payment. The idea is to help defray burial costs, but this small dollar amount will not offset too much of the expenses from a funeral home. Still, it is a nice idea. The real benefit for the surviving spouse is that they will be eligible for full spousal retirement benefits as if the worker were still living. This benefit is available to the surviving spouse once he or she has reached the normal retirement age. He or she can also receive a reduced benefit as young as age 60 (not 62) or as young as age 50 if he or she is disabled.

Another layer of benefit for the surviving spouse will apply if he or she is also caring for a minor child of the deceased worker. The children must be eligible for dependent children's benefits and be either younger than age 16 or be disabled themselves. If a surviving spouse is caring for a dependent child of the deceased, then the surviving spouse is eligible to receive spousal benefits at any age as long as the requirements on the child remain met.

Dependent children of the deceased worker are also eligible for benefits provided that they are unmarried and either younger than 18 or younger than 19 if they are still in high school. The age requirement is waived if the dependent child was disabled before he or she turned 22. There are even some special circumstances where stepchildren, grandchildren, and adopted children of a deceased worker can qualify for benefits. These special scenarios are beyond the scope of this textbook, but know that they exist.

There is also a survivor's benefit for dependent parents of a deceased fully insured worker. The dependent parents must be at least 62 years old to qualify. The other caveat is that the parents must meet the standard Internal Revenue Service (IRS) dependency test, which states that the deceased worker must have been paying at least 50 percent of the dependent parent's support. Also, a family maximum applies to the total dollar amount that a family can receive if there are two or more individuals receiving survivor's benefits.

How Is the Actual Benefit Calculated?

Social Security benefits are based on the employee's **average index monthly earnings (AIME)**. To find a worker's AIME, the SSA will begin by listing all annual wages earned by an employee and then indexing them with an adjustment factor similar to inflation. It would be unfair to compare wages earned 25 years ago with wages earned last year. The SSA uses the highest grossing 35 years of indexed wage history. They then divide the cumulative wages from the highest grossing 35-year window by 420 (35 × 12 = 420 months in a 35-year window), and voilà...AIME. The SSA provides AIME to all workers on an annual basis. They will mail a statement to each worker's home address, and the information is also available on their website.

Benefits paid are based on the AIME. The actual monthly Social Security benefits paid are technically known as the **primary insurance amount (PIA)**. The calculation of PIA is very straightforward. For 2014, begin by taking 90 percent of the first $816 of AIME, then take 32 percent of any AIME that falls between $4,917 and $816, then take 15 percent of any AIME above $4,917. Remember that AIME is a monthly compensation figure. Table 20.1 shows how the PIA would be calculated for a worker whose AIME is $7,000 (an average annual salary of $84,000).

The worker illustrated in Table 20.1 will have a monthly Social Security benefit of $2,359.17, which means that he or she will replace 33.70 percent ($2,359.17/$7,000) of his or her AIME (proxy for preretirement income) using Social Security benefits!

Early Retirement and Social Security

From the perspective of the SSA, *early retirement* means applying for benefits any time before a worker reaches the early retirement age. In practice, workers begin to consider this option at age 62.

Table 20.1 AIME calculation example

Threshold percentage	Amount of AIME	Benefit
90%	$816	$ 734.40
32%	$4,101 ($4,917 – $816)	$1,312.32
15%	$2,083 ($7,000 – $4,917)	$ 312.45
	Cumulative benefit (PIA)	$2,359.17

Most people would love to retire as early as possible, but there is a catch. Receiving Social Security benefits before the normal retirement age will result in a reduced benefit. The absolute earliest that someone could begin to apply for benefits is age 62 (48 months prior to their normal retirement age). If the worker is applying for an early benefit for himself or herself, then the benefit will be reduced by 5/9th of 1 percent for each month before the normal retirement age limited to 36 months. A further reduction is 5/12th of 1 percent for each month before the normal retirement age for the next 24 months. Consider the plight of the worker in the previous example who had a PIA of $2,359.17 at the normal retirement age. What would happen if she chose to retire instead four years (48 months) early? The answer is shown in Table 20.2.

If the worker shown in Table 20.2 decided to retire four years early, then the reduced monthly benefit (PIA) would be $1,769.38 ($2,359.17 – $589.79), and this reduction in benefit is permanent except under a special scenario, which you will learn about in the second to last section in this chapter. The desire to retire early could materially impact this worker's ability to enjoy a comfortable retirement. At this point, he is weighing the benefit of retiring early with the loss of monthly income in retirement. That is essentially a very nice car payment!

However, if the spouse of this worker is applying for an early benefit, then the benefit will be reduced by 25/36th of 1 percent for each month before the normal retirement age limited to 36 months, and a further reduction of 5/12th of 1 percent for each month before the normal retirement age for the next 24 months. Consider how things would work for the person we have used so far in examples if we assume that it is a spouse filling for spousal benefits. Assume that the spouse would otherwise have a PIA of $1,912.47 at the normal retirement age. The spousal benefit will be lower than the actual worker's. What would happen if a spousal

Table 20.2 Early retirement reduction example (Taxpayer)

Percentage reduction	Applicable months	Total percentage reduction	Dollar reduction in PIA
5/9th of 1%	36	20%	$471.83
5/12th of 1%	12	5%	$117.96
	Cumulative reduction	25%	$589.79

Table 20.3 Early retirement reduction example (Spouse)

Percentage reduction	Applicable months	Total percentage reduction	Dollar reduction in PIA
25/36th of 1%	36	25%	$478.12
5/12th of 1%	12	5%	$95.62
	Cumulative reduction	30%	$573.74

filer chose to retire instead four years (48 months) early? The answer is in Table 20.3.

The spousal benefit is more negatively impacted (30 percent reduction instead of 25 percent reduction) than the early benefits of the actual worker. The recipient of the spousal benefit would receive $1,338.73 ($1,912.47 – $573.74).

Deferred Retirement and Social Security

Some individuals are very passionate about what they do. They would prefer to work as long as possible. Others delay filing for Social Security simply because they are good at math. Either way, there is added value to delaying retirement beyond the normal retirement age.

For those who choose to delay retirement beyond the normal retirement age, the SSA has arranged a financial incentive. They will increase the delayed filer's PIA by 8 percent per year for every year that they delay receiving benefits. The SSA will make pro-rata adjustments up to age 70. The incentive to delay is only available for fully insured workers. It is not available for spousal benefit filers.

Obviously, if someone is able to delay retirement, it is best for his or her monthly cash flexibility. As long as the fully insured worker is in good health, this can be an excellent option for them to consider. The benefits of delaying will be realized only if taxpayers either have enough income that they last until age 70 without tapping into their retirement savings or they have a substantial nest egg accumulated.

Another way to think about deferred (or delayed) retirement is using the analogy of a guaranteed inflation-adjusted 8 percent annuity. Where else can a retiree get this kind of guaranteed return? Some would certainly question the guarantee, given the current status of the Social Security trust fund and American politics. The long-term viability will certainly change over time, and there will likely be changes to the payroll tax rates for Social Security, to the normal retirement age, and perhaps even to the level of benefits themselves. But, do not forget that the population of Social Security recipients is a huge voting force in America, and a complete revocation of the system is not likely as long as the American government can still write checks.

The Earnings Test

Can a Social Security recipient have a job during retirement? Absolutely! With so many Americans heavily reliant on Social Security for their retirement income, it may be very wise to also work a part-time job. The complication is that those who work while also receiving *early* Social Security retirement benefits will be subject to an **earnings test**, which may result in a reduction of PIA from the SSA. The reduction only applies to those receiving retirement benefits before the normal retirement age (early retirement). The amount that the monthly check is reduced by is not gone forever. In baseball terms, it is benched. The amount that is removed from the PIA due to the earnings test in early retirement is then adjusted back into the PIA after normal retirement age.

Social Security benefits are reduced by one dollar for every two dollars over the income limit established by the SSA. For 2014, this limit is $15,480 for those who attain normal retirement age sometime after 2014 and $41,400 for those who reach normal retirement age during 2014. Consider the previous example of a worker who should receive a reduced early retirement benefit of $1,769.38. If he also worked and earned $20,000 during the year, he would have an earnings test reduction in the monthly benefits equal to $188.33 {[($20,000 – $15,480)/2] then divided again by 12 to get the monthly number}. This individual would receive an adjusted $1,581.05 ($1,769.38 – $188.33) each month until the year in which he would reach normal retirement age. In that year, the earnings test adjustment would be based on an income limit of $41,400, and assuming the additional income remains at $20,000, there will not be any adjustment in the year in which this worker reaches the normal retirement age. Once the taxpayer reaches the normal retirement age, there will no longer be any restrictions on the amount of income that can be earned, and the benefit will be restored to $1,769.38 **PLUS** an upward adjustment factored by the SSA for each year where the earnings test reduced the benefits.

It is important to understand that the earnings test only applies to earned income. It does not apply to pension benefits or distributions from retirement savings accounts.

Applying for and Taxation of Benefits

A worker who is planning to retire should plan to file for Social Security benefits three months in advance of when he or she will actually need to receive the payments. This is an arm of the federal government and there will be a delay in the processing because there are so many people being covered by the Social Security system. Benefits can be paid retroactively for up to six months. Consider a worker who retires on his 66th birthday and is so focused on his new freedoms that he forgets to file for benefits until two months later. With the three-month potential processing lag, he would potentially miss out on five months of benefit checks that he otherwise would have received, had he been proactive in filing for his benefits. The SSA will provide retroactive payments to cover those five months. Had this new retiree waited six months to file for benefits, then he would be nine months behind (6 months for procrastination and 3 months for the processing lag), and he would only receive six months of retroactive benefits.

An argument can be made to ignore the retroactive payments and to just calculate the payments as a deferred retirement, which would result in an increased monthly benefits check indefinitely. It will be up to the new retiree to figure if the retroactive payments or the higher monthly payment would be more beneficial. If the retiree is in rapidly failing health, the retroactive payment may make the most sense. Otherwise, the increased benefit from deferred retirement should be strongly considered.

Applying to begin benefits is relatively straightforward. One question commonly asked is: How can someone know what benefits they are entitled to in advance of retiring so that they can logically consider their readiness for retirement? The SSA sends an annual mailing (after a taxpayer reaches age 25) to alert taxpayers to their current AIME and PIA status. The SSA also has a section on the website where taxpayers can create an account to monitor their benefits. The website will also provide custom "calculators" to help a worker project retirement scenarios from the perspective of Social Security. It is important to check this information periodically to make sure that the SSA has not missed compensation that should increase the AIME.

Social Security benefits were intended to be a retirement safety net for those who do not have other means of paying for retirement living expenses. However, many individuals, who also have other assets on which they can live, receive benefits. The IRS has structured taxation of Social Security benefits in a way that follows the logic just discussed.

A retiree who is single and receiving retirement benefits from Social Security will apply the tax schedule shown in Table 20.4 to their Social Security benefits.

From this schedule, you can see that after a retiree's adjusted gross income (AGI) rises above $25,000, a portion of their Social Security income becomes taxable as ordinary income. Common items that will create AGI for a retiree are interest on bank deposits or certificates of deposits, realized capital gains in taxable investment accounts, distributions from pensions and IRAs (reported on a Form 1099-R), and possibly a part-time job. Sometimes, the amount of money that is withdrawn from an IRA in retirement is enough to put a retiree over either the $25,000 threshold or the $34,000 threshold. This should be monitored by either the taxpayers or their financial professional. The maximum amount of Social Security benefits that could be taxable is 85 percent.

Married retirees have a higher threshold schedule. The taxability schedule in Table 20.5 applies to a married retiree's Social Security benefits.

Table 20.4 *When are social security benefits taxable for a single taxpayer?*

AGI income range	Percentage of benefits taxed
Under $25,000	0%
$25,000–$34,000	50%
Over $34,000	85%

Abbreviation: AGI, Adjusted gross income.

Table 20.5 When are Social Security benefits taxable for a married taxpayer?

AGI income range	Percentage of benefits taxed
Under $32,000	0%
$32,000–$44,000	50%
Over $44,000	85%

Abbreviation: AGI, Adjusted gross income.

Should a Taxpayer Take Early Social Security Benefits?

And now for the $100 million question…should a taxpayer file for early Social Security retirement benefits? Everyone would love to retire as young as possible and begin to enjoy a different pace of life with perhaps more focus on volunteering and family. But, this is not available for everyone. It is imperative to thoroughly evaluate each early retirement scenario on a case-by-case basis. It may be workable for one taxpayer and not for another.

You have already learned that filing for Social Security benefits early will result in a permanently reduced monthly check (PIA). Figure 20.1 shows that early benefits result in a reduction in benefits of roughly 7 percent per year. For every year that workers decide to keep working past age 62, they are essentially earning a 7 percent increase in PIA for each year that they keep working. This thought pattern works up to the normal retirement age at which point the increase in benefits is now 8 percent per year for deferred retirement. This is an interesting way of thinking of this scenario. Hopefully, it makes logical sense to you that by not taking a reduced benefit today, the retiree will receive a higher benefit later. This is an easy way to earn 7 percent more benefits by not taking early benefits and possibly an 8 percent growth strategy if the taxpayer surpasses the normal retirement age and stretches out to age 70!

Sometimes an early retirement is the result of an involuntary termination. Business conditions change and layoffs do occur. If a layoff affects someone who is able to qualify for early retirement from Social Security, this might be a tempting option. Some forced retirees in this situation are not planning on remaining in retirement. They are transitional…they are looking for a new job, but they need some money to get them through

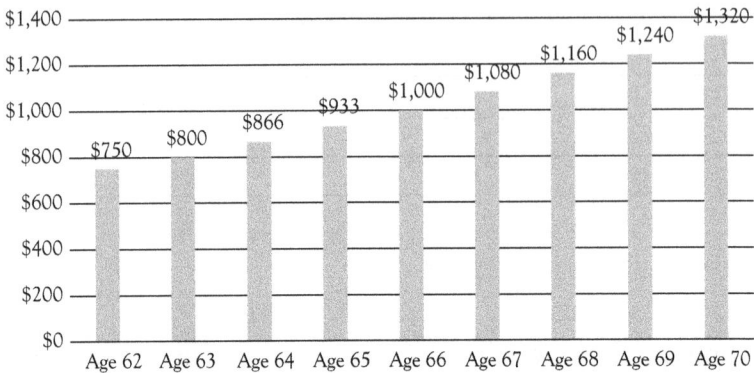

Figure 20.1 Schedule of Social Security benefits assuming $1,000 PIA at normal retirement age of 66

Source: Social Security Administration
Abbreviation: PIA, Primary insurance amount.

until the new job is secured. In this instance, the forced retirees have a **unique payback option** where they could apply for early retirement benefits and then within one year, they could repay all benefits received without interest, and then benefits would be suspended until they reapply for benefits at their *planned* retirement. Their actual retirement benefits will then be based upon when they reapply for benefits and not on the reduced early retirement amount. This option assumes that the taxpayer has the discretionary cash flow to repay the benefits received.

According to the American Association of Retired Persons (AARP), 41 percent of men and 46 percent of women elect to retire early at age 62. They also reveal that 14.3 percent of men and 9.7 percent of women wait to collect a full benefit at their respective normal retirement age.[7] Early retirement, it seems, is chosen by many workers who are eager to retire and change priorities.

Table 20.6 highlights the fact that patience (in terms of filing for Social Security benefits) does have a cost. It is estimated that if someone waits until age 70 to file when they otherwise would have taken benefits at age 66 (their normal retirement age), then they would need to collect the higher benefit level until roughly age 84 before they would be ahead by taking the deferred benefits. If a taxpayer is in very good health, then

Table 20.6 Retirement break-even ages

Age to begin benefits	Relative comparison age	Break-even age range
66	62	Between 77 and 78
70	62	Between 80 and 81
70	66	Between 83 and 84

Source: Charles Schwab[8]

this might be a worthy gamble. If longevity is in question or at least uncertain, then deferred retirement benefits might not be the best option to select.

Supplemental Security Income

Supplemental Security Income (SSI) is a secondary layer of retirement income for Americans who meet a specific criterion. They must be below a certain income range, which is determined by each state, *and* they must be (1) age 65 or older, (2) disabled, or (3) legally blind. While SSI benefits are administered by the SSA, the funds do not come from the Social Security trust fund. Payment for SSI benefits comes directly from the budget of the U.S. Treasury. These payments could be as high as $721 for an individual and $1,082 (2014 limit) for a married couple, and this value is in addition to any Social Security payments being received.[9] This category of retirement income is designed to help those who have very little means to care for themselves.

Recipients of SSI benefits must maintain "limited resources." This means that they cannot own more than $2,000 worth of assets for an individual or $3,000 if they are a married couple. The SSI recipient's home and one car are not included in this resource limit. This basically means that SSI beneficiaries cannot maintain a bank account larger than these resource thresholds and still receive the additional benefits.

There is one notable exception to the limited resources mandate. The SSI beneficiaries could have a special needs trust (SNT) established for their benefit. An SNT must be established by someone other than the SSI benefit recipient. This could be a parent or some other relative perhaps.

Also, an SNT must be irrevocable, and it must stipulate that any sum left in the SNT after the SSI recipient's death can be remitted to Medicaid to cover any end-of-life expenses paid by the state.[10]

Discussion Questions

1. Social Security is arguably the most important retirement system in America, yet some workers are not covered under Social Security. Who are these people?

2. Some people say that Social Security creates moral hazard. Why would they say such a thing?

3. Stacey earned compensation totaling $11,000 from a single employer between January 1 and April 1. She then stopped working to care for her mother who was in failing health. How many quarters of coverage does Stacey earn for this taxable year?

4. A certain woman has been out of the workforce for the last 10 years as she has been focusing on raising three children. She has recently decided to reenter the job market. How long will she need to work before her spouse would be eligible for surviving spouse benefits, should that unfortunate circumstance become necessary?

5. What is the earliest age at which a retired worker is eligible to receive Social Security benefits?

6. One of your uncles, who was born in 1948 tells you that he is planning to retire with full Social Security benefits this year at age 65. What advice would you give your uncle?

7. A certain couple divorced five years ago. They were married for eight years and neither has remarried. The ex-wife is now 66 years old and interested in applying for Social Security. What are her options?

8. A tragic car accident claimed the life of a devoted husband and father. The survivors are a 45-year-old wife, a 24-year-old mentally disabled child who has been disabled from birth, a 21-year-old college student, and an 18½-year-old who will be graduating high school in another 10 months. What are the survivor's benefits available to this family, assuming that the deceased father was fully insured?

9. Below is a series of indexed annual salaries for an individual. He began with a $45,000 indexed salary straight out of college and

had annual increases of 3 percent with the exception that every seven years he changed jobs and received a salary increase larger than 3 percent. What is this individual's AIME?

$45,000.00	$55,000.00	$67,500.00	$87,500.00	$112,500.00
$46,350.00	$56,650.00	$69,525.00	$90,125.00	$115,875.00
$47,740.50	$58,349.50	$71,610.75	$92,828.75	$119,351.25
$49,172.72	$60,099.99	$73,759.07	$95,613.61	$122,931.79
$50,647.90	$61,902.98	$75,971.84	$98,482.02	$126,619.74
$52,167.33	$63,760.07	$78,251.00	$101,436.48	$130,418.33
$53,732.35	$65,672.88	$80,598.53	$104,479.58	$134,330.88

10. Using the AIME you calculated in the previous question, what is this individual's PIA (using 2014 AIME bend points), assuming that he retires at the normal retirement age?

11. What would happen if the individual whose PIA you just calculated needed to retire at age 63 instead of the normal retirement age of 66?

12. A married client who has been retired for several years has an annual pension from his previous employer equal to $25,000 per year. The combined required IRA distribution for this couple is $12,500. They have taxable capital gains income of $4,500 from their non-IRA account. They have combined Social Security benefits of $35,000. They are considering taking an additional IRA distribution of $10,000 to gift money to their only child. What advice do you have for them relative to their Social Security benefits?

13. A worker born in 1953 is currently planning to file for deferred Social Security benefits at age 68. How much benefit could he expect to receive if his PIA at his normal retirement age would equal $2,473.49?

14. A taxpayer was forced to "retire" (layoff) at age 63. She filed for early Social Security benefits and begins to receive a check for $1,976.43. Six months later, she is able to find a part-time job where she can earn $1,700 per month. This is not enough to cover the living expenses and so she needs to keep receiving Social Security benefits as well. The SSA finds out that she now has a part-time job. What will happen to the monthly Social Security benefits?

CHAPTER 21

Retirement Needs Analysis

Introduction

Once individuals have decided to make retirement planning a priority, they need to move beyond which plan type is best for them to save with and instead focus on developing a projection of their personal retirement snapshot. Any model for making forecasts is only as good as its inputs. As is said of nutrition...garbage in, garbage out. Assumptions need to be made for retirement age, life expectancy, retirement spending levels, inflation, and investment returns. All five assumptions involve both a degree of science and a degree of finesse. Retirement spending levels is perhaps the easiest to estimate, although each variable is a moving target. It matters most what the assumptions are closest to retirement, but they are also extremely valuable during the accumulation years in determining how much needs to be saved. All five of these variables will be explored in this chapter.

Learning Goals

- Understand the likelihood of retiring at the normal retirement age
- Understand how to establish a life expectancy assumption
- Describe the different psychological standard of living factors for clients in different stages of their careers
- Describe the replacement ratio approach for planning a retirement lifestyle
- Describe the expense method approach for planning a retirement lifestyle
- Describe the impact of inflation on retirement
- Understand how retirement planning investment assumptions can be formed

The Retirement Age Assumption

According to Gallup, the average retirement age is now up to age 61.[1] In Chapter 9, you learned that early retirement presents certain challenges to the new retiree. Gallup also asked various groups of people at what age they plan to retire. In 2013, 37 percent of respondents said that they expect to retire older than age 65, 26 percent said that they expect to retire at age 65, and another 26 percent said that they expect to retire younger than age 65. PNC's latest Perspectives on Retirement Survey revealed that nearly 60 percent of survey respondents retired from the workforce sooner than they had expected.[2] The reality is that almost half of workers retire sooner than they otherwise had planned.

It is interesting to note the differences between the response and the age of the respondent in Gallup's survey. The youngest adult participants in this study show the highest expectation of retiring early, while those closest to retirement are overwhelmingly tipped in favor of a deferred retirement. These older Americans can see how their plan (or lack thereof) has played out, and reality is more apparent to them. Still, the average age is 61 years…

The incidence of early retirement is partly due to some outliers who are wealthy enough that their needs are well provided for. Others have retirement forced upon them as a result of a layoff or some other life event, like a health issue. This is the involuntary retirement issue.

Those who do retire early will have several issues to contend with. You learned in Chapter 20 that those who take early retirement will have reduced Social Security benefits. The actual reduction will be amplified because not only will they have early reduction penalties, they will also contend with the possibility of a lower average index monthly earnings (AIME). The Social Security payment [primary insurance amount (PIA)] is based on AIME, and AIME goes up as gross wages go up. The last years of a worker's career are usually their highest earning years and cutting those years short also cuts AIME short. This same factor could also affect final average compensation (FAC) used in the defined benefit (DB) calculations if the employer offers a DB plan. In theory, the workers' home mortgage should be paid off by their late 50s, and this would then translate into additional savings potential during those final years

of employment. This is a problem to miss. The other issue that is sometimes overlooked is medical insurance coverage. The worker has been
accustomed to an employer providing coverage. Medicare is not available
until normal retirement age; so early retirement can also create an issue
of where medical coverage will come from at a time when coverage may
be most needed.

Life Expectancy Assumptions

In general, life expectancies are increasing somewhat, but they are increasing at a higher rate for men than for women. For a long time, women
have had a higher life expectancy than men, and this trend does persist,
but the gap is narrowing. Having a college degree significantly increases
life expectancy.[3] You are making the right choice!

The Centers for Disease Control has found that those who live in the
North appear to have longer lives than those in the South.[4] The reasons
for this are irrelevant to this discussion. The salient point is that the state
of residency will help to direct a planner to selecting a life expectancy
figure to be used in the retirement planning process. If someone wants to
move from Oregon to retire in Alabama, tell them to look out, although
Alabama is a very fun state!

One way to examine the trend in life expectancies is to consider the
most extreme age category—centenarians. Census data from 1900 to
1950 shows a somewhat steady decline in the number of centenarians.[5]
However, the trend reversed and has been regularly increasing to the
point where we now have 53,364 centenarians recorded as of the 2010
census data. This same census report also shows that for every 100 female
centenarians, there were only 20.7 men.[6] According to this report from
the U.S. Census Bureau, females are most likely to become centenarians.
Persons are also more likely to become centenarians if they are widows
or widowers (81.54 percent of centenarians), if they have a high school
degree or *less* (69.86 percent of centenarians), and if they are not veterans
(94.69 percent of centenarians).[7]

The growth in those becoming centenarians is important, but the
growth of those living into their 90s is also important to understand.
There are now nearly two million Americans in their 90s, and the size of

this population subset has nearly tripled in the last three decades.[8] The point is that many people are outliving the average life expectancy for their gender. A planner can make educated guesses whenever they begin to work with a client, but the life expectancy should be revised when someone approaches age 65 to capture the more current government statistics and to have greater insight into health concerns faced by the client. In general, financial professionals need to make an extended assumption of life expectancy and stress-test a few alternate ages. If a healthy 65-year-old client has a life expectancy of 81, then plan on something like 87 while stress-testing various ages into their 90s. Plan for the worst and hope for the best…

Retirement Standard of Living

Everyone wants to have the highest standard of living possible. For some, *standard of living* means vacations and fancy items, but for others it means flexibility to help family members and charitable organizations. The ways in which people spend their retirements are as diverse as the American culture itself. A client's proximity to their actual retirement age will greatly influence their expectations for their retirement standard of living.

Clients who are closer to actual retirement are often called *late-career clients*. These late-career clients are typically enjoying the highest annual earnings of their working career. This concept of peak earnings is great because it enables the highest level of savings, especially assuming that all debts have been paid in full. It also creates a challenge because a person's expectations for retirement lifestyle are anchored in recent experience. This means that those who are soon to retire will base their retirement standard of living expectations on their most recent salary level. This can set an unrealistic expectation especially if they have only enjoyed this higher salary level for a few years.

The next stage of client is known as a *mid-career client*. These clients are somewhere in the middle of their working lives. These clients will be basing their retirement living expectations on a projected career path and projected raises. Projections can be way off. There is nothing wrong with dreaming, but financial needs analysis for retirement planning works best when the assumptions are as realistic as possible. Mid-career clients need some help stress-testing alternative scenarios.

The final stage of client is the *early-career client*. These clients are least focused on retirement, but they may come to a financial professional to help them create a savings plan. These clients have the highest degree of estimation in their projections because they have the longest time to work before retiring. The financial professional's goal for these clients should be to help them develop a personal budget that places heavy emphasis on saving at least 10 percent of their take-home pay.

Both mid-career and early-career clients should have their financial plan completely revised a few different times during their working careers to help them revise their savings and spending habits as needed.

Approaches to Retirement Income

There are two core methods used to assess a client's income needs during retirement. The first is called the replacement ratio approach, and the second is called the expense method.

The **replacement ratio approach** is very easy to understand. It is merely the percentage of preretirement income that the client desires to replace in retirement. Their income level in their final working years will greatly influence this decision. Most clients will need a replacement ratio of between 60 and 80 percent to maintain an approximately level standard of living. That means that if the client was golfing three days per week before retirement, then they should be able to continue the same lifestyle. *Adding frequent golfing (or traveling) is not maintaining a standard of living… this is altering (or perhaps increasing) their standard of living.*

Why would someone be able to maintain their preretirement standard of living with only 60 to 80 percent of their preretirement income level? A retired client will benefit from both reduced taxes and reduced expenses during retirement. From the tax side of the equation, a retiree will no longer be paying Federal Insurance Contributions Act (FICA) taxes (unless they maintain a part-time job). They will also receive some tax-free income because a meaningful portion of Social Security income is tax-free. Withdrawals from individual retirement accounts (IRAs) and pensions are usually not taxed by state and local governments. Some areas even provide reduced property taxes for seniors through income level-based rebate programs. From the vantage point of expense reduction, the retiree will save on work-related expenses such as clothing, eating out, and fuel for their car. Hopefully, their home is completely paid off, thus eliminating monthly mortgage payments. Retirees also receive senior-only discounts at many venues including movies, restaurants, and some hotels. *The big expense reduction comes from no longer saving for retirement.* If the retiree was saving $15,000 per year during their preretirement years, then this is $15,000 that will automatically not need to be replaced during retirement.

Figure 21.1 displays the replacement ratios for the Social Security portion of a client's retirement income. These calculations are based on the PIA formula previously discussed in Chapter 20. Note that a taxpayer who earned an average salary of $30,000 per year will receive a replacement ratio of 50.35 percent, while someone who earned an average salary of $80,000 will only have a replacement ratio of 34.04 percent. The second client will have a larger dollar amount as a monthly Social Security check, but that dollar amount represents a smaller percentage of preretirement income. Whatever preretirement income is not replaced by Social Security income will need to be replaced by inheritances, personal savings (employer sponsored or otherwise), and possibly some level of employment during retirement.

The only way to know what one is spending is to track expenses first and then create a budget to plan how personal finances will be allocated.

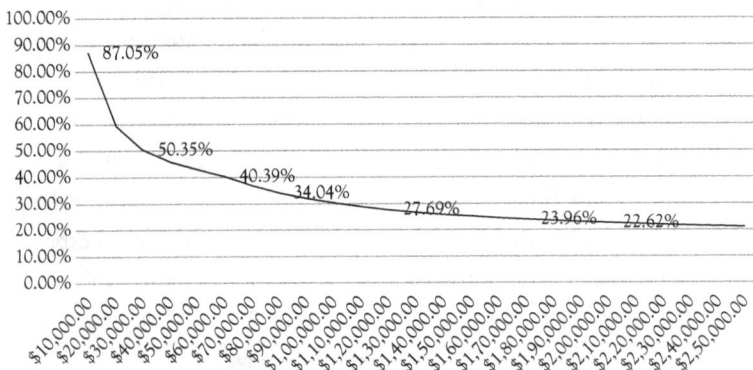

Figure 21.1 Replacement % at normal retirment age for Social Security income only

Note: Author's calculation based upon the 2014 primary insurance amount (PIA) formula.

Budgeting has a negative connotation, but it really is nothing more than a spending plan. Everyone loves to spend money. Why not plan it out! The **expense method** is essentially building a year-by-year budget for retirement. As previously discussed, some common expenses that decline typically in retirement are mortgage expenses, clothing expenses, and transportation-related costs. There are some areas that will increase in retirement. Medical expenses usually rise in retirement as more services are needed. Utility costs also tend to rise. Retirees are home more often; so heating and cooling bills may rise. In accordance with Murphy's Law ("Anything that can go wrong, will go wrong"), home maintenance issues also tend to increase in retirement. This is partly because people are home more and can pay more attention to maintaining their primary residence. Recreation, entertainment, and travel expenses also tend to increase as retirees are fulfilling lifelong dreams while their health still enables them to experience these activities and visit family.

Inflation Assumptions

We all know that inflation is the rate at which prices increase over time. Another way to view this is as a retiree's time-adjusted spending ability. An item that costs $1,000 today will not cost $1,000 in 10 years. Social Security has an annual adjustment factor called the **cost of living adjustment (COLA)**, but other retirement income sources will need to be manually adjusted for inflation unless a retiree has purchased an annuity with an explicit inflation adjustment feature.

It is easy to understand why inflation is vital for retirement planning projections, but determining a number to use is a somewhat subjective moving target. Inflation from 1914 to 2013 has averaged 3.34 percent per year. Inflation for the last 40 years (1973–2013) has averaged 4.32 percent, and inflation for the last 20 years (1993–2013) has averaged 2.45 percent.[9] Wow, what a range! If a taxpayer used the most recent 20 years, they might underestimate the true inflation potential. There are many factors that must be considered. Factors such as in which subsectors of the economy, like medical care and services, do retirees tend to spend more money. Medical inflation tends to be higher than mainline inflation. The Bureau of Labor Statistics also breaks down inflation into medical inflation. Medical inflation averaged 3.9 percent during the last 20 years (1993–2013), and it averaged 6.1 percent in the last 40 years (1973–2013).[10] The cost of medical care has been increasing at a more rapid pace than general inflation.

The Bureau of Labor Statistics has recognized the different types of expense categories embraced by retirees. They have created an experimental data set, which they call the CPI-E (CPI-U is the consumer price index for all urban consumers). The idea is to weight more heavily the influence of housing costs and medical costs on the general level of inflation. This data set may one day be used to establish COLA for Social Security if it encounters the right political tailwinds. From December 1982 through December 2011, the observed CPI-E rose 3.1 percent per year while normal inflation (CPI-U) rose 2.8 percent per year.[11] The idea of CPI-E is a step in the right direction, but more research is needed to find an inflation measurement that truly captures a retiree's spending.

Another consideration is that as people age, they are not able to be as independent as they once were. The logical conclusion of this fact is that retirees should consume more services than goods. The Bureau of Labor Statistics shows that from February 2013 to February 2014, the headline inflation rose only 1.1 percent, while services inflation rose 2.4 percent.[12] This is an ongoing trend that the cost of services inflate more rapidly than the cost of goods.

Clearly, the inflation rate assumption used in forming retirement planning projections needs to be customized to each retiree. Higher expected usage of medical services will necessitate a higher inflation assumption. Most planners use 4 percent as the base level for inflation and then adjust upward if more medical services are required. Some regions will have higher or lower inflation rates as well. It is better to overestimate the inflation rate than to undershoot. A conservative (higher) inflation assumption will provide the retiree with the most realistic scenario possible.

Investment Assumptions

Perhaps the most difficult assumption to make in projecting retirement scenarios is a reasonable rate of return on investments. There are so many variables to consider that this really is very complex. The good news is

Table 21.1 Historical investment returns

Time period	Stocks	10-year Treasury	60–40 mix favoring stocks
1928–2013	11.50%	5.21%	8.98%
1964–2013	11.29%	6.97%	9.56%
2004–2013	9.10%	4.69%	7.34%

Source: Stern School of Business at New York University[13]

that longer time horizons (people in their 30s and 40s planning for retirement) can be more forgiving than shorter time horizons.

One major consideration is asset allocation—the percentage breakdown between stocks and bonds. Conventional wisdom would tell a retiree to have a very large percentage of their portfolio invested in fixed income (bonds), but in a lower interest rate environment, that is not as wise as it once was. There are many questionnaires that can be used to help someone assess their ideal allocation, but this should best be determined with the assistance of a well-trained investment needs advisor.

The first three columns in Table 21.1 come from data compiled by the Stern School of Business at New York University. The final column is simply this author's mix of 60 percent stocks and 40 percent bonds. A return assumption between 7 and 9 percent should be fine, assuming that a client has a longer time horizon and would be allocating a mix between stocks and bonds.

In general, more conservative return assumptions provide for more achievable retirement planning projections. Return assumptions higher than 8 percent may necessitate more risk-taking than the retirement saver should be exposed to. One idea is to use 8 percent (or slightly higher) as the return assumption during working years and then shift to 6 to 7 percent during retirement. This would permit more risk-taking during the accumulation years and less risk-taking during the payout years. Placement in the 7 to 9 percent range should be based upon the cost of failure. If the cost of taking too much risk and failing is very high, then the investor should be even more conservative and use a return assumption closer to 6 percent. In this scenario, the cost would be too high if failure might mean needing a part-time job in retirement or delaying retirement to make up for poor investment choices. If the cost is low, meaning an investment loss will not really impact the individual's plans, then they can probably take more risk and therefore aim for a return assumption of 8 percent or even higher.

It is often suggested that investors should be riskier in their investment approach while they are younger, have the ability and willingness to accept more risk, and are building toward a specific dollar-level goal. If younger clients have a lower risk tolerance, then they should begin with a lower risk strategy. Investing in higher risk assets is not a guarantee of higher returns. Sometimes, investment choices simply do not play out as expected and the lower risk strategy may actually produce a better result.

A colleague at Penn State Erie, Dr. Brian Boscaljon, has suggested that at the point when a client reaches their target asset base, the risk level should be toned down to preserve the desired wealth level.[14] This is an outstanding idea that deserves application in practice. Most investors hit a certain wealth level and then change their goal to some higher level. That is like playing football and constantly moving the end zone. It is much safer to use the method suggested by Dr. Boscaljon.

There has also been debate over where it is best to hold fixed income versus equity investments. Some have theorized that it is best to hold fixed income investments, which make a regular taxable income payment, within a retirement account. This strategy would shelter the regular interest payments from ordinary income tax rates until retirement. Applying this strategy would also suggest to hold equity (stock) investments outside of tax-sheltered accounts. The thinking is that the investor could then choose when to realize a capital gain and have better control over taxation. The other side of the argument is that equities will likely appreciate much more significantly over time, and holding them within an IRA (or other tax-sheltered account) is best because they will grow the most in a deferred way. Both sides have a valid argument, and financial professionals should be aware of the issues involved with their client's unique situation.

Discussion Questions

1. Is it true that the normal retirement age derives its name because that is when most people tend to retire?

2. What are some of the risks posed by early retirement?

3. How should a life expectancy be chosen for a given client?

4. What trends are visible in the life expectancy data presented in this chapter?

5. What is the recommended range of replacement ratios? Why would the range be less than 100 percent?

6. Does everyone receive the same replacement percentage from Social Security?

7. Why is it not recommended to simply use the long-term inflation average of 3.34 percent as the inflation assumption in retirement planning projections?

8. What is the recommended method for selecting an investment return rate?

CHAPTER 22

Housing, Medicare, and Long-Term Care Concerns

Introduction

Regardless of the level of wealth attained, every retiree will deal with issues like where to live, how to provide for healthcare needs, and how to manage end-of-life care situations. Housing options could include staying where they are, but they may need to consider how they can monetize their home and still live there if the need exists. They should also understand the various planning options available to them through Medicare. Moreover, they should understand what can be done if they retire before age 65, when Medicare coverage begins.

It has been said that the only two guarantees in life are death and taxes. As retirees approach the inevitability of death, they should understand the planning options available to them. They can predetermine how care should be administered if or when death becomes a reality. They can also use insurance products to minimize the sometimes savagely expensive nature of end-of-life care.

Learning Goals

- Identify the common options for downsizing a client's housing situation
- Describe alternatives to downsizing
- Understand the potential concerns to consider relative to out-of-state retirement
- Identify ways that a house could be used as a financial asset and still remain the primary residence
- Describe the various benefits and restrictions available within Medicare

- Identify a solution to an early retirement gap in healthcare coverage
- Understand the purpose of long-term care (LTC) insurance
- Identify the different types of advance directives and how they could be useful

Introduction to Housing Issues

All retirees have one thing in common…they all need to live somewhere. The problem is that housing costs can become a significant burden if they are not carefully monitored. Recent research suggests that retirees and soon-to-be retirees aged 54 to 74 spend an average of 32.8 percent of their monthly income on housing-related expenses, and those over age 75 spend an average of 36.7 percent.[1] This is a substantial percentage of a fixed budget! These expenses could be mortgage payments, property taxes, and repairs or upgrades. Sometimes a change in their housing situation becomes necessary.

When a client is considering a change in housing situation, one of the biggest challenges to overcome can be the psychological attachment to the house. This is especially true if he or she has lived in the same house for a long time and is either a widow or has perhaps raised kids in that house. Many people remain in their long-time primary residence longer than financial prudence would otherwise dictate due to this challenge.

Many factors need to be considered when considering staying in a long-time primary residence in retirement (later-stage retirement in particular). One factor is the suitability of the structure to retirement living needs. Are the bathrooms able to accommodate an aging retiree's needs? Are there any stairs in the house that provide access to necessary areas like bedrooms, kitchens, living rooms, bathrooms, and laundry facilities? Another factor is strictly financial. The house may be mortgage-free, but can the retiree maintain the house? There will be property taxes, utilities' bills, and exterior maintenance (like lawn care and snow removal). There may be issues like roof replacement, furnace or air conditioner replacement, or appliances that fail. Murphy's Law usually drops several of these factors on a surviving spouse within a relatively short period after the first spouse passes.

Another issue that could affect a housing decision is the condition of the neighborhood. Neighborhoods sometimes deteriorate over time in terms of both physical condition and moral fabric. What was once a very safe neighborhood may no longer be so.

The final straw may fall to financial necessity. The financial well-being of a retiree may be dependent upon accessing the equity in their home for living expenses. One option to tap into this equity pool is to outright sell the house. You will learn about these options in the next section in Retirement Housing Options and Relocation Issues.

From an income tax perspective, homeowners can sell their primary residence, assuming that they lived there for two out of the previous five years, and exclude $250,000 of the gain from capital gains taxation. Married couples who file a joint tax return can exclude $500,000 of gain. This is a significant tax benefit and can lead people to consider a primary residence as a good investment. This is not always the case, but that is a different discussion altogether.

Retirement Housing Options and Relocation Issues

Financial professionals are often called upon to assist their clients in all areas of their financial lives including the decision to remain in their long-term home or to downsize. One venue that retirees might downsize to is called a **life care community**, which is a group of structures that begin with apartment living and culminate in skilled nursing care if the retiree's needs progress that far. When retirees decide to enter a life care community, they will pay one lump-sum payment to the company that hosts the facility. They will then pay an ongoing monthly fee that typically remains unchanged regardless of the level of care received. The facility operator will then draw upon the initial lump-sum payment if the retiree progresses into higher care levels. The lump sum is sometimes refundable to the retiree's heirs or the retirees themselves if they leave the facility through death or decision before they use the lump sum to pay for higher levels of care.

Some life care communities will charge a higher initial lump sum to offer a refundable feature. For example, a life care community called Shell Point in Fort Myers, Florida, offers a certain 700-square foot apartment for $1,652 per month.[2] Without a refundable lump-sum option, the initial lump sum is as low as $151,000, but with a 90 percent refundable feature, the initial lump sum required jumps to a minimum of $270,290. *It is imperative to check closely the financial health of the life care community operator before turning over the initial lump sum on the chance that fraud is lurking in the background.* Unfortunately, one must always be on the lookout for those looking to separate the unsuspecting from their money. This is most prevalent among the elderly.

Another place where a retiree might choose to downsize is called **age-restricted housing**. Age-restricted housing could be simply a large apartment complex or a series of patio homes with a central community building, which offers amenities like hairdressers, groceries, craft rooms, swimming pools, fitness centers, libraries, cooking classes, or even access to a private golf course. Part of the allure is almost like moving back into a college dorm where there are numerous other people in the retirees' age range who may be interested in similar activities. For some, this sense of community is enough to peak their interest. There are two different options for age-restricted housing communities. In one scenario, all residents must be 62 or older. In the other variation, the benchmark is set at 55 years. In this second scenario, 80 percent of the residents must be older than 55 years. These age-restricted communities could be a problem if a taxpayer has children who may need to move back home after college or some other life event. They may not be able to move back home due to the age restrictions of the community. Also, housing in age-restricted communities is generally much smaller.

Some clients will want to relocate to another state when they retire to be closer to relatives or simply to be in a climate more suited to their preferences or needs. This decision needs to be considered very carefully because it is difficult to undo. There are certainly moving expenses to factor into the equation, but there is much more. Some states have very different taxation schemes for retirees (income taxes, property tax rebates). A big tax difference that is sometimes overlooked is the difference in inheritance taxation. The client should also consider available support structure such as access to medical care.

Alternative Housing Choices

The natural alternative to relocation and downsizing is simply to remain in the same house. This choice might require some creative solutions, but it may be best in the long term. Could guardrails and possibly automatic lifts be added to stairs? Could flooring be altered to make the house easier to maintain and less of a tripping hazard? Could the laundry, bedroom, bathroom, and eating area all be situated on the same floor? Could a service be hired to maintain the lawn and remove snow during the winter? If all these items could be addressed and the neighborhood is not a problem, then remaining in a long-term primary residence might be the best solution. This enables the retiree to not address the psychological nuances of choosing to sell a house associated with so many memories.

If the retiree is experiencing financial difficulty, then there are a few creative solutions to enable to remain at home and still tap the equity. The first creative solution is called a **sale-leaseback agreement**. In this type of arrangement, retirees will sell their house to someone else, but enter into a contract to rent it from them for a certain period of time, which is typically a lifetime lease (a long as the retiree is alive or physically able or both). In this way, they are accessing all of the equity, staying in the house longer, and shifting maintenance issues to the new owner. The other product of creative finance is called a **reverse mortgage**. This is a nonrecourse loan, which means that other retiree assets are safe from this creditor. The homeowners will receive payments while they remain in their house. The payments could take one of three forms: a lump sum based upon the age, a credit line accessible as needed, or a set monthly cash advance. Essentially, a loan balance will accrue in exact reverse of how the homeowner paid for their house in the first place. A homeowner must be at least 62 years old to access this option, and older retirees are permitted to borrow significantly higher percentages of the home's appraised value because their life expectancy is shorter. You might be wondering what happens to the remaining home equity if there is any equity left when the retiree either passes or decides to move. In a reverse mortgage, the excess equity belongs to either the retirees or their heirs, whichever is applicable.

Medicare Options

Medicare has the reputation of being very complex to navigate. To help add structure, it has been broken up into four parts: Part A for hospital coverage, Part B for doctor's bills, Part C for managed care alternatives, and Part D for prescription drug benefits.

Medicare Part A provides eligible retirees with inpatient hospital coverage. To be eligible for Part A coverage, a retiree must be in one of three categories: (1) at least 65 years old and either eligible for Social Security benefits or have chosen to defer Social Security benefits, (2) at least 65 years old and opted out of Social Security during their working career, or (3) someone who does not qualify on their own for Social Security benefits, but they are at least 65 years old and married to a fully insured spouse who is at least 62 years old. Those who are at least 65 years but do not meet these requirements can opt into the Medicare program by paying a monthly fee which is up to $426 per month.

Once eligibility is satisfied, the retiree will receive full access to benefits. Medicare Part A benefits are viewed in terms of **benefit periods**, which is the duration of an illness requiring hospitalization. Each benefit period holds a maximum of 90 days, and there is a requirement that at least 60 days must separate each benefit period. All Medicare recipients receive 60 lifetime **reserve days,** which are best explained in the context of an example. Pretend that a Medicare Part A-covered taxpayer (Bill) becomes ill and requires hospitalization. The illness lasts for less than 90 days, and so the entire hospital stay is covered by Medicare. Bill then has another illness 61 days later. A new benefit period has begun, and the next 90 days will be covered by Medicare. However, if Bill had only remained in the hospital for 20 days with a 45-day break before another hospital stay of 90 days, then potentially he would have a problem. Because the break was not for more than 60 days, these two events are considered to be the same benefit period, and 110 days of hospitalization exceeds the 90 threshold. This means that Bill would need to pay personally for 20 days of hospitalization. This could be an enormous expense! However, Medicare allows him 60 lifetime days that could be used to provide care at Medicare's expense. Bill could elect to have these 20 days come out of his reservoir of 60 lifetime days, and then the entire stay will be covered. After those 60 lifetime days have been used, then any extended stays are Bill's responsibility. There is no limit to the number of benefit periods in a lifetime, only a limitation on the number of days in a benefit period and the number of days that must separate benefit periods.

Medicare Part B covers lab tests, physician visits, and outpatient surgeon's fees. An emergency room visit is considered an outpatient hospital service unless the patient requires admittance to the hospital. It will also cover certain supplies, like a wheelchair, that are deemed medically necessary for recovery and treatment. Prescription drugs administered in an outpatient setting are typically not covered by Part B...you need part D for that. Some therapy is also covered. Part B is available for those who qualify for Part A coverage, but it does require a premium paid by the recipient. The premium starts at $104.90 per month and goes up as the retiree's income level [adjusted gross income (AGI)] goes up. The premium is deducted from monthly Social Security benefits. Some services that are specifically excluded from Medicare Part B include cosmetic surgery, dental care, vision coverage, hearing aids, and orthopedic shoes (sometimes used for diabetics).

Medicare Part C is a managed care alternative program, which is sometimes called a **Medicare Advantage plan**. A Part C participant will pay a Part B premium and perhaps a bit more to a private insurance company, and the Part C plan will replace Parts A, B, and D. The federal government will pay a fee to the insurance company, and the recipients will receive their coverage through the private insurance company instead of Medicare itself. Medicare Advantage plans will typically provide extended coverage in exchange for a limited service area. If a retiree does not plan on doing much travel, then this could be a good option. Medicare Advantage plans are different from a **Medigap Policy**, which is a supplemental insurance policy that can be purchased to fill in missing puzzle pieces with Part A and Part B.

Medicare Part D is a voluntary prescription drug benefit. To be eligible for Part D, retirees must be enrolled in Part B and then they are able to choose from a variety of Part D plans. Each Part D plan requires payment of an insurance premium. All varieties of Part D must offer at least a base (standard benefit) plan, which starts with a maximum out-of-pocket deductible of $310 (2014 limit); then the Part D participant would pay a 25 percent copay up to a total drug cost of $2,850. After this threshold, Medicare will pay nothing until out-of-pocket costs exceed $4,550 at which point the Medicare recipient will enter "catastrophic coverage," which means that they will pay the greater of a 5 percent copay or a $2.65 for a generic drug or a $6.60 for a brand-name drug. The gap in coverage between $2,970 and $4,750 is known as **the donut hole**. The Patient

Protection and Affordable Care Act of 2010 attempted to fix the donut hole by mandating that those who fall into the hole must be offered a 50 percent discount on brand-name drugs and a 7 percent discount on generic drugs until the donut hole has been passed. The legislative goal is to eliminate the donut hole by 2020.

The Usefulness of COBRA in Retirement Planning

How do people handle a scenario where they retire before age 65 (when Medicare eligibility begins) or if involuntary termination forces early retirement? Some people who retire before age 65 have a spouse who is still working, and coverage can be obtained through the spouse's employer. If this is not the case, then alternatives need to be considered. One such alternative was provided in 1986 through an amendment to the Employee Retirement Income Security Act (ERISA), which provided for ongoing group health coverage in the event of preretirement health coverage disruption.

The Consolidated Omnibus Budget Reconciliation Act of 1985 (COBRA) coverage could be applied to someone in their 30s who experiences a temporary healthcare coverage disruption, but it can be applied equally to an early retiree who is younger than the 65-year threshold for Medicare enrollment.

For COBRA coverage to apply, a taxpayer must have experienced either voluntary or involuntary termination of employment. The former employer must employ at least 20 people and also offer ongoing coverage, meaning that they did not discontinue coverage for all employees. Employees could also qualify for COBRA coverage if the employer cuts their hours below the employer's threshold for providing employer-subsidized healthcare coverage.

In general, COBRA coverage provides access to group insurance rates for an additional 18 months after severance of employment. The taxpayers will be responsible for paying their own insurance premiums, but the COBRA-provided group rates will be less than individual coverage by itself.

In place of COBRA coverage, recent retirees may find that they can be added to a spouse's healthcare coverage if their spouse is still covered by an employer-sponsored plan. Retirees who are in a very low-income situation may also qualify for Medicaid, which is completely different from Medicare.

LTC Insurance

With a population that is not just aging but living longer in general, end-of-life care is a very important and potentially a very costly consideration. End-of-life care can decimate an otherwise well-planned estate. The insurance industry's solution to this problem is called **LTC insurance**.

There are several categories of end-of-life care that need to be discussed. The first category is called **skilled nursing care**. This is a fancy term for a nursing home. Another category is called **assisted living,** which requires some nursing access but also a great deal of personal independence. **Home healthcare** is essentially skilled nursing care provided within the recipient's home. These first three categories of end-of-life care are the intended beneficiaries of LTC insurance. **Intermediate care** is a step between intensive care and basic hospital care. This may be a temporary stay at a skilled nursing facility to recover before going home. **Custodial care** is for ongoing help with basic nonmedical functions like walking and getting out of bed. **Adult day care** sounds like a prank, but it is actually a very useful adult babysitting service to give primary caregivers a much-needed break. What if a person with Alzheimer's is living at home with the spouse and the spouse needs a break to run errands or go to appointments? Adult day care is a tremendous blessing for this caregiver.

LTC insurance may offer a reimbursement plan where they simply pay all LTC-qualified expenses. They may also offer an *indemnity policy* where they only pay a certain daily benefit. Because of the lower level of benefit, indemnity policies are less expensive than reimbursement policies.

Long-term care insurance policies are completely customizable. They become more expensive as more bells and whistles are added. They also become more expensive as the policy covers the insured person for a longer period of time. Most LTC policies will have an imbedded **elimination period**, which is a period of time when benefits are not paid. The idea is that if someone needs intermediate care for only a few days, then the policy will not provide coverage, but if the needs last longer than the elimination period, which could be very short or as long as perhaps 90 days, then the LTC insurance policy will begin to pay benefits. Shorter elimination periods translate into higher insurance premiums. Some policies offer coverage for only a set period of time, perhaps three to five years, while others offer lifetime coverage. Obviously, longer periods of potential coverage equate to higher premiums. Another factor that will increase premiums is the presence on an inflation adjustment feature. Some policies do not have an inflation adjustment. Those that do will charge higher premiums.

To be eligible to receive benefits, insured persons either need to not be able to provide themselves with typically two out of six **adult daily living (ADL) functions** or be cognitively impaired (typically Alzheimer's or dementia). The six ADLs are eating, bathing, dressing (clothing not Thanksgiving), transferring from bed to a chair, using the toilet, and continence in general.

LTC insurance contracts are guaranteed renewable, which means that once a person has been approved, they must be renewed annually. The insurance premiums will remain level over the life of the loan. The only exception to this rule is if the insurance company changes the premium level for everyone in the same rate class. This does happen in practice and should be explained fully to clients before they purchase LTC insurance products.

Advance Directives

You have probably heard of tragic stories where individuals have a serious health threat, which requires them either to be put on a feeding tube or full life support to prevent them from dying. Sometimes, this is done because the patient has a reasonable probability of surviving, but usually this is done because family members are struggling with letting the loved one go, and the life support is maintained to prolong the goodbye. I don't know about you, but when it is my time to go...just let me go. Advance directives were created to solve this challenge.

One type of advance directive is called a living will. A **living will** is a formal legal document (similar to but different from a Last Will and Testament), which informs medical caregivers of the patient's wishes, should life support become necessary. A patient can tell the caregivers specifically not to use any form of life support. One step in this process that is vital is communication. The patient who has a living will should discuss this document with the spouse and kids. This would not be a good surprise. Also, be sure that all of the patient's doctors have a copy of the living will. The document does no good if the caregivers are not aware of its existence.

Another advance directive is a **do-not-resuscitate order**. This is an order written by a doctor declaring a patient's desire not to receive cardiopulmonary resuscitation (CPR) if he or she stops breathing or if the heart stops. This order only affects CPR. It does not prohibit a healthcare professional from administering medication. This is usually a decision made by those who see series health issues as a somewhat immediate concern. People do not typically make this blanket statement as soon as they retire (like they usually do with a living will), although it is certainly possible.

The third type of advance directive is called a healthcare **power of attorney (POA)**. This is a formal legal document that allows another person to make all decisions related to the healthcare needs of a given patient. In the event of a health emergency, the healthcare POAs must be available to consult with physicians because they are the only persons with legal authority to make the difficult decisions. Some clients will choose to have two or more children share the POA responsibilities. They do this so that no child feels less valuable than another, but this is a recipe for disaster. What if one child wants to keep the parent alive on life support while the other does not? Who do the doctors obey? Consensus decision-making is better left for nonemergency decisions where one decisive choice is needed. It is best to have only one POA. It is also best to discuss openly within the family not only who the POA should be, but also the healthcare wishes of the client. Clear communication can potentially minimize arguments between the surviving children when the client has passed away.

Whichever advance directive is used, assuming one is used at all, it is imperative that good communication exists within the family. It is also imperative that the doctors be made aware of any existing plans. An advance directive is only permanent once clients have lost their mental ability to function. As long as they are of *sound mind*, the client can alter any existing healthcare advance directives.

Discussion Questions

1. What factors should be considered by someone who is planning to remain in his or her long-term residence (home) rather than relocate?

2. What factors should be considered by a client who is planning to relocate out of state?

3. Describe a sale-leaseback transaction.

4. Describe a reverse mortgage.

5. If a client decides to enter into a reverse mortgage contract and the value of the reverse mortgage loan at the retiree's death exceeds the value of the house itself, then what happens to the excess loan balance? What if the value of the house exceeds the value of the loan?

6. Can retirees access Medicare benefits if they file for early retirement benefits?

7. Is it true that there are an unlimited number of reserve days, but a limited number of benefit periods?

8. Bill is hospitalized for 75 days; then he goes home for four months before being hospitalized for an unrelated illness for an additional 37 days. How will Medicare treat these two periods of hospitalization?

9. What if Bill were hospitalized instead for 75 days, and then he goes home for four weeks before being hospitalized for an unrelated illness for an additional 37 days. How will Medicare treat these two periods of hospitalization?

10. Can a 65-year-old who is fully insured simply apply for Part D benefits?

11. Describe Medicare Part C.

12. Describe the donut hole. Has it been fixed?

13. How does COBRA coverage help to solve the problem of pre-Medicare postretirement healthcare coverage concerns?

14. How is an indemnity long-term healthcare policy different from a reimbursement policy? Which one would you expect to be more costly?

15. A client tells you that he has a living will. Who should have a copy of this document and why?

16. A different client tells you that they have established a healthcare POA with both of their children listed as the co-POAs. What advice would you provide them?

CHAPTER 23

Retirement Distribution Planning

Introduction

Throughout people's working careers, they make periodic contributions into their retirement accounts. At some point, they will retire and need to withdraw money. Retirees need to understand the potential tax implications of this process. They also need to understand a few special rules that could save taxes over the long term.

The American government permits tax-deductible contributions under certain plan types. This is done to encourage the participants to save so that they are not solely reliant upon Social Security for their retirement well-being. However, the government does want to eventually generate taxable income for retirees so that they limit the length of the tax deferral period. They accomplish this by establishing an age when the retiree must begin to withdraw money and the government even provides the retirees a formula for the amount of their required minimum distribution (RMD). A well-established distribution plan is as important as a well-structured saving plan.

Learning Goals

- Explain the general tax treatment of retirement distributions
- Understand the §72(t) early withdrawal rules
- Identify the various methods of recovering cost basis
- Understand what counts as a qualified Roth IRA distribution
- Determine if a certain retirement account balance is eligible and advisable to be rolled over into another tax-deferred plan
- Describe the rollover options for the beneficiary of a retirement asset

- Understand the potential application of the net unrealized appreciation (NUA) rule to an employer-sponsored retirement plan
- Understand the RMD rules
- Describe how the RMD rules apply to a deceased participant

General Tax Treatment of Distributions

If a taxpayer does not properly understand and adjust for the tax implications of taking distributions from their retirement savings accounts, then they may pay taxes that they otherwise did not need to pay.

The general rule is that all distributions from retirement savings accounts will be taxed as ordinary income (normal tax rate schedule) unless some special rule applies. One notable special rule that should not be violated, if at all possible, relates to early distributions. Any distribution from a retirement savings account before the taxpayer turns 59½ will incur a 10 percent early withdrawal penalty above and beyond the applicable ordinary income tax rates.

Ordinary income taxes and early distribution limitations both apply to deductible contributions. There is a special rule for nondeductible contributions that will be explained thoroughly in the Recovery of Cost Basis section in this chapter.

The early distribution penalty is also known as a **72(t) penalty**. This is merely the IRS section that creates the 10 percent penalty. However, the 10 percent penalty amplifies into a 25 percent penalty for savings incentive match plans for employees (SIMPLEs) if the early distribution occurs within the first two years of the employee's participation. It should also be understood that most hardship withdrawals are subject to the 72(t) penalty. The only hardship withdrawals that do not involve a 10 percent penalty are withdrawals related to disability, certain medical expenses, and a qualified domestic relations order.

There are some notable exceptions to the 72(t) early withdrawal penalty. The first exception is for a beneficiary who is required to take distributions from an inherited IRA. This beneficiary may be younger than 59½, but he or she can escape the 10 percent penalty because it was inherited. The second exception is in the event of disability. This exception dovetails

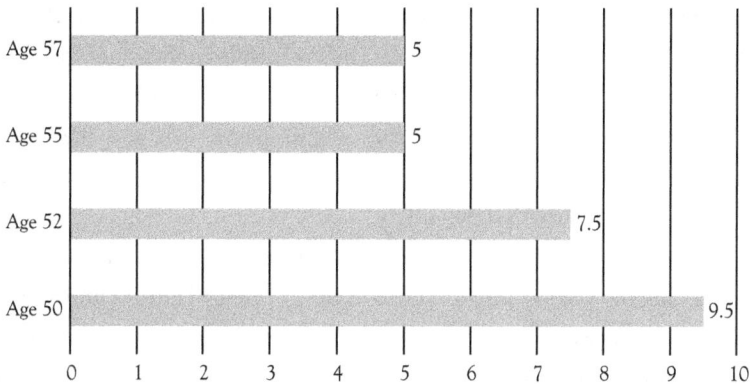

Figure 23.1 Length of SOSEP depends upon starting age

Abbreviation: SOSEP, Series of substantially equal payments.

with the disability-inspired hardship withdrawal previously mentioned. The third exemption is commonly called a **72(t) distribution** by financial practitioners. This exemption is also called a **series of substantially equal payments (SOSEP)**. Basically, taxpayers who need to take an early withdrawal could begin to take distributions without the 10 percent penalty if they establish a series of payments based upon a special formula. There are online calculators available to help a client establish the payment amount.

A 72(t) distribution must last for the longer of five years or until the taxpayer reaches age 59½. Figure 23.1 illustrates that someone who is 57 when he or she begins a 72(t) distribution will need to withdraw funds for five years (until age 62), while someone who begins a 72(t) distribution when they are 50 will need to take distributions for 9½ years (until they reach age 59½). With a 72(t) distribution, the distributions cannot deviate by even a penny from the calculated distribution amount for the entire period of required distributions. Any alteration in the distribution amount will result in all distributions (retroactively) being deemed early distributions and therefore assessed with a 10 percent retroactive penalty. Not the desired result!

The 72(t) Special Exception

There is a special exception for qualified plan participants or those with a 403(b). For this special exception to apply, the assets must remain in the qualified plan or 403(b). This means that the assets cannot be rolled over immediately into a traditional IRA. The exception applies only to those who have separated from service (terminated employment) after age 55. If the taxpayer meets these two basic requirements (age and the assets remain in the original plan), then distributions can be made from the account without the 72(t) penalty.

Consider a client who is 56 years old and has just been a victim of downsizing (he just lost his job). He is instantly plunged into an unplanned financial reality as well as an emotional roller coaster. This taxpayer's financial advisor recommends that he rollover his 400,000-dolar 401(k) into a traditional IRA to provide for greater investment flexibility (more investment choices). If the taxpayer follows this advice, then he will not be able to take penalty-free distributions. If he does proceed with the rollover, then his best option is to establish a 72(t) distribution to escape the penalties. One practical idea is to split the $400,000 into two separate traditional IRAs. The first IRA would have only enough money in it to fund a 72(t) distribution that exactly meets the taxpayer's needs. The other money could remain in a second IRA and continue to compound, free from the constraints of a 72(t) distribution schedule. There is no requirement that all traditional IRAs registered in a taxpayer's name be used to calculate a 72(t) distribution. This calculation is based on an account-by-account basis.

There are also a few notable 72(t) penalty exceptions that apply *only to IRAs*. A penalty-free withdrawal can be made from an IRA to pay for qualified postsecondary (college) education expenses. There is also a unique caveat that permits penalty-free withdrawals up to $10,000 for the purchase of the IRA owner's first house. A third penalty-free category available only to IRA owners is for health insurance premiums for those receiving unemployment benefits.

Consider a client who is 45 years old and wants to take a $25,000 hardship withdrawal from her 401(k) to pay for a child's college education. What is the 72(t) application for this scenario? Recall that the only hardship withdrawals that do not involve a 10 percent penalty are withdrawals related to disability, certain medical expenses, and a qualified domestic relations order. Qualified postsecondary education expenses to not qualify for penalty-free treatment. A 10 percent 72(t) penalty will be assessed on this hardship withdrawal. If this client wanted to make the distribution from an IRA, then the penalty would be waived.

Recovery of Cost Basis

In Publication 551, the Internal Revenue Service (IRS) defines **cost basis** as the original cost paid for an item.[1] The concept is that the original cost was paid for with money that has already been taxed once, and it would be counterproductive to tax it a second time. Cost basis therefore becomes an amount of money that is in a taxable situation but not taxed.

What might create a cost basis to accrue in a retirement account? There are two likely candidates. The first one is nondeductible contributions. Recall that nondeductible contributions are made from after-tax money. If they did not accrue as cost basis in taxable account, then double taxation would occur. The second candidate is the cost of pure insurance that was included on employees' W-2 if they purchased a life insurance product within their employer-sponsored retirement account.

There are four different distribution scenarios when cost basis will become very valuable. The first scenario is with a lump-sum distribution that is not rolled over into an IRA. In this instance, the entire cost basis is recovered immediately. Consider a client with a 401(k) with a $150,000 balance and $25,000 of nondeductible contributions. This client would have $125,000 ($150,000 – $25,000) of taxable income in the year of the distribution.

The next two scenarios both involve a rollover. In one rollover option, a client can roll over all deductible contributions as a first step. The second step is to take a tax-free distribution of all nondeductible contributions to recapture the cost basis all at once. Consider the client with $150,000 in a 401(k) and $25,000 of cost basis. She could elect to roll $125,000 into a traditional IRA and then receive a $25,000 tax-free distribution. The second rollover option is to roll all assets, both deductible and nondeductible contributions, into a traditional IRA. Again, consider our client with a $150,000 balance in the 401(k) and a $25,000 cost basis. If the client rolls the entire $150,000 into a traditional IRA, then she will need to calculate a prorated cost basis recovery every time a distribution is taken. Let us further assume that this client already has a second IRA with a $100,000 balance. The client keeps both IRAs separate and decides to take a $10,000 distribution from the recently rolled-over IRA. The pro rata cost basis recovery is determined using Formula 23.1.

$$\text{Distribution} \times \frac{\text{Cost basis remaining}}{\text{Total value of ALL traditional IRAs}} \qquad (23.1)$$

Applying Formula 23.1, we find that the actual dollar amount of pro-rata cost basis recovery will be $1,000 [$10,000 × ($25,000/$250,000)]. This means that the $10,000 distribution will result in $9,000 of taxable income and $1,000 of tax-free cost basis recovery. The remaining cost basis in the IRA is now $24,000 ($25,000 − $1,000). This number will become the numerator for the pro-rata cost basis recovery calculation the next time a distribution is needed. The important note to this process is that the denominator in this equation ($250,000) must include all traditional IRAs owned by this taxpayer.

The last possible cost basis recovery option is reserved for those who annuitized (turned their retirement plan into an annuity with a series of payments). These clients will also use a pro rata cost basis recovery calculation, but this one is different from the discussion in the preceding text. Consider a client who has a 403(b) and decides to annuitize his balance when he retires next month (on the 65th birthday). By annuitizing, this client will no longer have an account where he can take ad hoc distributions if a need arises. However, he will have a guaranteed (by the financial health of the insurance issuing company) series of payments during retirement. Assume that the payments are designed to last for 25 years (300 months) and that the client has a cost basis in the 403(b) of $40,000. The cost basis recovery is $133.33 ($40,000/300) per monthly payment. If this client's monthly annuity payment were $1,133.33, then he would enjoy $133.33 tax-free and the other $1,000 would be received as fully taxable income. Once the client recovers all of the cost basis (perhaps cost basis is specifically designed to be recovered faster than the annuity term), then all distributions become fully taxable.

Qualifying Roth IRA Distributions

A **qualifying Roth IRA distribution** will be available after one of three trigger events occurs. The first *trigger event* is the attainment of age 59½. The second trigger is the occurrence of either death or disability before age 59½. The third and final trigger event is an exception for a $10,000 distribution for a first-time homebuyer.

Once a trigger event has occurred, qualifying distributions are tax-free from a Roth IRA *only if* the distribution does not violate a special five-year rule. Roth IRAs make a big deal about the fifth anniversary of when the first contribution was made into the taxpayer's first Roth IRA. All Roth IRAs are aggregated together for purposes of calculating the five-year anniversary. An important caveat is that Roth 401(k) plans are not aggregated with Roth IRAs for this purpose. The path of least resistance, should the five-year anniversary become an issue, is to wait until the Roth 401(k) is rolled over into a Roth IRA before beginning distributions. The clock for the five-year time frame begins on January 1st of the year in which the first contribution is made to a Roth IRA. The whole purpose for this rule is to avoid taxpayers contributing to a plan in retirement, enjoying tax-free compounding for only a few years, and then receiving tax-free distributions. Roth IRAs are intended to be longer term retirement savings instruments.

Consider a client who contributes first to a Roth IRA on April 14, 2012. The five-year anniversary is measured by tax year, and therefore, this taxpayer's five-year anniversary will occur on December 31, 2017. After this anniversary date, the Roth IRA owner can take qualifying (tax-free) distributions, assuming a trigger event has also occurred.

A **nonqualifying Roth IRA distribution** will occur if taxpayers are either younger than 59½ years OR if they need to violate the five-year rule for whatever reason. The application of this rule is straightforward. Taxpayers can withdraw their after-tax, nondeductible Roth IRA contributions at any time, but they cannot distribute any earnings on those contributions without paying a 10 percent 72(t) penalty for early distributions. Roth 401(k) plans have another unique rule. With a Roth 401(k), nondeductible contributions must be prorated in the same manner as a traditional IRA. The solution to this rule is to roll over the Roth 401(k) into a Roth IRA assuming that the taxpayers are eligible for a rollover. They are only eligible to roll over an employer-sponsored plan if they have severed employment with that sponsoring employer.

Consider a client who is 55 years old. She began contributing to a Roth IRA four years ago and has already turned the $21,000 of contributions into a very nice $40,000 current account balance. In one scenario, this client needs to immediately withdraw $15,000 to purchase a piece of land. She has access to the $15,000 without 72(t) penalties because this amount is less than the total contributions. In another scenario, the tax-payer needs to withdraw the entire $40,000 for the land purchase. In this case, the taxpayer will have $21,000 of tax-free distribution and $19,000 that is both taxed and assessed at 10 percent 72(t) penalty.

Rollovers

Rollover is a technical term used to describe the movement of money from one plan type into another plan. This sounds like an amendment, but the difference is that a rollover is a case-by-case process and is not done for all participants in the plan. The most common rollovers are from either a 401(k) or a 403(b) into a traditional IRA. To rollover the balance in an employer-sponsored plan, the participant must first sever service with the employer. A 401(k) cannot be rolled into a traditional IRA while the employee still works for the sponsoring employer.

Recall that direct rollovers are between two retirement plan custodi-ans. For example, a participant might transfer his or her 401(k) at Van-guard into a traditional IRA at TD Ameritrade. In the instance of a direct rollover, the money has 60 days to leave the first custodian and arrive in the participant's traditional IRA at the new custodian. If the 60-day window is violated, then an early distribution may be declared. This time frame was established to prevent any funny business in the transfer pro-cess. This time window is typically not a problem because most transfers now take place electronically. However, if the 60-day window is breached for no fault of the participant, then the participant can request a waiver from the IRS.

The big problem is when a taxpayer chooses, knowingly or unknow-ingly, to elect an indirect rollover. In this case, a check comes to the par-ticipant from the first retirement custodian (i.e., 401(k) vendor), and then it is the taxpayer's responsibility to deposit the money into the new traditional IRA. In this instance, the IRS mandates that the first cus-todian must withhold 20 percent for taxes and send that money to the Department of the Treasury. The problem is that the taxpayer must come up with the money that was paid to the IRS from an outside source to deposit the money into the new traditional IRA to avoid being deemed as an early withdrawal.

Consider a client who has $100,000 in a 401(k) at Vanguard and unknowingly elects an indirect rollover. Vanguard will send this taxpayer a check for $80,000 and they will simultaneously send a check to the Department of the Treasury (bill collector for the IRS) for $20,000. The taxpayer will get this money back when he files his tax return, but he will wait for that to occur. In the meantime, he must deposit the full $100,000 into a traditional IRA to avoid any unplanned actual taxation or 72(t) penalties if the rollover occurs before age 59½. The taxpayer will need to lend himself $20,000 from another source to make the full indirect rollover happen, and then he will be reimbursed when tax time comes around…in theory.

There are a few situations where a rollover is not permitted. The first situation is when the client has begun to take government-mandated withdrawals, which you will learn about later in this chapter. The mandated withdrawals cannot be rolled over because that would violate the intention of requiring a withdrawal to begin with. The second situation involves 401(k) hardship withdrawals. These hardship withdrawals cannot be rolled over. The third situation is when a SOSEP has been established for an account. It does not matter is the SOSEP is established as a life annuity or as a 72(t) distribution. Either way, the presence of a SOSEP will remove the option of rollover.

It is very useful to ask: What is the purpose? The purpose of a rollover is to permit an extended period of tax-favored compounding. By selecting a rollover option, the taxpayer will effectively extend the tax-favored compounding from the point of retirement (or simply severance of employment) as long as possible.

Beneficiary Rollovers

In the previous section, you learned about rollovers as they are applied to retirement account owners. Those who inherit an IRA are also able to apply the rollover principle in a different form. These are called **beneficiary rollovers**. Spouses who inherit an IRA are in a unique situation.

They have two options. The first option is to roll their deceased spouse's IRA into an IRA in their own name. The asset is then treated as if it always was owned by the surviving spouse. The second option is to leave the IRA in the now deceased person's name. In this sense, the spouse steps into the decedent's shoes. The primary reason for choosing option 2 would be if the surviving spouse is younger than 59½ while the decedent was older than 59½. In this case, the younger surviving spouse could access death benefit distributions without the 10 percent 72(t) penalty.

Nonspousal beneficiaries are a whole other scenario. They must roll the decedent's IRA into a **beneficiary IRA** in the name of whoever inherited the asset. The new owner of a beneficiary IRA will need to take withdrawals from the account effective immediately. There is no longer an age 59½ limitation. The IRS has waited long enough to be able to tax that money. The owner of the beneficiary IRA will need to establish what the government's required distribution is for them and proceed to follow the mandated schedule.

There is another very important issue for beneficiary IRAs. Under normal circumstances, assets held within an IRA are usually exempt from bankruptcy proceedings. The United States Supreme Court has recently ruled that this protection does not extend to beneficiary IRAs unless the beneficiary is a *spousal* beneficiary[2]. This means that a nonspousal beneficiary who inherits an IRA and subsequently files for bankruptcy could see the inherited IRA consumed by bankruptcy creditors.

NUA Rule

There is a very special rule known as the **NUA rule** that applies to employer-sponsored retirement accounts when the participant owns employer stock within their plan. The application of this rule involves the participant receiving a lump-sum distribution of ONLY the employer stock and the remainder being rolled over into a traditional IRA. These shares will now be held in a nonqualified account registered in the participant's name without the limitations of an IRA. If this rule is applied, then upon distribution of the lump sum of employer stock, the cost basis (original cost) of the employer stock is taxed as ordinary income. A 10 percent 72(t) penalty will apply if the taxpayer is younger than 59½ when they apply this rule! The value of the employer stock between the cost basis and the price of the stock at the time it is distributed is taxed at long-term capital gains rates when the asset is ultimately sold. Any additional appreciation or depreciation in the stock will also receive capital gains treatment. These capital gains may be long term or short term depending on how long the taxpayer holds the shares after distributing them from their retirement account.

This is an amazing opportunity for participants with a reasonable amount of employer stock in their employer-sponsored retirement plan. As you no doubt could guess, there are caveats. The first caveat is that the NUA rule cannot be applied to either a simplified employee pension (SEP) or a SIMPLE. The idea is that SEPs and SIMPLEs are used by small businesses, and the IRS does not want the small business owner to escape taxation on the small business that they built by applying the NUA rule. This rule is intended for publically traded companies. The second caveat is that application of the NUA rule will negate the ability for the participant's estate to use stepped-up basis on these shares.

Stepped-up basis is a tremendous benefit for an inherited nonqualified account. Assume that a taxpayer has $200,000 in a nonqualified account, and the cost basis in the account is $50,000. If this taxpayer chose to liquidate the taxable account herself, then she would pay capital gains taxes on $150,000 ($200,000 − $50,000). However, if this same individual holds the assets until death and the account is inherited by someone else, then the inherited account will have a new basis of $200,000 and not $50,000. This is known as stepped-up basis, and it is a tremendous value! If the $200,000 is a joint account between a husband and wife, and one of them passes away, then the surviving spouse receives partial stepped-up basis. He or she will receive 50 percent of the original cost basis and 50 percent of the date-of-death value as the new basis. In this example, the new partial stepped-up basis will be $125,000 [(50% × $200,000) + (50% × $50,000)].

Required Minimum Distribution

Required minimum distribution, which is the government's mandated distribution amount, is commonly called simply **RMD** by practitioners.

You are already aware that distributions can be taken without the 72(t) penalty after a client reaches age 59½. At some point, the federal government wants taxpayers to begin taking distributions and therefore receiving taxable income. The government splits their required distributions into three categories. The categories are for traditional IRAs, Roth IRAs, and qualified plans.

Within a traditional IRA, taxpayers are required to begin taking withdrawals from their account after they turn 70½. What is with the half birthdays! In 1962, when the first retirement account (Keogh) was being born, the age of 60 was selected by Congress because it corresponded with the normal retirement age at that time. Someone brought up that the insurance industry's actuaries use 59½ as an *insurance age-equivalent number* of years in place of 60. Therefore 59½ was rubber-stamped by Congress as the official age, and it has not been changed since. The magic number of 70½ probably stems from two sources. National retirement plans all the way back to the first plan offered by Germany in 1889 have used 70 as a benchmark retirement age. Congress probably used 70½ not because of insurance equivalency, but to keep it logically consistent with the 59½ already on the books.

The government has a series of tables that are used to calculate a client's RMD amount. In practice, a financial professional will use an RMD calculator to find the value. The dollar amount provided by an RMD calculator must be withdrawn by December 31 of each year, or the government will impose a 50 percent penalty on the amount that was not withdrawn. The RMD calculation is based upon the previous year's ending balance and the age of the taxpayer and possibly the age of the beneficiary if he or she is more than 10 years younger than the taxpayer.

There is a special rule for the taxpayer's first year of RMD—the year in which they turn 70½. In this first year, they can delay taking RMD until the next April 1. This is known as the **required beginning date (RBD)**. If a taxpayer waits until the April 1st following their 70½ "birthday," then they may be taking two year's distributions as taxable income in the same year. Consider a client who turns 70½ in October of 2014 and has 2014 RMD of $5,642.13. This taxpayer could wait to receive the 2014 RMD until April 1, 2015. The $5,642.13 distribution is then taxable income for tax year 2015 even though it was a 2014 RMD distribution. Distributions are taxed in the year in which they are physically distributed. This client will also need to take a 2015 RMD distribution in tax year 2015. This means that by delaying their RMD, this client has created a double taxable distribution in their first year.

As was previously mentioned, Roth IRAs do not have an RMD amount associated with them. The government does not mandate any specific withdrawal from a Roth IRA until the Roth IRA is inherited by the Roth IRA owner's heirs. At the point of inheritance, the RMD requirement will be applied in the same manner as a traditional IRA (using the previous year's ending balance and an RMD calculator). The benefit of not mandating RMD is that Roth IRA balances can continue to compound tax-free for longer periods of time. This potentially creates a larger estate than would otherwise have existed.

There is a special rule that applies to qualified plans. The RBD can be postponed until the April 1 following retirement IF the participant remains working past age 70½ and also assuming that the assets remain in the qualified plan until distributions begin. This special rule is only available to those who are not 5 percent owners in the employer.

Distribution Issues for a Deceased Participant

There are unique distribution rules that apply when a participant dies. This discussion assumes that the participant dies *after* the RBD. For the tax year in which the participant dies, the RMD is calculated as if he or she were still living. The RMD must be distributed to the deceased participant's estate before the account can be transferred to any beneficiaries. After the RMD has been satisfied, the disposition of the account will depend on who the beneficiary is.

Spousal beneficiaries typically roll the decedent's IRA into their own IRA of the same type (traditional into traditional and Roth into Roth). However, a spousal beneficiary could leave the account in the decedent's name. They might do this if the decedent was older than 59½, thus enabling 72(t) penalty-free distributions, and the surviving spouse is younger than 59½. Other than for this reason, there is no need to leave the account in the decedent's name.

Nonspousal beneficiaries, like a child, grandchild, or other relative, will establish a new beneficiary IRA (or beneficiary Roth IRA). In either case, the nonspousal beneficiary is required to receive RMD distributions factored based on the new owner's life expectancy. Note that a nonspousal beneficiaries cannot roll a deceased participant's account into their own traditional IRA; they must open a separate *beneficiary* traditional (or Roth) IRA.

It is also possible to have a nonperson beneficiary, like a trust or a charity. The RMD for a nonperson beneficiary is factored based on the decedent's life expectancy (ignoring that they already expired) from government tables.

What happens if the participant dies *before* the RBD? Spousal beneficiaries will typically roll the deceased participant's account into their own IRA and then follow RMD rules as they would if it were simply their own asset. A nonspousal beneficiary will roll the account over into a beneficiary IRA and then take RMD based upon the beneficiary's life expectancy from a government table. The big difference is for a nonperson beneficiary. A nonperson beneficiary will need to withdraw the entire account balance (and therefore incur taxable income) over a five-year window. This becomes an issue if there are multiple beneficiaries and one is a nonperson entity. This issue is discussed in the next section.

Other Distribution Issues

If multiple beneficiaries exist for the same deceased participant's account, then the rules state that the oldest beneficiary (or the one with smallest distribution period) will establish the distribution period for all beneficiaries. This can be a problem if a participant establishes a spouse and a charity (or a trust) both as beneficiaries on the same retirement account. The spouse will then be forced to distribute all assets within five years and pay a great deal in taxes that might otherwise have been avoided.

There is no way to alter the beneficiaries on an account after a participant has died, but the IRS does provide a loophole. For the purposes of calculating RMD amounts, the IRS will calculate RMD based upon all beneficiaries who have not been paid out as of September 30 following the participant's death. As long as the nonperson's portion of the retirement account has been transferred to the new owner by the September 30 deadline, the other beneficiaries can follow their own distribution rules based upon their status as spousal or nonspousal beneficiaries. This also works for nonspousal beneficiaries. Basically, all beneficiaries should have their own account established by the September 30 deadline to avoid force RMD amounts that are more accelerated than need be.

Sometimes, taxpayers will use a trust as a portion of their estate plan. This instrument enables the taxpayers to control posthumously how their assets are distributed and even apply special thresholds for beneficiaries to meet (like levels of educational attainment or age thresholds) before money is distributed by the trustee. The trust will become irrevocable (unable to be altered) after the taxpayer has died. If a trust inherits retirement account assets, then the various beneficiaries' ages are used to determine the RMD amounts.

Certain participants chose to annuitize their retirement accounts. In this case, RMD is calculated in a different manner. RMD compliance is tested when the annuity payments begin. Insurance companies are aware of this special rule, and they factor this requirement into calculating the annuity amount to begin with. The annuity payments must start before the RBD.

Another important nuance of RMD calculation is that all IRAs are aggregated for determining RMD compliance. Consider a taxpayer who has three separate traditional IRAs each with $200,000 in them. He also has an RMD amount of $21,794.17 based upon his age and the oldest beneficiary. He can aggregate the IRAs in terms of taking the required $21,794.17 out of only one IRA and leaving the other two untouched. It is also possible to aggregate 403(b) accounts. It is not possible to aggregate qualified plans. This is one reason why qualified plans are often rolled into a traditional IRA after retirement occurs.

Discussion Questions

1. A 72(t) penalty amounts to a 10 percent penalty for all plan types.
2. Are all hardship withdrawals exempt from a 72(t) penalty?
3. What are the three generic exemptions to a 72(t) penalty?

4. What is the tenure requirement for a 72(t) distribution (SOSEP), should that be applied to an account?

5. What special 72(t) exemption is available to qualified plan participants?

6. What special 72(t) exemptions are available only for traditional and Roth IRA owners?

7. An IRA owner has nondeductible contributions of $25,000 in his traditional IRA, which is valued at $300,000. He plans to take a distribution of $20,000 and understands that the nondeductible contributions have created a tax-free cost basis. He thinks that the full $20,000 will be tax-free. Is he correct?

8. Reconsider the IRA owner who has nondeductible contributions of $25,000 in his traditional IRA, which is valued at $300,000. He still plans to take a distribution of $20,000. What is his cost basis recovery?

9. A client needs to withdraw money from her Roth IRA. She is 49 years old and has contributed $57,000 into a Roth IRA, which is now worth $242,000. What are her options if she needs to withdraw $32,000 to purchase a new car? What if she needed to withdraw $65,000 to pay for an executive MBA degree?

10. With respect to the five-year rule, are all Roth IRAs and Roth 401(k)s aggregated in meeting the test of tenure?

11. Why might a spousal beneficiary keep an IRA in the now deceased spouse's name?

12. Are applications of the NUA rule free from 72(t) penalties?

13. Name two significant limitations imposed by the NUA rule.

14. A client of yours applies the NUA rule. He had a cost basis of $57,000 and the employer stock was worth $233,000 when they applied the rule and removed the stock from the umbrella of a tax-advantaged plan. The client waits two years until the stock's value is $311,000 before selling. Describe the tax implications and when the taxes will be paid.

15. This same client applies the NUA rule with a cost basis of $57,000 and the employer stock was worth $233,000 when they applied the rule and removed the stock from the umbrella of a tax-advantaged plan. However, when the client sells the stock two years later, its

value has declined to $174,000. Describe the tax implications and when the taxes will be paid in this circumstance.

16. Is it true that a client must begin taking RMDs by the time they reach age 59½?

17. A client reached the RBD on April 24, 2013. He elected to apply the April 1 rule. What does the tax situation look like in 2013 and in 2014?

18. A client dies at age 75 and leaves an IRA to heirs. With respect to RMD, what must happen before the IRA is distributed?

19. A client dies before the RBD. With respect to RMD, what happens if the spouse inherits the IRA?

20. A client dies before the RBD. With respect to RMD, what happens if the children inherit the IRA?

CHAPTER 24

Managing Distribution Options

Introduction

Investors often have unrealistic expectations about the amount of money that their retirement savings could generate. Someone with a $250,000 account balance might approach retirement thinking that he or she could withdraw $2,000 per month to supplement lifestyle demands. Is this realistic? The short answer is no in our current interest rate environment if he or she wants the account to be sustainable for a long period of time. Clients need to understand the level of income they could expect from their savings as they prepare mentally for retirement.

They also need to understand the withdrawal options they have available to them beyond the required minimum distribution (RMD). Trained financial professionals are very valuable both to a retirement saver and to a current retiree because they are familiar with the various planning options.

No two clients are alike. Some have tremendous resources while others have just enough to meet their minimum lifestyle standards. Both the middle class and upper class have some unique planning issues that a financial professional needs to understand.

Learning Goals

- Understand the range of sustainable withdrawal rates, given the interest rate environment
- Describe what happens when a participant has a relatively low balance in a qualified plan and then terminates employment
- Identify a few annuity-based distribution options
- Understand the distribution options unique to individual retirement accounts (IRAs) and 403(b) plans

- Identify the key retirement planning concerns for a middle-class client
- Identify the key retirement planning concerns for wealthier clients

Sustainable Withdrawal Rates

What percentage rate can retirees plan to withdraw from their tax-advantaged retirement savings and have the highest probability of not running out of money? This is the $100 million question. Academics and practitioners have different opinions. Some financial professionals tell their clients that they can get them 6 to 8 percent cash flow every year in retirement. This is usually a sales tactic to simply close the deal, and the client will not find out until it is too late that reality is very different from 6 to 8 percent per year with reasonable access to their principal and no back-end constraints. Sometimes, annuities are used to accomplish this monumental goal. Retirees need to understand that distributions from the annuity are partly a managed payout of their principal and partly investment growth. They will typically have nothing left at the end of the annuity payment period unless certain options are purchased when the annuity is sold to them.

Conventional wisdom once focused on 4 percent as the proper distribution rate. This thought process is hinged upon a mix of 50 percent stocks and 50 percent bonds. The reality is that in a low interest rate environment, like the one currently available in the American economy, this may be too aggressive an assumption. Some academic research papers recently have suggested that the probability of not outliving one's assets is achieved more realistically in a low interest rate environment with a 2.5 to 3.0 percent distribution rate.[1]

One investment notion about low interest rate environments is that low interest rates on bonds, treasuries, certificates of deposit, and savings accounts will drive investors to riskier assets. This is partly the purpose of the current low interest rate regime. Investors will not be able to meet even a 3 percent interest rate threshold without taking more investment risk or increasing their duration, which can be a big problem in a potentially rising interest rate environment. The mechanics and uses of duration are beyond the scope of this book, but understand that a low duration is best in a potentially rising interest rate environment. One strategy that some advisors have used is to couple dividend-paying stocks with longer term call option contracts. This strategy should be used only by those who completely understand all aspects of what could bring success or defeat. This strategy could potentially produce sustainable returns above 4 percent, but it is because there is more investment risk being deployed.

Qualified Plan Distribution Options

In general, qualified plans have limited distribution options. The standard option is full distribution availability upon attainment of the normal retirement age, which will be adjusted over time, but is currently 66 years for those born between 1943 and 1954. There are exceptions for those who die before reaching the normal retirement age or for those who become disabled. Some plans offer early retirement options, and there is usually an exception for this feature as well.

One distribution feature that is unique to qualified plans is known as **involuntary cash-outs**. An involuntary cash-out means that the employer can force an employee to take a mandatory lump-sum distribution without the participant's choice of timing or form of distribution. The good news is that a lump sum can be rolled into an IRA, but it is the idea of being forced to do something that many participants dislike.

There are two thresholds that are very important for the notion of involuntary cash-outs. The first is $5,000. If a participant's plan balance is less than $5,000 at the time that employment is terminated, the company has the right to force an involuntary cash-out. This means that if the participant's balance is greater than $5,000 he or she must be offered all distribution options available within the plan. The second threshold is $1,000. If the participant's balance is below $1,000, the company will typically just send the participant a check in the mail. This could potentially create a 72(t) penalty albeit on a very small plan balance. If the participant's balance falls between $1,000 and $5,000, the balance will be issued as a lump-sum distribution and rolled into an IRA.

In-service withdrawals are also an option. They are hardly ever used in defined benefit plans, and are used infrequently in defined contribution plans. Recall that the two plan types where in-service withdrawals are most commonly found are 401(k) accounts and profit-sharing plans.

Optional Forms of Distribution

What choices do participants have in terms of taking a distribution, assuming the involuntary cash-out option is not applied to them? In Chapter 23, you learned about the rollover option, which is really just a lump-sum distribution. This is the most commonly chosen form of distribution. However, there are several other forms of distribution available to participants.

A participant could select a life annuity distribution option if the employer makes this choice available. A **life annuity** is a stream of payments that last for the entire life of the participant (called the annuitant with annuities). When the annuitant dies, the benefits stop being paid. It is that simple. If a taxpayer retired at age 66, selected a life annuity option, and died at age 70, then the heirs would be left without any value. This option is not ideal for someone who is married, because the surviving spouse could be left disadvantaged. One solution to this problem is to pay for an option to guarantee the payments for a certain period of time. If this option is chosen, the monthly payments will be lower than without the option enabled. Payments would proceed either for the life of the annuitant or for a certain period of time (perhaps 25 years). Consider our client who retires at age 66. Instead of a straight life annuity, he selects a life annuity with 15-year period certain. He still dies at age 70, but his heirs will receive payments until the year in which the retiree would have turned 86. On the 20th anniversary of when payments began, all payments will stop.

Another optional form of payment is called a **joint and survivor annuity (JSA)**. This option is essentially the *qualified joint and survivor annuity* (QJSA) that you already learned about. Conceptually, this is a joint life annuity with the survivor receiving a potentially reduced payment. Payments made under a JSA will be lower than payments made with a life annuity. This decreased payment compensates the insurance company for making additional payments to the surviving spouse. As with a QJSA, a JSA can be established with any percentage of continuing benefits desired. Most participants typically pick some number between 50 and 100 percent for the surviving spouse. Higher percentages for the surviving spouse translate into lower payments for the participant.

There is also an option called an **annuity certain**, which will pay benefits for a specified time period and then stop. This could also simply be called a period-certain annuity. This is different from a *life annuity with* a period-certain add-on (a *rider* in insurance parlance). There is no life payment context with an annuity certain. Payments will last for a specified period of time and then stop. If our participant retires at age 66 and selects a 25-year period-certain option, then payments will continue until this retiree reaches age 91. Payments will then stop. If the retiree lives longer than age 91, he or she will not receive any benefits.

Another option, which is not as widely used, is known as an **installment payment**. This is essentially the same concept as an annuity certain with the exception that an insurance company does not manage the payments as with an annuity certain. The employers will manage the payments themselves. The payments are scheduled to be made for a certain period of time, but they could stop earlier if the plan assets encounter headwinds in the stock market, or the company goes bankrupt. This is a riskier option for the retiree.

Some companies offer an additional benefit to their employees, which is called **subsidized benefits**. In this instance, the company might make additional benefits available to a married participant who chooses a JSA. The participant might not need to reduce the monthly benefit amount from the value of a straight life annuity to pay for the JSA option. The employers may elect to pay this difference themselves and leave the participant with a normal benefit check. Sometimes, companies will also subsidize early retirement by not reducing benefits from what the participants would have received if they had remained employed until reaching the normal retirement age.

IRAs and 403(b)s

As you have already learned, an IRA offers considerably more distribution flexibility than a qualified plan. Distributions are entirely discretionary at all times. That is not to say that they are penalty-free at all times.

You have already learned how the 72(t) penalty is applied to preage 59½ distributions from IRAs. A savings incentive match plan for employees (SIMPLE) is funded with an IRA, but its 72(t) penalty is elevated to 25 percent during the first two years after plan installation. Recall that exceptions to the 72(t) penalty exist for distributions made because of a participant's death or disability. Exceptions also exist to pay certain medical expenses. These exceptions apply to simplified employee pensions (SEPs) and SIMPLEs as well. Three additional exceptions are available only for traditional or Roth IRA owners. These exceptions are for medical insurance premiums for the unemployed, postsecondary education expenses, and the first-time home purchase exemption, which is capped at $10,000.

RMD rules are also a factor. Traditional IRAs, which are often the rollover target from qualified plans, have a mandatory distribution schedule after the participant turns 70½. This is not the case for Roth IRAs, which enables them to compound earnings for a long period of time to build estate value.

In general, a 403(b) has more options for distributions than a qualified plan, but fewer options than an IRA. These plan types do not permit discretionary withdrawals at any time, but they do permit in-service withdrawals under certain circumstances. As a point of difference relative to IRAs, plan loans *are* permitted within a 403(b) account. A second point of distinction is that unlike IRAs, 403(b) plans are subject to the QJSA rules. It is fairly likely that a qualified plan will be directly rolled over into a traditional IRA, while a 403(b) is often converted into a stream of payments using some form of annuity. Just like IRAs, a 403(b) is subject to 72(t) early withdrawal penalties and ordinary tax rates for all withdrawals.

Planning for the Middle Class

According to the U.S. Census Bureau, the median household income in America for 2012 was $51,017.[2] The American *middle class* will fall within a range of roughly $25,000 on either side of this number ($26,017 to $76,017). The middle class has enough money to function comfortably in most U.S. cities, but the truly sobering part is that this is roughly the same median household income as 1995.[3] The American middle class is not making much progress...

A recent Wells Fargo study showed that 59 percent of the middle class is focused more on paying current bills than on preparing for retirement.[4] The same study shows that only 52 percent of middle class workers aged 25 to 75 declare that they are confident that they will have enough money for retirement. A different study published by Forbes suggests that 37 percent of those in the middle class plan on working until they die.[5] This is a morbid thought, but it illustrates that the middle class needs tremendous help with budgeting and retirement planning. The previously mentioned Wells Fargo study also found that only 29 percent of survey respondents from the middle class have a formal written retirement plan. They need help from a financial professional!

Those in the middle class are most likely to be reliant upon an employer-sponsored plan for retirement well-being. The presence of an employer-sponsored plan, like a 401(k) or a profit-sharing plan, will couple with Social Security to provide most of a middle-class worker's retirement. An obvious exception is for those who plan to receive a meaningful inheritance. *Plan* is the operative word. Until the inheritance has been received, it is only an idea. The estate they plan on inheriting may be soaked up by long-term care or other end-of-life needs, unless proper estate planning has been undertaken by the benefactor of the estate.

Middle-class Americans are especially vulnerable to the dangers of pre-retirement distributions. When times get tight, it is tempting to establish a series of substantially equal payments as a 72(t) exception. This is the wrong move to make because it erodes potential retirement income. Plan loans are also dangerous to middle-class workers. An immediate need (or desire) may be more likely like the sirens in Greek mythology who lured unsuspecting sailors to their demise. The American culture is very focused on consumption. Excessive current consumption is the sworn enemy of middle-class retirement savers.

The decision of when to retire can have a significant impact on a middle-class American's financial health. The closer persons get to retirement, the more they begin to realize that reality dictates they need to work up to and in some cases beyond the normal retirement age. Members of the middle class should not even consider taking early Social Security benefits, unless they have amassed meaningful assets. They should be focused on working until the normal retirement age and even up to the limit of receiving extra benefits (currently age 70) if they are physically able.

The primary insurance amount formula is slanted purposely in favor of the lower and middle class. Recall that income replacement percentages are larger with lower income levels. Those in the middle class will have a higher percentage of their preretirement earnings replaced by Social Security benefits than will those in the upper class.

Planning for Wealthy Clients

When people think of a wealthy client, they are typically thinking about the upper fringes of the upper class. Technically, the upper class begins at about $100,000 with the upper middle moniker bestowed upon those that fall between the textbook definitions of middle and upper class. In nonspecific terms, a *wealthy* client is someone who has enough money that worry over sufficient retirement income is not even a passing thought.

This group of people is generally more concerned about estate planning than savings strategies and spending plans. Estate planning is a very diverse area and is beyond the scope of this book. The primary goal of estate planning with a trust is either to minimize taxation or to control posthumously how assets are distributed more thoroughly than a will alone can accomplish. The person who places money in a trust is called a grantor. The grantor can stipulate who gets paid by a trust and under what circumstances. A common stipulation is that an heir will receive partial payments at different age levels (often beginning around 25), once certain levels of schooling have been achieved. The money deposited into a trust can also help avoid taxes, sometimes in creative ways. If you are interested in learning more about this topic, then you should read *Estate Planning Made Easy* written by David T. Phillips and Bill S. Wolfkiel.

One mechanism for minimizing taxation is to use an **irrevocable life insurance trust (ILIT)**. This is a special type of trust where an irrevocable (nonreversible) trust is established with a trust other than the grantor. The grantor makes annual contributions to the trust, which are then used by the independent trustee to purchase a life insurance policy. Because the grantor does not have any control or the ability to alter the structure of either the trust or the life insurance policy, which is owned by the ILIT, the ultimate death proceeds will be outside of the grantor's estate. This is very important! If the beneficiary of the life insurance were to be the grantor's estate, then the value of the life insurance would be assessed as an estate tax. Being outside of the estate shelters the proceeds from estate taxes. The death proceeds can then be used by the ILIT trustee to pay the estate taxes covering the grantor's other assets and leave the heir with a tax-free pile of goodies. If there are any excess insurance proceeds beyond the estate taxes, the money can be paid to the heirs of the grantor if the trust document permits.

Another factor for the wealthy is that they do not need the RMD distributions. They may ignore the RMD rules if they have a Roth IRA or they may wish to deposit the traditional IRA RMD distributions into a nonqualified account after taxes have been paid (because RMD distributions from a traditional IRA are fully taxable).

Discussion Questions

1. What investment withdrawal rate is prudent for conservative investors? Why this number?

2. An employee has only $978 in the employer-sponsored plan when his employment is terminated. What will happen to his account balance?

3. An employee has $4,978 in the employer-sponsored plan when her employment is terminated. What will happen to her account balance?

4. An employee has only $6,978 in the employer-sponsored plan when her employment is terminated. What will happen to her account balance?

5. What is the difference between a life annuity and an annuity certain?

6. Would a life annuity or a life annuity with a period certain have a higher dollar payment for the retiree?

7. A company offers their employees an installment payment option in their retirement plan. What should an employee know before choosing this option?

8. A middle-class single female is employed as a manager in a hospital system in rural Pennsylvania. She earns $75,000 per year. She is

63 years old and is considering when to retire. She has a DB plan that will replace 25 percent of her preretirement income, and she has $300,000 in a 403(b) account. She is wondering if she can comfortably retire in the near future. Digging deeper, you find out that she has no home mortgage and wants to relocate to Raleigh, North Carolina, to be near her children. How would you advise her?

9. A promising young engineer in his early 30s has decided to change jobs. At his former employment, he had a DB plan with an accrued vested balance of $4,000, and the plan document specifies that any vested balance has all options available to it. He also has a 401(k) with a $22,000 balance. This rising star has come to you for advice on what do with the benefits from the former employer. He discloses that he will not be eligible for the new employer's plan for one year. What should this young engineer do?

10. An executive in her mid-50s approaches you for retirement advice. She has accumulated retirement savings of $6.7 million. This executive is married with two children who are both managers in Fortune 500 companies. This executive enjoys working and plans to work until age 70. What issues should this executive be considering?

Appendix

	PLAN YEARS				
	2014	2013	2012	2011	2010
401(k) salary deferrals (calendar year limit)	$17,500.00	$17,500.00	$17,000.00	$16,500.00	$16,500.00
401(k) catch-up contributions	$5,500.00	$5,500.00	$5,500.00	$5,500.00	$5,500.00
403(b) salary deferrals (calendar year limit)	$17,500.00	$17,500.00	$17,000.00	$16,500.00	$16,500.00
Compensation cap	$260,000.00	$255,000.00	$250,000.00	$245,000.00	$245,000.00
415(c) contribution limits	$52,000.00	$51,000.00	$50,000.00	$49,000.00	$49,000.00
415(b) contribution limits	$2,10,000.00	$2,05,000.00	$2,00,000.00	$1,95,000.00	$1,95,000.00
SIMPLE salary deferrals (calendar year limit)	$12,000.00	$12,000.00	$11,500.00	$11,500.00	$11,500.00
SIMPLE catch-up contributions	$2,500.00	$2,500.00	$2,500.00	$2,500.00	$2,500.00
SEP salary deferrals (lesser of 25% of comp OR)	$52,000.00	$51,000.00	$50,000.00	$49,000.00	$49,000.00
IRA maximum deductible amount	$5,500.00	$5,500.00	$5,000.00	$5,000.00	$5,000.00
IRA catch-up contributions	$1,000.00	$1,000.00	$1,000.00	$1,000.00	$1,000.00
457(b) eligible deferrals limit (calendar year)	$17,500.00	$17,500.00	$17,000.00	$16,500.00	$16,500.00
Highly compensated employees own 5% or prior year compensation exceeding…	$1,15,000.00	$1,15,000.00	$1,10,000.00	$1,10,000.00	$1,10,000.00
Key employee is officer making…	$1,70,000.00	$1,65,000.00	$1,65,000.00	$1,60,000.00	$1,60,000.00
OR 1% owner making…	$1,50,000.00	$1,50,000.00	$1,50,000.00	$1,50,000.00	$1,50,000.00
OR 5% owner without compensation limits					
Social Security taxable wage base	$1,17,000.00	$1,13,700.00	$1,10,100.00	$1,06,800.00	$1,06,800.00
Social Security tax rate	6.20%	6.20%	4.20%	4.20%	6.20%
Medicare tax withholding rate	1.45%	1.45%	1.45%	1.45%	1.45%
Self-employed FICA withholding	12.40%	12.40%	8.40%	8.40%	12.40%
Self-employed Medicare withholding	2.90%	2.90%	2.90%	2.90%	2.90%

Abbreviations: FICA, Federal Insurance Contributions Act; IRA Individual retirement account; SIMPLE, Savings Incentive Match *Plan* for Employees.

Notes

Chapter 1

1. Qualy (2012, April 26).
2. St. Louis Federal Reserve Bank (2014, April 1).
3. Harris Interactive (2011, February 2).
4. Bureau of Labor Statistics (2013, September).
5. AFL-CIO (2014, March 19).

Chapter 2

1. Vernellia R. Randall, Fall 2013, "ERISA as a Barrier to Compensation for Injuries," *University of Puget Sound Law Review,* access on March 19, 2014, http://academic.udayton.edu/health/02organ/manage01f.htm
2. Sarah Holden, Peter Brady, Michael Hadley, November 2006, "401(k) Plans: A 25-Year Retrospective," *Investment Company Institute Research Perspective,* accessed on June 18, 2014, http://www.ici.org/pdf/per12-02.pdf

Chapter 4

1. Bureau of Labor Statistics (September 2013).
2. Burr (January 3, 2013).

Chapter 5

1. Internal Revenue Service (2013, March).
2. Internal Revenue Service (this is general information on the IRS's website. The last date updated was March 28, 2014).
3. Internal Revenue Service (2013, March).
4. Greene (2012, December 6).
5. Internal Revenue Service (2013, March).
6. Internal Revenue Bulletin: 2013-50 (2013, December 9).
7. Internal Revenue Code §1042(e) (this is just a section of the IRS Code. There is no date provided).
8. Miller (2010, March).

Chapter 6

1. Employee Benefit Research Institute (2009).

Chapter 11

1. John Ehrhardt, Zorast Wadia, March 2014, Milliman 100 Pension Fund Index, accessed on March 30, 2014, http://us.milliman.com/uploadedFiles/Solutions/Products/pfi-assets/pfi-march-2014.pdf
2. Brendan McFarland (January 17, 2014).

Chapter 12

1. US Department of Labor (November 2013).
2. US Department of Labor (September 2006).
3. US Department of Labor (February 2012).

Chapter 13

1. United States v. Windsor (2013, June 26).

Chapter 16

1. IRS Publication 2553 (Revised December 2013).
2. IRS Tax Topic 556 (Last Update February 27, 2104).

Chapter 17

1. TIAA CREF (no date is provided on their website, it is just general information available on their website).
2. Dale (2014, April 2).
3. IRS Announcement 2014–15 (no date listed on the IRSs website for Announcement 2014–15).

Chapter 18

1. Securities Exchange Commission (September 2011).

Chapter 19

1. Seburn (1991, December).
2. Finke et al. (2013, January 15).

3. Gould (2013, December 9).
4. Small Business Administration Office of Advocacy (2012, September).
5. Hegewisch and Williams (2013, September).
6. Arias (2014, January 6).
7. Wang et al. (2013, July 10).
8. Lee and Tang (2013, November 5).
9. Embrey and Fox (1997).
10. Elan (2011, December 30).
11. TIAA-CREF (2012, December 12).
12. Retirement Statistics (2014, January 1).
13. Bureau of Labor Statistics (2013, December).

Chapter 20

1. Social Security Administration (2014, April 2).
2. Social Security Administration (2014, April 2).
3. Social Security Administration (no date provided on SSA website).
4. Social Security Administration (no date provided on SSA website).
5. Rugy (2012, May 22).
6. Social Security Administration (2014, March).
7. Quinn (2013, October).
8. Spiegelman (2013, May 24).
9. Social Security Administration (no date provided on SSA website).
10. Just Health (no date provided on the website).

Chapter 21

1. Brown (2013, May 15).
2. Sabatini (2013, October 14).
3. Tavernise (2012, September 20).
4. Chang et al. (2013, July 19).
5. Caplow et al. (2014, April 9).
6. Meyer (2010, December).
7. Kincel (2014, April).
8. Yen (2011, November 17).
9. McMahon (2014, March 18).
10. Bureau of Labor Statistics (this website holds data that is updated every month by the BLS).
11. Bureau of Labor Statistics (2012, March 2).
12. Bureau of Labor Statistics (2014, May 15).
13. Stern School of Business at NYU (2014, January 5).
14. Boscaljon (2013, Spring).

Chapter 22

1. National Center for Policy Analysis (2014, February 11).
2. Shellpoint Retirement Community Pricing Schedule (this website is general pricing information with no date provided).

Chapter 23

1. IRS Publication 551 (2001, July).
2 Clark et ux. v. Rameker, Trustee, et al, June 12, 2014, United States Supreme Court, accessed on June 18, 2014, http://www.supremecourt.gov/opinions/13pdf/13-299_6k4c.pdf

Chapter 24

1. Finke (2013, January 15).
2. US Census Bureau (2013, September 17).
3. Kochhar (2014, January 27).
4. Wells Fargo News Release (2013, October 23).
5. Touryalai (2013, October 25).

References

AFL-CIO. n.d. "Pensions," http://www.aflcio.org/Issues/Retirement-Security/Pensions (accessed March 19, 2014).

Arias, E. January 6, 2014. "National Vital Statistics Report." *Centers for Disease Control*, http://www.cdc.gov/nchs/data/nvsr/nvsr62/nvsr62_07.pdf (accessed April 6, 2014).

Boscaljon, B. Spring, 2013. "Defining an Individual's Critical Wealth Level." *Journal of Wealth Management*, pp. 17–28.

Brendan McFarland. n.d. "Funded Status of *Fortune*1000 Pension Plans Estimated to Have Improved Significantly During 2013," http://www.towerswatson.com/en-US/Insights/Newsletters/Americas/insider/2014/funded-status-of-corporate-pensions-improved-significantly-during-2013 (accessed March 30, 2014).

Brown, A. May 15, 2013. "In U.S., Average Retirement Age Up to 61." *Gallup Economy*,.http://www.gallup.com/poll/162560/average-retirement-age.aspx?utm_source=alert&utm_medium=email&utm_campaign=syndication&utm_content=morelink&utm_term=Business%20-%20Economy (accessed April 9, 2014).

Bureau of Labor Statistics. December 2013. "Labor Force Projection to 2022: The Labor Force Participation Rate Continues to Fall." *Monthly Labor Review*, http://www.bls.gov/opub/mlr/2013/article/labor-force-projections-to-2022-the-labor-force-participation-rate-continues-to-fall.htm (accessed April 6, 2014).

Bureau of Labor Statistics. March 2, 2012. "Consumer Price Index for the elderly," http://www.bls.gov/opub/ted/2012/ted_20120302.htm (accessed April 12, 2014).

Bureau of Labor Statistics. n.d. "National Compensation Survey: Employee Benefits in the United States, March, 2013," http://www.bls.gov/ncs/ebs/benefits/2013/ebbl0052.pdf (accessed March 21, 2014).

Bureau of Labor Statistics. n.d.a. "CPI-U Medical Care Data," http://data.bls.gov/timeseries/CUUR0000SAM?output_view=pct_12mths (accessed April 9, 2014).

Bureau of Labor Statistics. n.d.b. "CPI-U Table 7," http://www.bls.gov/news.release/cpi.t07.htm (accessed April 9, 2014).

Bureau of Labor Statistics. November, 2010. "Program Perspectives." 2, no. 6, http://www.bls.gov/opub/btn/archive/program-perspectives-on-defined-contribution-plans-pdf.pdf (accessed April 5, 2014).

Burr, B. n.d. "Ford Sells $2 Billion in 30-Year Bonds to Help Fund Defined Benefit Plans," http://www.pionline.com/article/20130103/ONLINE/130109970 (accessed March 21, 2014).

Caplow, T.; L. Hicks; and B.J. Wattenberg. "The First Measured Century: An Illustrated Guide to Trends in America 1900-2000," http://www.pbs.org/fmc/book/1population4.htm (accessed April 9, 2014).

Chang, M.-H.; H. Athar; P.W. Yoon; M.T. Molla; B.I. Truman; and R. Moonesinghe. July 19, 2013. "State-Specific Healthy Life Expectancy at Age 65 Years – United States 2007-2009," *Centers for Disease Control's Morbidity and Mortality Weekly Report,* http://www.cdc.gov/mmwr/preview/mmwrhtml/mm6228a1.htm (accessed April 9, 2014).

Dale, A April 2, 2014. "Shielding Inherited IRA Assets," *The Wall Street Journal,* http://online.wsj.com/news/articles/SB10001424052702304441304579477150954100222?mod=dist_smartbrief (accessed April 12, 2014).

Elan, S. December 30, 2011. "Financial Literacy Among Retail Investors in the United States." *Library of Congress, Federal Research Division,* http://www.sec.gov/news/studies/2012/917-financial-literacy-study-part2.pdf (accessed April 6, 2014).

Embrey, L.; and J. Fox. 1997. "Gender Differences in the Investment Decision-Making Process." *Association for Financial Counseling and Planning Education,* https://afcpe.org/assets/pdf/vol825.pdf (accessed April 6, 2014).

Employee Benefit Research Institute. n.d. "Nondiscrimination, Minimum Coverage, and Participation Requirements for Pension Plans," http://www.ebri.org/pdf/publications/books/fundamentals/fund12.pdf (accessed March 21, 2014).

Finke, M.; W. Pfau; and D. Blanchett. n.d. "The 4% Rule is not Safe in a Low Yield World," http://www.preservationfinancial.net/PDF/4_Percent_Rule_Dead.pdf (accessed April 5, 2014).

Finke, M.; W.D. Pfau; and D.M. Blanchett. n.d. "Rule is Not Safe in a Low Yield World," http://www.preservationfinancial.net/PDF/4_Percent_Rule_Dead.pdf (accessed April 11, 2014).

Gould, P. December 9, 2013. "While Many Pre-Retirees Plan to Work Longer, They May Underestimate Life Expectancy and Don't Have a Financial Plan in Place," *Society of Actuaries Press Release,* http://www.soa.org/News-and-Publications/Newsroom/Press-Releases/Society-of-Actuaries-Release-New-Survey-Report-on-Retirement-Risks.aspx (accessed April 12, 2014).

Greene, K. December 6, 2012. "Benefits Leaders Reins in 401(k)s," *The Wall Street Journal,* http://online.wsj.com/news/articles/SB10001424127887323316804578163722900112526?mg=reno64-wsj&url=http%3A%2F%2Fonline.wsj.com%2Farticle%2FSB10001424127887323316804578163722900112526.html (accessed March 21, 2014).

Harris Interactive. n.d. "Number of Americans Reporting No Personal or Retirement Savings Rises," http://www.harrisinteractive.com/NewsRoom/HarrisPolls/tabid/447/mid/1508/articleId/684/ctl/ReadCustom%20 Default/Default.aspx (accessed March 19, 2014).

Hegewisch, A.; and C. Williams. September 2013. "The Gender Wage Gap: 2012," http://www.iwpr.org/publications/pubs/the-gender-wage-gap-2012-1/ (accessed April 6, 2014).

Internal Revenue Bulletin: 2013-50. December 9, 2013. "Reduction or Suspension of Safe Harbor Contributions," http://www.irs.gov/irb/2013-50_IRB/ar07.html (accessed March 21, 2014).

Internal Revenue Code §1042(e). n.d. http://www.irs.gov/pub/irs-drop/rr-00-18.pdf (accessed March 21, 2014).

Internal Revenue Service. March, 2013. "Section 401(k) Compliance Check Questionnaire: Final Report," http://www.irs.gov/pub/irs-tege/401k_final_report.pdf (accessed March 21, 2014).

Internal Revenue Service. n.d. "Retirement Topics—Hardship Distributions," http://www.irs.gov/Retirement-Plans/Plan-Participant,-Employee/Retirement-Topics—Hardship-Distributions (accessed March 21, 2014).

IRS Announcement 2014-15. n.d. http://www.irs.gov/pub/irs-drop/a-14-15.pdf (accessed April 4, 2014).

IRS Publication 2553. n.d. http://www.irs.gov/pub/irs-pdf/i2553.pdf (accessed April 3, 2014).

IRS Publication 551. July, 2001. "Basis of Assets," http://www.irs.gov/pub/irs-pdf/p551.pdf (accessed April 11, 2014).

IRS Tax Topic 556. n.d. http://www.irs.gov/taxtopics/tc556.html (accessed April 3, 2014).

Just Health. n.d. "What is Limited Resources under SSI?" http://justhealth.info/content/what-limited-resources-under-ssi (accessed April 14, 2014).

Kincel, B. April, 2014. "The Centenarian Population: 2007-2011," http://www.census.gov/prod/2014pubs/acsbr12-18.pdf (accessed April 9, 2014).

Kochhar, R.; and R. Morin. January 27, 2014. "Despite Recovery, Fewer Americans Identify as Middle Class," http://www.pewresearch.org/fact-tank/2014/01/27/despite-recovery-fewer-americans-identify-as-middle-class/ (accessed April 12, 2014).

Lee, Y.; and F. Tang. November 5, 2013. "More Caregiving, Less Working: Caregiving Roles and Gender Differences." *Journal of Applied Gerontology*, http://jag.sagepub.com/content/early/2013/10/29/0733464813508649.abstract (accessed April 6, 2014).

McMahon, T. March 18, 2014. "Historical Inflation Rate," http://inflationdata.com/Inflation/Inflation_Rate/HistoricalInflation.aspx (accessed April 9, 2014).

Meyer, J. December 2010. "Centenarians 2010," http://www.census.gov/prod/cen2010/reports/c2010sr-03.pdf (accessed April 9, 2014).

Miller, S. March, 2010. "The ESOP Exit Strategy." *The Journal of Accountancy*, http://www.journalofaccountancy.com/issues/2010/mar/20092046.htm (accessed March 21, 2014).

Milliman's Pension Funded Index. n.d. http://us.milliman.com/Solutions/Products/Pension-Funding-Index/# (accessed March 30, 2104).

Moore, R. February 14, 2014. "Does Your Employee Retirement Education Include Information About Carrying a Mortgage into Retirement?" http://www.ncpa.org/media/how-a-mortgage-impacts-retirement-income (accessed April 12, 2014).

National Center for Policy Analysis. February 11, 2014. "Seniors Spending More on Credit Cards, Mortgages," http://www.ncpa.org/sub/dpd/index.php?Article_ID=24088 (accessed April 12, 2014).

Qualy, J.M. April 26, 2012. "Financial Freedom Victim or Victor?" *Lecture at the University of Missouri*, http://pfp.missouri.edu/documents/news/FS4_qualy.pdf (accessed March 19, 2014).

Quinn, J. October, 2013. "When to Claim Social Security Benefits?" *AARP Bulletin*, http://www.aarp.org/work/social-security/info-10-2013/when-to-claim-social-security-benefits.1.html (accessed April 9, 2014).

Randall, V.R. n.d. "ERISA as a Barrier to Compensation for Injuries," http://academic.udayton.edu/health/02organ/manage01f.htm 9 (accessed March 19, 2014).

Retirement Statistics. n.d. http://www.statisticbrain.com/retirement-statistics/ (accessed April 6, 2014).

Rugy, V. May 22, 2012. "How Many Workers Support One Social Security Retiree?" *Mercatus Center at George Mason University*, http://mercatus.org/sites/default/files/worker-per-beneficiary-analysis-pdf.pdf (accessed April 8, 2014).

Sabatini, P. October 14, 2013. "Workers are Retiring Earlier Than Expected." *The Buffalo News*, http://www.buffalonews.com/business/retirement/workers-are-retiring-earlier-than-expected-20131010 (accessed April 9, 2014).

Seburn, P. December, 1991. "Evolution of Employer-Provided Defined Benefit Pensions," *Monthly Labor Review*, http://www.bls.gov/mlr/1991/12/art3full.pdf (accessed on April 5, 2014).

Securities Exchange Commission. n.d. "Investor Alert: Self-Directed IRAs and the Risk of Fraud," http://www.sec.gov/investor/alerts/sdira.pdf (accessed April 4, 2014).

Shellpoint Retirement Community Pricing Schedule. n.d. http://www.shellpoint.org/pricing/contractA.html (accessed April 10, 2014).

Small Business Administration Office of Advocacy. September, 2012. "Frequently Asked Questions About Small Business," http://www.sba.gov/sites/default/files/FAQ_Sept_2012.pdf (accessed April 5, 2014).

Social Security Administration. April 2, 2014. "Social Security Basic Facts," http://www.ssa.gov/pressoffice/basicfact.htm (accessed April 8, 2014).

Social Security Administration. March, 2014. "Monthly Statistical Snapshot, February 2014," http://www.ssa.gov/policy/docs/quickfacts/stat_snapshot/ (accessed April 8, 2014).

Social Security Administration. n.d. "SSI Federal Payment Amounts for 2014," http://www.ssa.gov/OACT/cola/SSI.html (accessed April 14, 2014).

Social Security Administration. n.d. "When to Start Receiving Retirement Benefits," http://www.ssa.gov/pubs/EN-05-10147.pdf (accessed April 13, 2014).

Social Security Administration. n.d.a. "Life Expectancy for Social Security," http://www.ssa.gov/history/lifeexpect.html (accessed April 8, 2014).

Social Security Administration. n.d.b. "Actuarial Life Table, 2009," http://www.ssa.gov/OACT/STATS/table4c6.html (accessed April 8, 2014).

Spiegelman, R. May 24, 2013. "When Should You Take Social Security?" http://www.schwab.com/public/schwab/nn/articles/When-Should-You-Take-Social-Security (accessed April 13, 2014).

St. Louis Federal Reserve Bank. n.d. "Personal Savings Rate," http://research.stlouisfed.org/fred2/data/PSAVERT.txt (accessed March 19, 2014).

Stern School of Business at NYU. n.d. "Annual Returns on Stock, T. Bonds, and T. Bills: 1928-current," http://pages.stern.nyu.edu/~%20adamodar/New_Home_Page/datafile/histretSP.html (accessed April 10, 2014).

Tavernise, S. September 20, 2012. "Life Spans Shrink for Least Educated Whites in the U.S." *The New York Times*, http://www.nytimes.com/interactive/2012/09/21/health/a-troubling-trend-in-life-expectancy.html?ref=us (accessed April 9, 2014).

TIAA CREF. n.d. "Bankruptcy Protection for Retirement Plans and IRAs," http://www1.tiaa-cref.org/public/advice-planning/education/saving-for-retirement/family-matters/bankruptcy_iras/index.html (accessed April 12, 2014).

TIAA-CREF. December 12, 2012. "Women More Likely Than Men to Follow Financial Advice," https://www.tiaa-cref.org/public/about/press/about_us/releases/articles/pressrelease440.html (accessed April 6, 2014).

Touryalai, H. October 25, 2013. "Work Until You Die? More Middle Class Americans Say They Can Never Retire." *Forbes*, http://www.forbes.com/sites/halahtouryalai/2013/10/25/work-until-you-die-more-middle-class-americans-say-they-can-never-retire/ (accessed April 12, 2014).

United States v. Windsor. June 26, 2013. http://www.supremecourt.gov/opinions/12pdf/12-307_6j37.pdf (accessed April 2, 2014).

US Census Bureau. September 17, 2013. "Income, Poverty and Health Insurance Coverage in the United States: 2012," http://www.census.gov/newsroom/releases/archives/income_wealth/cb13-165.html (accessed April 12, 2014).

US Department of Labor. n.d. "Default Investment Alternatives Under Participant-Directed Individual Account Plans," http://www.dol.gov/ebsa/newsroom/fsdefaultoptionproposalrevision.html (accessed March 30, 2014).

US Department of Labor. n.d. "Fifth Third Bancorpet al. vs. John Dudenhoeffer et al.," http://www.dol.gov/sol/media/briefs/dudenhoffer(A)-11-01-2013.pdf (accessed April 4, 2014).

US Department of Labor. n.d. a "Meeting Your Fiduciary Responsibilities," http://www.dol.gov/ebsa/publications/fiduciaryresponsibility.html (accessed March 30, 2014).

Wang, H.; A. Schumacher; C. Levitz; A. Mokdad; and C. Murray. July 10, 2013. "Left Behind: Widening Disparities for Males and Females in US County Life Expectancy, 1985-2010." *Population Health Metrics,* http://www.pophealthmetrics.com/content/11/1/8 (accessed April 6, 2014).

Wells Fargo News Release. October 23, 2013. "Middle Class Americans Face a Retirement Shutdown; 37% Say, 'I'll Never Retire, but Work Until I'm Too Sick or Die, a Wells Fargo Study Finds," https://www.wellsfargo.com/press/2013/20131023_middleclasssurvey (accessed April 12, 2014).

Wiatrowski, W. December 2012. "The Last Private Industry Pension Plans: a Visual Essay," *Monthly Labor Review,* http://www.bls.gov/opub/mlr/2012/12/art1full.pdf (accessed April 5, 2014).

Yen, H. November 17, 2011. "Reaching Age 90 is More Likely Than Ever, Census Finds," *The Huffington Post,* http://www.huffingtonpost.com/2011/11/17/reaching-age-90-more-likely-americans_n_1099822.html (accessed April 9, 2014).

Index

ACP test. *See* Actual contribution
  percentage test
Actual contribution percentage (ACP)
  test, 45, 64, 81
Actual deferral percentage (ADP) test,
  44–45, 54, 64, 81
Actuarial cost method, 106
ADL. *See* Advance determination
  letter
Adoption agreement, 63
ADP. *See* Actual deferral percentage
  test
Advance determination letter (ADL),
  15
Advance directives, 260–261
Affiliated service groups, 69–70
Age weighting, 80–81
Aggregation rules, 68–69
AIME. *See* Average index monthly
  earnings
Alternative minimum taxes (AMT), 174
AMT. *See* Alternative minimum taxes
Annuity certain, 285
Average benefits test, 66
Average index monthly earnings
  (AIME), 227, 240

BLS. *See* Bureau of Labor Statistics
Break-in-service rule, 92
Brother-sister-controlled group,
  aggregation rules, 69
Bureau of Labor Statistics (BLS), 4

Cash balance (CB) plan, 21–22
Catch-up contribution, 24
CB. *See* Cash balance plan
COBRA. *See* Consolidated Omnibus
  Budget Reconciliation Act of
  1985
COLA. *See* Cost of living adjustment
COLI. *See* Corporate-owned life
  insurance

Compensation, 77
Consolidated Omnibus Budget
  Reconciliation Act of 1985
  (COBRA), 258–259
Constructive receipt rule, 156–157
Contribution limit test, 64
Corporate-owned life insurance
  (COLI), 163–164
Cost basis, 267
Cost of living adjustment (COLA),
  245–246
Coverage, eligibility, and participation
  rules
  affiliated service groups, 69–70
  aggregation rules, 68–69
  "21-and-1" rule, 68
  family attribution, 69–70
  initial core concepts, 63–64
  leased employees, 70–72
  410(b) minimum coverage test,
    64–66
  planning opportunities, 67–68
  401(a)(26) testing, 66–67
Crisis of financial unawareness
  financial awareness, 3–5
  individual retirement account
    (IRA), 7–8
  nonqualified deferred
    compensation, 7–8
  tax-advantaged plan attributes,
    5–6
  tax-advantaged plans, general
    requirements of, 7
Cross testing, 79–80

DB. *See* Defined benefit plan
DC. *See* Defined contribution plan
Death
  incidental death benefit rule,
    99–102
  preretirement death planning,
    98–99

Defense of Marriage Act (DOMA), 138
Deferred retirement, 94–95, 229–230
Defined benefit (DB) plan, 19, 21–22
  vs. DC plans, 23–25
  final average compensation (FAC),
    32
  flat amount per year of service
    method, 34
  flat benefit method, 34
  flat percentage of earnings method,
    33
  formulas to determine benefits
    paid, 31–34
  life annuity, 32
  pension-type plan *vs.* a profit-
    sharing-type plan, 30
  special types, 34–35
  unit benefit formula, 32
  10 year certain and continuous, 33
  years-of-service cap, 31
Defined contribution (DC) plan, 19,
    22–23
  401(k) compliance testing, 44–46
  vs. DB, 23–25
  employee stock ownership plan
    (ESOP), 48–50
  401(k) plan, 41–44
  prior year testing, 45
  profit-sharing plans, 40–41
  stock bonus plans, 47–48
Department of Labor (DOL), 12, 122
Designing benefit offerings
  age weighting, 80–81
  compensation, 77
  cross testing, 79–80
  integration with social security,
    78–79
  nondiscrimination requirements,
    75–77
  plan types, common choices for,
    81–82
  voluntary after-tax contributions,
    82–83
Disability benefits, 102
Distribution options. *See also*
    Retirement distribution
    planning
  IRAs, 285–286
  middle class, planning for, 286–288

optional forms of, 284–285
  qualified plan distribution options,
    283–284
  403(b)s, 285–286
  sustainable withdrawal rates,
    282–283
  wealthy clients, planning for,
    288–289
DOL. *See* Department of Labor
DOMA. *See* Defense of Marriage Act
Due diligence, 20

Early retirement, 93–94, 227–229
Earnings test, 230–231
Economic benefit rule, 155–156
Economic Growth and Tax
    Relief Reconciliation Act
    (EGTRRA), 36
EGTRRA. *See* Economic Growth and
    Tax Relief Reconciliation Act
Employee census, 21
Employee plans compliance resolution
    system (EPCRS), 139
Employee Retirement Income
    Security Act (ERISA), 11–12,
    58, 85, 154
Employee stock ownership plans
    (ESOPs), 4, 22, 23, 48–50,
    148
Employee stock purchase plans
    (ESPP), 176–177
EPCRS. *See* Employee plans
    compliance resolution system
Equity-based compensation
  business, 170–171
  employee stock purchase plans
    (ESPP), 176–177
  incentive stock options (ISO),
    174–176
  nonqualified stock options
    (NQSO), 172–174
  overview of, 169–170
  preliminary concerns, 171–172
  special equity-based plan types,
    177–179
ERISA. *See* Employee Retirement
    Income Security Act
ESOPs. *See* Employee stock
    ownership plans

ESPP. *See* Employee stock purchase
    plans
ETF. *See* Exchange-traded fund
Exchange-traded fund (ETF), 83
Executive bonus life insurance,
    167–168
Expense method, 245

FAC. *See* Final average compensation
Fact-finding process, 20
Family attribution, 69–70
Federal Insurance Contributions Act
    (FICA), 222
FICA. *See* Federal Insurance
    Contributions Act
Fiduciary bond, 129
Fiduciary responsibility
    collateral benefit, 121
    disclosures and requirements,
        123–124
    discretionary authority, 120
    exclusive benefit rule, 121
    fiduciary conflict mitigation,
        121–123
    fiduciary duty, 120–121
    fiduciary-prohibited transactions,
        125–128
    limiting fiduciary liability, 128–129
    participant-directed investing,
        124–125
    self-dealing, 126
    standard of prudence, 122
    third-party administrators (TPAs),
        120
Final average compensation (FAC),
    32, 56, 82, 240
Financial awareness, 3–5
Financial unawareness, crisis of, 3–7
Flat amount per year of service
    method, 34
Flat benefit method, 34
Forfeiture provisions, 160–162
Forfeiture, substantial risk of, 155
415(b) benefit limit, 23
410(b) minimum coverage test,
    64–66
403(b) plans, 5
    Small businesses and nonprofits,
        58–59

457 plans, 7, 166–167
401(a)(26) testing, 66–67
Funded status, 106
Funding
    at-risk plans, 107
    common trust fund, 111
    cushion amount, 107
    DB plan, 106–108
    DC plan, 109–110
    fiduciary responsibility, 111
    fully insured plans, 108–109
    funding target, 107
    guaranteed insurance contract
        (GIC), 110
    instruments, 110–112
    irrevocable, 110
    prefunded, 107
Funding issues, 163

GIC. *See* Guaranteed insurance
    contract
Golden handshake, 159
Guaranteed insurance contract (GIC),
    110

HCEs. *See* Highly compensated
    employees
Highly compensated employees
    (HCEs), 56, 64, 75, 78, 154
Holistic view
    employer-sponsored plans,
        214–215
    financial professional, role of,
        211–212
    of retirement planning, 210–211
    retirement planning process, steps in,
        212–214
    women, 215–216
Housing issues
    alternative housing choices,
        254–255
    overview, 252–253
    and relocation issues, 253–254
100-1 rule, 100

ILIT. *See* Irrevocable life insurance
    trust
Incentive stock options (ISO),
    174–176

Individual retirement account (IRA),
    4, 7–8, 53. *See also* Roth IRAs
  active participants, 184–187
  emerging IRA opportunities,
    199–200
  funding instruments, 195–197
  handling excess contributions,
    191–192
  overview of, 182–183
  prohibited investments, 199–200
  rollovers and Roth conversions,
    189–191
  Roth IRAs, 187–189
  self-directed IRAs, 197–198
  traditional, 183–184
Individual retirement annuity, 196
Inflation assumptions, 245–246
Informally funded, 163
Initial concerns
  DB *vs.* DC plans, 23–25
  defined benefit (DB) plan, 19,
    21–22
  defined contribution (DC) plan,
    19, 22–23
  Keogh plan, 25–26
  preliminary concerns, 20–21
Initial core concepts, 63–64
Installment payment, 285
Integration level, 78
Internal Revenue Service (IRS),
    12, 143
  exclusive benefit rule, 16
  involuntary termination, 17
  private letter ruling, 15
  proposed regulation, 15
  prototype, 17
  regulations, 15
  revenue rulings, 15
  summary plan description (SPD),
    15–16
  voluntary termination, 17
Investing
  assumptions, 246–248
  general considerations, 114–116
  guidelines, policies, and objectives,
    112–114
  separate account GIC, 116
  stable value fund, 116

  synthetic GIC, 116
  time horizon, 114
  unrelated business income tax
    (UBIT), 115
Involuntary cash-outs, 283
Involuntary termination, 148
IRA. *See* Individual retirement
    account
Irrevocable life insurance trust (ILIT),
    288
IRS. *See* Internal Revenue Service
ISO. *See* Incentive stock options

Joint and survivor annuity (JSA),
    284
JSA. *See* Joint and survivor annuity

Keogh plan, 25–26
Key employees, 56

Lack thereof, 3–5
Leased employees, 70–72
Life annuity, 32, 284
Life expectancy assumptions,
    241–242
Limited liability company (LLC), 9
Living will, 260
LLC. *See* Limited liability company
Long-term care (LTC) insurance,
    259–260
  adult daily living (ADL) functions,
    260
  adult day care, 259
  assisted living, 259
  custodial care, 259
  elimination period, 259
  home healthcare, 259
  intermediate care, 259
  skilled nursing care, 259
LTC insurance. *See* Long-term care
    insurance

Medicare
  benefit periods, 256
  medicare advantage plan, 257
  medigap policy, 257
  options, 255–258
  reserve days, 256

Money purchase pension plans
(MPPPs), 22, 35–36, 76
Moral hazard, 223
MPPPs. *See* Money purchase pension
plans

Net unrealized appreciation (NUA)
rule, 47, 272–273
NHCEs. *See* Nonhighly compensated
employees
Nondiscrimination requirements, 75–77
Nonelective contribution, 46
Nonhighly compensated employees
(NHCEs), 44, 59, 65
Nonqualified deferred compensation
plans, 7–8
benefit security, 164–165
company-owned life insurance,
163–164
constructive receipt rule, 156–157
design considerations, 162–163
economic benefit rule, 155–156
executive bonus life insurance,
167–168
forfeiture provisions, 160–162
funding issues, 163
objectives of, 158–159
457 plans, 166–167
vs. qualified plans, 154–155
specific types of, 159–160
top-hat exemption, 166
wage-based taxes, 157–158
Nonqualified stock options (NQSO),
172–174
Nonqualifying Roth IRA distribution,
269
Nontax-advantaged savings *vs.*
tax-advantaged plans, 6
Normal retirement age (NRA), 92–93
NQSO. *See* Nonqualified stock options
NRA. *See* Normal retirement age
NUA rule. *See* Net unrealized
appreciation (NUA) rule

Parent-subsidiary-controlled group,
aggregation rules, 69
PBGC. *See* Pension Benefit Guaranty
Corporation

PBO. *See* Projected benefit obligation
Pension Benefit Guaranty Corporation
(PBGC), 12, 35, 142
Pension Protection Act (PPA), 11, 14
Pension-type plan *vs.* a profit-
sharing-type plan, 30
Percentage test, 65
Phantom stock, 177
PIA. *See* Primary insurance amount
Plan installation
administration requirements,
136–137
common errors, 137–138
compliance issues, 138–139
new plan, 134–135
qualified domestic relations order
(QDRO) interacts, 137–138
summary plan description (SPD),
135
Plan loans
actual contribution percentage
(ACP) testing, 89
actual deferral percentage (ADP)
testing, 89
defined benefit (DB) plan, 86
ERISA, 87
individual retirement account
(IRA), 86
Internal Revenue Service (IRS), 88
nonhighly compensated employee
(NHCE), 89
overview, 86–87
rules and administration, 87–90
401(k)s, 86
403(b)s, 86
savings incentive match plans for
employees (SIMPLEs), 86
simplified employee pensions
(SEPs), 86
Plan terminations
alternatives to, 142–143
DB plan, 145–146
DC plan, 144
distress termination, 145
distribution options, 146–147
in-kind distribution, 145
limits on, 143–144
by operation of law, 148–149

partial termination, 148
qualified termination administrator,
    149
reasons for, 141–142
reversion of excess plan assets, 146
single premium annuity contract
    (SPAC), 147
standard termination, 145
POA. *See* Power of attorney
Post-ERISA trends, 13–14
Power of attorney (POA), 261
PPA. *See* Pension Protection Act
Primary insurance amount (PIA),
    227, 240
Profit-sharing retirement plans
    (PSRPs), 22, 40–41, 78
brokerage window, 44
exchange-traded funds (ETFs), 44
hardship withdrawal, 42
highly compensated employees
    (HCEs), 40
vs. pension-type plan, 30
safe harbor events, 42
Projected benefit obligation (PBO),
    106
PSRPs. *See* Profit-sharing retirement
    plans

QDI. *See* Qualified default investment
QDRO interacts. *See* Qualified
    domestic relations order
    (QDRO) interacts
QJSA. *See* Qualified joint and
    survivor annuity
QPSA. *See* Qualified preretirement
    survivor annuity
Qualified default investment (QDI),
    125
Qualified domestic relations order
    (QDRO) interacts, 137–138
Qualified joint and survivor annuity
    (QJSA), 98
Qualified plan, 4
vs. other plans, 5
Qualified preretirement survivor
    annuity (QPSA), 98
Qualifying Roth IRA distribution,
    268–270

Rabbi trust, 165
Ratio test, 65
Reallocation forfeiture, 91
Required minimum distribution
    (RMD), 273–275
Restricted stock, 178
Retirement age assumption, 240–241
Retirement age selection
deferred retirement, 94–95
early retirement, 93–94
normal retirement age (NRA),
    92–93
Retirement distribution planning
beneficiary rollovers, 271–272
cost basis, recovery of, 267–268
for deceased participant, 275–276
general tax treatment, 264–265
net unrealized appreciation (NUA)
    rule, 272–273
other issues, 276–277
qualifying Roth IRA distribution,
    268–270
required beginning date (RBD),
    274
required minimum distribution
    (RMD), 273–275
rollovers, 270–271
72(t) special exception, 265–266
Retirement income, 243–245
Retirement landscape
Employee Retirement Income
    Security Act (ERISA), 11–12
Pension Protection Act (PPA),
    11, 14
post-ERISA trends, 13–14
RMD. *See* Required minimum
    distribution
Roth IRAs, 187–189
backdoor Roth conversion, 200
conversions, 203–205
vs. deductible traditional IRA
    contributions, 202–203
vs. nondeductible traditional IRA
    contributions, 200–202
stepped-up basis, 201

Safe harbor contribution, 45
Salary reduction plans, 160

Savings incentive match plan for employees (SIMPLE) plans, 5, 21, 55–56, 82

SEC. *See* Securities and Exchange Commission

Secular trust, 165

Securities and Exchange Commission (SEC), 106

SEP plans. *See* Simplified employee pension plans

Series of substantially equal payments (SOSEP), 47, 265

SERP. *See* Supplemental executive retirement plan

SIMPLE plans. *See* Savings incentive match plan for employees plans

Simplified employee pension (SEP) plans, 5, 21, 82
  Small businesses and nonprofits, 53–55

Single premium annuity contract (SPAC), 147

Small businesses and nonprofits
  403(b) plans, 58–59
  SEP plans, 53–55
  SIMPLE plans, 55–56
  top-heavy rules, 56–58

SMM. *See* Summary of material modifications

SNT. *See* Special needs trust

Social security
  benefit calculation, 227
  and deferred retirement, 229–230
  and early retirement, 227–229
  earnings test, 230–231
  funding, 223–224
  inherent importance of, 221–223
  initial benefit issues, 224–225
  supplemental security income (SSI), 235–236
  survivor benefits, 226
  taxation of benefits, 231–233
  taxpayer, 233–235
  unique payback option, 234

Social Security Administration (SSA), 222

SOSEP. *See* Series of substantially equal payments

SPAC. *See* Single premium annuity contract

SPD. *See* Summary plan description

Special needs trust (SNT), 235

SSA. *See* Social Security Administration

SSI. *See* Supplemental security income

Stable value fund, 116

Standard of living, 242–243

Stock bonus plan, 22

Stock bonus plans, 4, 47–48

Straight DB plan, 21

Subsidized benefits, 285

Summary of material modifications (SMM), 136

Summary plan description (SPD), 15–16
  plan installation, 135

Supplemental executive retirement plan (SERP), 160

Supplemental security income (SSI), 235–236

Target benefit (TB) plans, 22

Taxable wage base (TWB), 78

Tax-advantaged plans
  attributes, 5–6
  categories of, 4
  general requirements of, 7
  vs. nontax-advantaged savings, 6

Tax Equity and Fiscal Responsibility Act of 1982 (TEFRA), 56

Tax-free inside buildup, 164

Taxpayer, 233–235

TB plans. *See* Target benefit plans

TEFRA. *See* Tax Equity and Fiscal Responsibility Act of 1982

Terminations. *See* Plan terminations

Third-party administrators (TPAs), 120

30,000-foot view, 3–7

Top-hat exemption, 166

Top-heavy rules
  death and disability planning, 97–102
  small businesses and nonprofits, 56–58

TPAs. *See* Third-party administrators
TWB. *See* Taxable wage base
"21-and-1" rule, 68

UBIT. *See* Unrelated business
        income tax
Unrelated business income tax
        (UBIT), 115

Vesting, 7
    general considerations,
        91–92
    required schedules, 90–91
Voluntary after-tax contributions,
        82–83

Wage-based taxes, 157–158

OTHER TITLES IN OUR FINANCE AND FINANCIAL MANAGEMENT COLLECTION

John Doukas, Old Dominion University, Editor

- *Managerial Economics: Concepts and Principles* by Donald Stengel
- *Your Macroeconomic Edge: Investing Strategies for the Post-Recession World* by Philip J. Romero
- *Working with Economic Indicators: Interpretation and Sources* by Donald Stengel and Priscilla Chaffe-Stengel
- *Innovative Pricing Strategies to Increase Profits* by Daniel Marburger
- *Regression for Economics* by Shahdad Naghshpour
- *Statistics for Economics* by Shahdad Naghshpour
- *How Strong Is Your Firm's Competitive Advantage?* by Daniel Marburger
- *A Primer on Microeconomics* by Thomas Beveridge
- *Game Theory: Anticipating Reactions for Winning Actions* by Mark L Burkey
- *A Primer on Macroeconomics* by Thomas Beveridge
- *Fundamentals of Money and Financial Systems* by Shahdad Naghshpour
- *An Executive's Guide for Moving from US GAAP to IFRS* by Peter Walton
- *Effective Financial Management: The Cornerstone for Success* by Geoff Turner
- *Financial Reporting Standards: A Decision-Making Perspective for Non-Accountants* by David Doran
- *Revenue Recognition: Principles and Practices* by Frank Beil
- *Applied International Finance: Managing Foreign Exchange Risk and International Capital Budgeting* by Thomas J. O'Brien
- *Venture Capital in Asia: Investing in Emerging Countries* by William Scheela
- *Global Mergers and Acquisitions: Combining Companies Across Borders* by Abdol S. Soofi and Yuqin Zhang

Announcing the Business Expert Press Digital Library

Concise E-books Business Students Need
for Classroom and Research

This book can also be purchased in an e-book collection by your library as
- a one-time purchase,
- that is owned forever,
- allows for simultaneous readers,
- has no restrictions on printing, and
- can be downloaded as PDFs from within the library community.

Our digital library collections are a great solution to beat the rising cost of textbooks. E-books can be loaded into their course management systems or onto students' e-book readers.

The **Business Expert Press** digital libraries are very affordable, with no obligation to buy in future years. For more information, please visit **www.businessexpertpress.com/librarians**. To set up a trial in the United States, please email **sales@businessexpertpress.com**.

www.ingramcontent.com/pod-product-compliance
Lightning Source LLC
Chambersburg PA
CBHW060325200326
41519CB00011BA/1836